To Rachel,
With best wishes!
Leslie Cohen

Trapped Inside
the Story
The biography of
Naomi Kalsky, born
Sonya Hebenstreit

By Leslie Cohen

Level 4 Press, Inc.

TRAPPED INSIDE THE STORY

Dedication

To Naomi Kalsky, nee Sonya Hebenstreit, who is a genuine heroine and a unique role model

This book is printed on acid-free paper.

Published by
Level 4 Press, Inc.
13518 Jamul Drive
Jamul, CA 91935
www.level4press.com

BISAC Subject Heading: HIS043000 HISTORY / Holocaust

ISBN: 978-1-933769-16-5

Printed in China

TRAPPED INSIDE THE STORY

A Fairy Tale

"Once there were two witches who used to hunt children and eat them. These witches had evil eyes, wild hair, and huge fangs. However, horrible as they were, the witches loved a little girl named Marisetchka, and they would never hurt her.

> Marisetchka-Dunetchka
> Beware of the witches!
> They may love you today,
> But they'll eat you for supper
> Tomorrow!

Marisetchka had a neighbor—a young boy named Ivasyk—who knew all about Marisetchka's evil friends, the witches. One day, Ivasyk found out that the witches were planning to capture him and cook him in a stew. However, on the day the witches set their trap for Ivasyk, he was ready.

The next morning, Ivasyk snuck out of his house and climbed a tall tree in his back yard, where he hid, listening to the witches talk. They made a huge campfire under the tree where Ivasyk was hiding. There, they feasted on fresh child stew, certain that they had roasted and eaten the body of Ivasyk.

After their banquet, they relaxed and joked under the tree. One of the witches got up and took the bowl of bones that she believed were the remains of Ivasyk. She scattered the bones all over the yard, screaming, "Away with you, you bones of Ivasyk-Kutasyk who is no more!" Then, the other witch heard a noise in the tree and looked up. She saw Ivasyk hiding there.

Ivasyk shouted to the witches from his perch in the tree, "I tricked you! Those aren't the bones of Ivasyk but those of your beloved Marisetchka-Dunetchka! If you don't believe me, just look under her pillow and you will see her breasts lying there!" Hearing this, the witches were infuriated. Their beloved Marisetchka was dead, and they had been tricked into eating her! "Wherever you try to hide, Ivasyk-Kutasyk, we will find you and destroy you!" they screamed. However, since the witches had eaten so much, they were too heavy to climb the tree. So, with their huge jaws and long, sharp teeth, they decided to gnaw at the tree trunk. They chewed and chewed and chewed until the tree collapsed.

Ivasyk-Kutasyk,
Run from the witches!
Ivasyk-Kutasyk,
Run for your life!

Hop from treetop to treetop,
Never daring to fall,
Or the witches will eat you
For supper tonight!

There was another tall tree just next to this one, and Ivasyk hopped from the lofty branches of one tree onto the branches of the other. Therefore, the witches went to the next tree, and started gnawing at the trunk, just as before. When the second tree collapsed and fell, Ivasyk hopped into a third tree, which was the last one in the yard. Ivasyk thought to himself,

"When they bring down this tree,
that will be the end of me!

But suddenly, when the evil witches had gnawed through the trunk of the third tree, it fell on top of them, killing them all, instantly. And thus, the young boy, Ivasyk, escaped the terrible fate of being cooked and eaten by the witches."

Broken Pieces of Childhood

As soon as Zoshka finishes telling me the story, I beg her, "Tell me again!"

On a good day, she puts her head back and laughs so hard that her big, big belly shudders.

"You can never get enough, can you, little Sonya?"

"Does that mean 'yes'?"

And she laughs again.

"Tell me again, please, please, please!"

And many times, she does.*

---

* Lvov, Poland: the 1930s

Along with the rest of the world, the people of Lvov suffered from the Great Depression throughout the 1930s. Businesses were ruined, people went bankrupt, and many people were paid for their labor in food, rather than money.

Before the Depression, Sonya's father, Israel, had owned his own bakery. Now he works for somebody else.

Fairy tale heroes come from humble origins. They meet many people who seem simple and unimportant at first, but those characters often reappear and play a different role from what may have been expected. Similarly, everyday objects and experiences sometimes take on a magical significance later in the story....

I can tell it's morning before I open my eyes. The aroma of fresh-baked bread wakes me up. And I smile as I open my eyes, knowing that the kitchen table is piled high with bread and rolls, and I can eat as much as I want for breakfast!

I hear the neighbor women talking with Mama, as they buy bread and rolls for their families.

"Good morning, Rechel."

"Hello, Esterel. How are you today? Is Ulek feeling any better?"

"Yes, thanks to that syrup you gave me. One nice, hot roll and he should be as good as new."

So Ulek was sick yesterday! That's why I didn't see him. Well, good for him, the big bully! I can never go out to play in the court-yard without having him tease me or pull my hair.

By the time I get out of bed and follow my nose into the kitchen, Mama is filling her huge baskets with warm rolls and loaves of bread, getting ready to go around to the local shop-keepers in our neighborhood. Those baskets are very heavy, but Mama is big and strong. While she packs the baskets, I choose a steam-

2

ing hot roll with crunchy *kummel* (caraway seeds), filling it with butter and cheese. My favorite breakfast is *pletzek*—a round, flat bread, with chopped onions and spices in the middle—but Father hasn't brought any home this morning.

"Here, have another, Zissel," Mama offers me, smearing it with a thick layer of butter.

"Talk to me in *Polish*, not *Yiddish*!" I stamp my foot. "And call me *Sonya*, not *Zissel!* Sonya is my *real* name!" I insist.

Mama chuckles and says, "My little daughter with the big ideas!"

Zoshka hands me a bowl of steaming hot "coffee," which is mostly made of boiled milk. She winks at me when Mama isn't looking and I smile up at her, as she wipes the butter off my chin.

"Come Zissel, let's go see a movie!" says Mama.

Way up front there's a family sitting around a table piled high with food. The food looks delicious, but I can't smell it. I want to get closer to them. Seeing all that food makes me hungry. So I get up and run toward the front of the movie house, calling to the family at the table:

"Hello! Look, I'm over here! I want some *pierogi,* (dumplings filled with mashed potatoes or stewed fruit) too!" I can hear Mama running after me down the aisle. She catches up to me and tries to pick me up, but I scream, "No, no, Mama! I want to sit with the family at the table and eat *pierogi!*"

She carries me out of the theater, kicking and crying.

"Zissel, *maidele*," (my little daughter) she says when we get outside, "it's a movie; it's not a real family. There's no food on the stage. It's just pictures."

But I don't believe her. "No, no!" I scream. "I saw the *pierogi* on the table. You can't fool me!"

I'm mad at her and I don't talk to her for the rest of the day.*

Zoshka is always at home with me. I love when we sit in the kitchen, peeling potatoes together, and she tells me stories in Ukrainian. She sings, too, in Ukrainian—long, long ballads about love—all in rhyme.

---

* Lvov, Poland: the early 1930s

Sonya's family, the Hebenstreits, is a typical Lvov family, living in a two-room apartment. The front room is a kitchen, with a cooking stove, a dining table, a credenza for storing dishes and food, and several *taborets*—low stools with storage space under their seats. It's lit by a bare light bulb that hangs from the ceiling. There are no refrigerators, no telephones, and—of course—no televisions!

The back room is the "salon." A heating stove is built into the middle of the room, with a chimney leading up to the roof. Chimney sweeps come to clean the chimney several times each winter. The back room serves as a bedroom for the whole family, with beds and nightstands along the walls.

The Hebenstreit Family

Standing in the field like a statue,
The maiden waits for her lover.
Riding 'cross the fields on horseback,
The Cossack jingles some coins.
He says, 'Here's for you and your mother:
Two kronen for beer and two for soap.
With the soap, you'll wash yourself,
So your beauty will not fade
And the beer will keep your mother
From noticing your belly.
The beer will keep your mother
From seeing how you bulge.'

"What's a *bulge*, Zosshu?" I ask.

"Oh, never mind! It's just a song," she answers.

I don't understand the words or remember them, but I love to hear the melody. And I'm learning to speak Ukrainian just like Zoshka!

When Zoshka is too busy for me, I'm bored and lonely. I wander around the apartment

5

humming the melodies and telling the simpler stories over and over to myself. But *shhhh!* quietly, so I don't wake Father.

Hippity-hop, hoppity-hop,
Little Zhabka jumped into the pot!

The poor little frog wasn't looking where he was going and he landed in a deep bucket of milk that the milkmaid had just put aside.

Well, the milk was still warm from the cow, and very rich and creamy, so at first Little Zhabka just lapped it up and swam around in it, thoroughly enjoying himself. But when he had had enough, he realized that he couldn't get out of the bucket! What was he going to do?

Hippity-hop, hoppity-hop,
Little Zhabka can't get out of the pot!

The poor little frog was so frightened that he started to thrash around wildly. He hopped and he jumped, he dived and he kicked, until the milk began to churn.

Hippity-hop, hoppity-hop,
Zhabka thrashed around in the pot!

So hysterical was Little Zhabka, he didn't think about what he was doing, he just kept kicking wildly.

Hippity-hop, hoppity-hop,
Zhabka churned the milk in the pot!

So the silly little frog was finally able to stand on top of the butter he had churned from the milk, and jump out of the bucket.

Hippity-hop, hoppity-hop,
Zhabka hopped away from the pot!

Once I saw a real frog and I remember how it hopped. So I hop around the salon, trying to imitate Zhabka. I'm very pleased with myself for being able to remember the whole story. But it's much more fun when Zoshka tells it. Why does she have to be so busy?

I have nothing to do at home and I'm bored, so Zoshka lets me sit next to her at the kitchen sink and I help her peel potatoes. We do this a lot when Mama is out. I like to sit next to Zoshka, peeling potatoes. She tells me stories and sings to me. But one day, Mama comes home while I'm helping Zoshka. I can tell she's angry when she sees what we're doing.

"I don't want Sonya peeling potatoes," she yells at Zoshka. "Let's hope that she can accomplish more than that with her life!"

Zoshka looks down and doesn't say anything, but I'm very disappointed. It's fun to peel potatoes with Zoshka! She tells me her stories over and over again, and she sings to me and tells me jokes in Ukrainian. Zoshka is more my friend than Mama, who seems so far above me. And Zoshka is soft and cuddly—not like Mama! Sometimes I grab fistfuls of Zoshka's skirt and snuggle up to her soft side. When I do that, she strokes my hair and never pushes me away. Mama never hugs me or lets me hug her—she's too important for that, and she's always busy working or taking care of our bills.

Sunday is Zoshka's day off, and she puts on her best dress to go to the Tzerkiev—the Russian Orthodox Church. Then she sits on her bed and curls her hair by heating a pair of tongs and twisting strands of hair around it. I love to watch her make herself pretty.

"When I grow up, I'm going to curl my hair, too!" I tell her.

"Oh, you have a long time to wait until then, little Sonya!"

Sometimes Zoshka takes me with her after church to visit her family. Her brother, Michael, and his wife, Michalova, live in an apartment building near ours. It's easy to walk to their apartment. Our house is only three stories tall, but Michael's apartment building seems to reach all the way to the sky. Maybe hundreds of families live there. I think there might even be a thousand people living on their street!

"It's so big, Zosshu," I say, "doesn't anybody ever get lost?"

Zoshka just laughs.

Sometimes there are other visitors, too. Michalova has two grown-up children: Olga and Kazhik. Olga is an old maid. She has an ugly face and a nasty temper just like her face. I try to stay away from her. Kazhik is Michalova's son from the time she was married before. He looks big and scary, but his wife, Stacha, is always nice to me, and they have a little boy named Yurek.

8

"Hello Sonya," Stacha says one Sunday. "What a pretty outfit that is!"

I'm wearing the expensive skirt that Mama had a seamstress make for me, with a matching jacket. The skirt is way too long for me, and Mama says I need to wear it for a few years, so I roll up the waist and put a belt around it, making a thick fold. I look down and shrug my shoulders, but I don't explain the bulge under my waistline because Mama said not to tell anybody. I can hear Michalova and Zoshka giggling, but Stacha says, "Never mind them. Why don't you come and play with the baby?"

Yurek is just learning to walk. He grabs my finger with his little hand and we walk around the room. I tell him the story about Zhabka, the little frog, and I show him how to hop.

"Hippity-hop, hoppity-hop,
Little Zhabka jumped into the pot!"

When Yurek falls down while trying to hop, we both laugh.

But it's not so much fun when Zoshka takes me to visit Michalova during the middle of the week. Michalova is a washerwoman, so the apartment is always full of laundry. She never sits down while we're visiting her. She talks to Zoshka while she works, and she sweats a lot. Doing laundry is hard work! At our house, Zoshka does the laundry. But we're only one family, so she doesn't have as much to do as Michalova.

Michalova's Apartment

One summer day, while Mama is out working, Zoshka and I have a wonderful surprise. Zoshka's grown-up daughter, Katerina, comes to visit! I've never seen her before. Zoshka says she lives far away.

Katerina is beautiful. She has big blue eyes, and when she smiles, she has dimples! She laughs and smiles all the time she's with us. Katerina has strawberry blonde hair, with a permanent wave. She's wearing a dirndl skirt and a flowered blouse. She looks just like a Krakowianka doll—the kind I wish Mama would buy for me. I can't take my eyes off her the whole time she's here. I've never seen any-one so beautiful.

Katerina's boyfriend brings her to visit us in a shiny black car. It's the first time I've met somebody who has his own car. In our neighborhood, we never see private cars. There are a few people with ladder wagons, pulled by a horse or a donkey, but no cars. All the neighbors come out to see it.

And Katerina brings presents for me and my little sister, Rosa. She gives us each a huge bar of chocolate with whole nuts in it—not like the broken pieces of chocolate I sometimes get

10

at the grocery shop. The chocolate bar is wrapped in a thin layer of gold paper. On the outside, it has brightly colored wrapping paper.

Mama comes home while Katerina is here. She's never seen Katerina before, either. She thanks Katerina for the chocolate bars, and warns Rosa and me not to eat the whole bar all at once. Rosa takes a few bites and puts hers away. But I nibble at mine all afternoon until I finish it. That night, I have a stomachache and I throw up.

My own family is nothing like Zoshka's. Father is a baker. He works all night and comes home to sleep all day, so I have to be very quiet if I go into the salon. Father is very quiet, and when he talks, he speaks Yiddish. He knows just a little Polish, and he speaks it very slowly, with lots of mistakes. He and Mama always speak Yiddish at home. Father calls Mama, Rechel— that's her Yiddish name—and she calls him Sroulik. That's the nickname for Israel. They both call me Zissel when we're at home. But I hate Yiddish and I don't answer them unless they speak to me in Polish.

Mama is the one who runs the household. She never sits still, except when she's reading the newspaper. She doesn't like housework. She says she can earn more money if she goes out to work and hires someone to take care of the house and watch us kids. So she sells bread and rolls for the same bakery that Father works at and Zoshka lives with us.

Mama especially likes to talk and laugh and joke with people—not children like me, but adults—and she has a lot of friends. Some of

11

them are the neighbors in our building, and some of them are Gentiles. Mama's Polish is good, and she can tell jokes and stories in Polish just as she can in Yiddish. But she doesn't tell fairy tales, like Zoshka. All of her stories are for grown-ups.

Sometimes, Mama takes me with her when she goes out. But she walks very fast and it's hard for me to keep up with her. It's nothing like walking with Zoshka, who is short and very fat, and moves slowly, like me.

Mama holds my hand tightly, and drags me after her. It's not that I don't want to go with her, but it's so hard to walk across the cobblestones! Each one is like a hill set into a valley, a castle surrounded by a moat. My tiny feet keep slipping into the cracks between the domes and getting stuck. I can hear the clippity-clopping of horse hooves against the cobblestones as Mama tugs me along, but I don't look up to see them. I have to look at my feet.

When we get to Zamarstynovska Street, there are no more cobblestones. Zamarstynovska is big and wide with huge trees on both sides. But our street, Kressova, is narrow and cobbled, and I'm always out of breath from trying to keep up with Mama.

It's late Friday afternoon, and Mama says we have to hurry to get home before *Shabbat.* Mama doesn't have the money to pay the rent. She holds my face up to the landlord.

"Look at this *schone maidele,* my beautiful little daughter. She's only five years old. You wouldn't want to kick her out into the street, would you?" she asks him. "Give us a few more days. I promise I'll pay you soon."

"I have my bills, too!" he says, but I notice his voice is very kind.

I feel so ashamed that I cry all the way home.

Mama is walking very fast. "Please try to keep up with me, Sonya," she says, dragging me along. "We need to get home before sundown."

At home, Mama heats water on the stove and fills a large tub with water in the kitchen to give me my bath before *Shabbat*. Then she and Father bathe in the tub, too. We always take a bath before *Shabbat*.

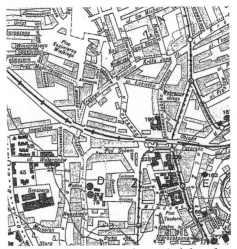

Map of Hebenstreit's neighborhood

Sometimes I don't mind the cobblestones so much. I love to go with Mama to visit her friend Lucia in Kleparov, even though it's a long, long walk. Lucia and her husband live in a small house with a big vegetable garden. There are

13

rows and rows of vegetables, and each different kind is a different shade of green, with different shaped leaves. Lucia picks the vegetables and ties them in bunches. She takes them to the outdoor market near Starozakonna Street (in English—Old Testament Street—named for the large Jewish community that has lived there throughout the history of Lvov). That's where she sells them. Mama buys some of each kind for our soup.

While Mama is chatting with Lucia, I walk around Lucia's vegetable garden, or play outside in the fields with the local children. Sometimes we play hopscotch, and sometimes we play circle games.

"Come, Sonya, you be the young girl from Krakow," the biggest boy tells me. He tells the other children which parts to play, too. Everybody stands in a circle and sings the story in rhymes, acting it out. The children who are playing the special parts—the beautiful young girl, the guard, the king and the executioner—stand inside the circle. We walk around and make hand gestures every time our name is mentioned. The others stand around us, singing and clapping. The next time we play, each player gives their part to someone else. So after we get our parts, the children form a circle and we all start chanting:

She's the beautiful young girl,
The beautiful young girl,
The beautiful young girl from Krakow!
She's gone into the field,
The king's own private field,
To collect the red leaves of the birch tree!

14

*"Hey, pretty maiden!" says the King's royal
guard,
"What are you doing here,
In the private fields of the king?"
"I'm picking red leaves," she says,
"Red leaves from the birch tree,
Red leaves to cook, to make my mother well."
"But you can't pick red leaves
In the field of the king,
You're stealing from the king,
And you'll be punished!" warns the guard.
The beautiful young girl
The beautiful young girl
The beautiful young girl from Krakow,
Goes home to her mother,
But her mother is still ill,
So she comes back again for the birch leaves.
The guard is very angry,
He brings her to the king,
The king is very angry,
"How dare you do this thing?"
"Get the executioner! Off with her head!"
The executioner comes with his heavy axe.
And the beautiful young girl,
The beautiful young girl,
The beautiful young girl from Krakow,
With tears in her eyes
Says her last goodbyes.
The church bells ring
And the angels sing:
"Don't be afraid, beautiful young maiden.
Don't be afraid to die.
"Don't be afraid, beautiful young maiden.
Your soul is already with God in heaven."
And the beautiful young girl,
The beautiful young girl,*

15

The beautiful young girl from Krakow
Bows her head
and goes to her death with dignity.

As they sing the part about the church bells ringing, every child raises his hands and makes the gestures of bells ringing. After it's my turn to play the girl from Krakow, I give my part to another girl, and we play again and again.

When Mama comes looking for me, I can see she's annoyed. She doesn't like me to play with the neighborhood kids in Kleparov.

"What a silly game!" she tells me.

But I like it!

Krakowianka Dolls

One day Mama says, "Let's go for a walk, just the two of us!" It's a warm, sunny spring day, and Mama takes me to the park in Lvov. It makes me feel very special that she's invited me to go with her. We sit on a bench and look at the scenery.

Mama tells me about her Gentile friends: Lucia, Anya, Katya, and Maria.

16

"I'm glad you speak Polish so well. It will help you study when you go to school. And you'll be able to make friends with the Polish children, too."

She never calls me Zissel any more—not even at home.

I love to go with Mama to the great outdoor market in Lvov. Every Thursday we go there to buy meat from the kosher butcher for our *Shabbat* meal. Mama says we're lucky to have enough money to have chicken for *Shabbat* dinner every week. Some families don't even have that, she tells me.

The market is a long way from home, on Starozakonna Street, in a Jewish neighborhood. We have to cross the Peltevna Bridge in order to get there. I love the market because it's so exciting. It's always full of people and everything is out in the street—not inside shops.

There are whole animals hanging on hooks—sides of beef, and chickens and geese and ducks. When I look at them, I think there are two different kinds of animals: the ones that live in barnyards or on farms, like in the stories that Zoshka tells me, and the ones that people buy in the markets and take home to cook and eat.

There's so much to see at the market that my eyes dart in every direction. And the whole street smells of spices—it's a wonderful aroma. There's always entertainment, too. There are sometimes clowns, magicians, or comedians. People crowd around the entertainers in a circle and afterwards, they throw coins.

17

Once we saw Breitbart, the famous Jewish weightlifter there. He put on a thrilling show. He took a very strong iron chain and passed it among the men.

"Here," he said, "Just try to break it!" But nobody could.

Then Breitbart took the chain and tore it apart, right in front of us!

Everyone clapped and cheered.

"Oh, that's nothing!" he told the crowd.

"Come on," he said, "follow me!"

And on a street near the market, he lay on the ground underneath a car and lifted it up. We couldn't believe his strength, even though we saw it with our own eyes! Mama and I went home very excited. We had seen a very famous man do something fantastic.

But even on a normal market day, there's always something special at the outdoor market.

Then one day, Mama asks me, "Are you ready to go to another movie, *maidele*?"

"Oh, yes!" I say. Now I'm older and I understand that movies aren't real.

So Mama takes me to see "Heidi," with my favorite actress—Shirley Temple. I know they're only pictures, but they look so real that I feel I could step right into the forest. But I don't say a word. I just sit quietly in my seat like everybody else.

The story makes me want to laugh sometimes and cry at other times. Heidi loses her mother and father, and she goes to live with her grandfather. I can't imagine what it's like to be an orphan. And I've never had a grandfa-
18

ther—all my grandparents died when my parents were very young. But Heidi's grandfather is a big, mean-looking man, who lives all alone in a wooden house in the forest, way up in the mountains. Everybody says he's a strange man—he doesn't like people and he almost never speaks. When Heidi's aunt brings Heidi to meet him, Heidi is scared just to look at him. I'm frightened, too. I think it's better that I never met my grandparents than to have a grandfather like that!

When Heidi's aunt leaves her there and says, "You're staying here! You have no other place to go!" I want Heidi to run after her. But the aunt refuses to take her back.

Heidi sits down at the table to have her first meal with her grandfather. She's miserable and she doesn't say a word. I hold my breath when Heidi's grandfather picks up a knife. Heidi is afraid that he's going to stab her with it, since so many people have told her what a strange man he is. I can feel Heidi's terror—and her relief when she sees her grandfather cut the cheese with the knife.

After that, Heidi meets Peter, a young shepherd. Peter tells Heidi about Clara, a wealthy young girl who can't walk and has to sit in a wheelchair. Clara lives in a mansion in the big city, and her governess brings her to the mountains sometimes to breathe the fresh air. When Heidi meets Clara, they immediately become great friends, and the lonely young cripple asks Heidi to come and live with her. Heidi goes home with Clara, but the governess doesn't like Heidi and makes her feel very unwelcome.

I'm thrilled with Heidi's friendships with Clara and Peter, and I feel as if I'm part of Heidi's world, too—like a distant friend or relative. All the way home, Mama and I talk about the film.

"Have you ever seen such a forest, Mama?" I ask her.

"Yes, Sonya, and you will too, some day. Near Rava Russka, where our family lives, there's a big forest. It's called Valkovice. And there are big, beautiful lakes there, too."

"Just like in the movie, Mama?" I ask.

"Just like that!"

One day, I'll go to visit the family in Rava Russka, and I'll see the forest.

That night when I go to bed, I'm still thinking about Heidi and her friends. I go over the scenes from the movie in my mind, wondering what will happen to Heidi and her friends after the movie is over. And I wonder what happened to Heidi's mother and father, why she was sent to live with her grandfather, and what her family life had been like when her mother and father were alive.

I fall asleep thinking how wonderful it must be to have such good friends, and how terrible it is to be an orphan.

When I grow up, I'm going to be a doctor and invent a medicine that will make people live forever!

I don't remember when my little sister Rosa was born, but she's been pestering me for as long as I can remember! She's very skinny, so Mama always saves the juiciest pieces of meat with the most fat for her. Those are just the pieces I want!

"A child needs to be round and fat—like Sonya—in order to be healthy," Mama says.

Why doesn't Mama give *me* the best pieces of meat? It isn't fair! And not only that, Rosa always gets an orange for a treat. Mama says oranges are a wonder drug. Sometimes she lets me buy an orange for a snack, but not every day. She sends me to the corner grocery store and I pick out one orange wrapped in sweet-smelling, crinkled paper. I sign my name in the shopkeeper's register. When the bill comes to Mama at the end of the month and it's too high, Mama tells me I have to stop buying oranges. But Rosa still gets one every day!

Once in a while as a special treat, Mama gives me five *groschen* to buy broken pieces of chocolate from the Pisinger chocolate factory. The chocolate has pieces of nuts and raisins in it. The grocer rolls a piece of newspaper into the shape of a cone and puts the small pieces into it. I nibble piece after sweet, delicious piece, as I cross the street. It's all gone before I get home. Chocolate is the most delicious thing I can imagine! Why do I have to wait so long from one time to another? It isn't fair!

When I was littler, Mama used to take me for walks in the beautiful park in the center of Lvov, just the two of us. I loved those walks. But now that Rosa can walk, she takes both of us. Mama walks between us and takes each one of us by the hand. That way we can't fight.

Once in a while, Father takes Rosa and me for a walk in the park on a Saturday afternoon. Those walks are very different from the walks we take with Mama. Mama is very careful with money and she buys us only one treat on any outing. But father never says "no" when Rosa asks for chocolates or hot roasted peanuts in a cone, or juice from a kiosk. I only ask for one treat, But Rosa keeps saying she wants something else, and Father never says "no." I tell Rosa, "You know you're not supposed to!" But she just sticks out her tongue at me and ignores what I say. I always feel guilty when Rosa and I go out with Father, knowing how angry Mama would be if she found out about everything he buys us. Mama always reminds us we have to be very careful not to waste money.

Mama and I both love Shirley Temple films. Shirley Temple is the most beautiful child I've ever seen! She has blonde curly hair, and dimples in her face. And she sings and dances! How could anybody be so perfect?

I remember the mansion that Heidi's friend Clara lived in. Her family was so rich that they had a telephone. I've never seen a real telephone, but when we get home from the movie, I make a play phone out of a piece of string and two tin covers from old shoe polish containers. I take it outside to the courtyard and play "telephone" with the kids from our building until Ulek comes along and grabs the tin from me, and pushes me very hard. I fall down and scrape my leg.

I run inside crying, and tell Zoshka, "Ulek pushed me down again! Go outside and yell at him, Zoshka. Make him give me back the telephone!"

Zoshka laughs at me and says, "Sonya, the more the two of you fight, the more I think you're going to grow up and get married! There's an old Ukrainian saying that goes: 'The harder they fight, the better they love!'"

I go into the salon and sulk. Why won't Zoshka help me? Doesn't she care? And will I really marry Ulek when I grow up? That's the worst thing that could ever happen to me, I think. Now I'm scared. Zoshka knows almost everything. What if she's right? What if I grow up and marry Ulek?

Mama's younger sister, Nechama, is a seamstress. Mama says she's going to live in Palestine as their other sister, Devorah, did. Nechama leaves during the coldest part of winter. Mama and I go to the train station to see her off. The day is so cold that my hands and my feet are numb. I'm crying very hard, so Mama puts her own gloves over my gloves, and the ticket-taker in the tram comes over to see what's wrong. He's a nice man, and he takes my hands in his own, blows on them, and rubs them very hard. It hurts me, but it makes the numbness go away. Then he says, "Stamp your feet hard like this, and pretend you're dancing." So I "dance" all the way to the train station.

When we finally get there, Nechama is ready to leave. She's sitting in her seat, and Mama speaks to her through the window. Mama lifts me up to say goodbye, too. Nechama waves goodbye to us and Mama says, "We may never see her again."

Mama's crying.

Sometimes I still think about my little baby sister, Malka. She looked just like a baby Shirley Temple, with her chubby, round face and curly blonde hair. And she was so sweet. Nothing like Rosa!

When Malka was learning to walk, I loved to watch her waddle around the apartment and see her yellow curls shake with every tiny footstep. Malka means queen, and my sister Malka's shiny golden ringlets were like a crown.

One night, Malka got a horrible earache. She cried all night long. Mama didn't get any sleep, and she didn't go to work the next morning. Even I woke up in the middle of the night because Malka was crying so loudly. Mama took Malka to the clinic and came home with medicine. But it didn't help. Malka still had a high fever and she kept crying. Mama walked around the room with her, bouncing her and singing to her. I tried to make Malka laugh, but she wouldn't even look at me.

Then pus started coming out of Malka's ears, and she started screaming. Finally, Mama asked a neighbor to bring the Yiddish folk doctor. But when he tried to look into Malka's ears, she shrieked even louder. She wouldn't let him touch her, so he sang:

> "*hostenyu, costenyu,*"
> *hostenyu, costenyu,*"

He chanted the Yiddish words for hocus-pocus over and over again. But Malka kept crying and pulling her ears. Then he recited some other prayers:

"hosti-costi, leben zolsti,"

he sang in Yiddish, meaning, "you will live a long life."

Finally, Mama took Malka to the hospital. She was gone a very long time. When she came home, she just said that one horrible word, "scarletina." Nobody had to tell me that scarletina means death. My beautiful baby sister Malka, who I loved so much, was going to die! I started crying, too.

But Mama said she would do anything to save Malka's life. So she went back to the hospital and asked the nurse what she would like for a gift.

"That's the only way to get things done," she told Father.

The nurse wanted shoes with pigskin soles, which were very comfortable, but also very expensive.

"I don't know where we're going to get the money," said Mama, but she went out and bought the pigskin shoes for the nurse. For days, Mama stayed at the hospital at Malka's side.

But a few days later she came home crying. "The world has turned black all around me," she said.

Father didn't say anything, but he was crying, too.

Mama tore her sweater and cut off a piece of her hair from the front of her head. She put a black cloth over the mirror in the salon.

A man came from the hospital to post a "quarantine" sign on our front door.

Our family sat *shiva*—the seven days of mourning—for my beautiful baby sister, Malka, who was only two years old! I never felt so sad before, and I'm sad whenever I remember it.

Once in a while, since Malka died, Mama hugs me and sits me on her knees. I love these times, and I wish she would do it more often, but Mama is always busy with something or other.

Then one day, she says, "Come, Sonya. I think you're old enough to learn how to darn socks."

Like all clothes, socks are very expensive. So, when our socks have holes in them, Mama darns them on a darning "mushroom." It's a small, round piece of wood with a long wooden handle. Mama pushes the small round part of the "mushroom" into the heel of the sock and holds on to the end of the handle. Taking a threaded needle, she shows me how to weave a new piece of material where the hole is. You have to go back and forth over and over again.

I watch for a long time, and then I try it, but it's very hard for me. My darning doesn't come out very well, so Mama fixes it.

"From now on," she tells me, "you can help me every time I darn the socks."

It's a challenge and I enjoy doing it, even though I don't do it well. I'm proud that Mama lets me help her.

"Zoshka, tell us a story!" I beg. "Rosa and I have nothing to do at home. We're bored!"

So Zoshka tells us the story of the two little cats:

26

Two little cats,
One skinny, one fat.
Two little cats,
One playful, one sad.

The happy cat was called Yi-aow
She was white and fat
She fell into a pot of milk
And she was very glad.
"Yi-aow! Yi-aow! What a lucky cat!"
"To fall into the milk like that!"
"Now I'll have all the milk I want!"
"Yi-aow, yi-aow and yum-yum-yum!"

But the skinny cat
Was black and sad.
He, too, fell into a pot of milk.
"Ni-aow, ni-aow he wailed and cried"
"I'd rather be anywhere but inside
This wet and sticky, very icky
Glop!"

I listen to Zoshka and afterward, I repeat the rhymes over and over to myself. But stupid Rosa picks up a brush and walks away, brushing her hair, while Zoshka is right in the middle of the story. What a stupid-head!

Late at night, when they think I'm asleep, Mama and Father talk to each other in Yiddish. One night, I hear Mama say, "We have to do something about Zissel. She fights with Rosa all of the time, and Zoshka complains about it. She even slaps them sometimes. And what's worse, Zissel sits around the house listening to

27

Zoshka's nonsense stories and peeling potatoes all day," Mama tells Father. "Imagine that— peeling potatoes! And you should hear some of the things Zoshka tells her: she sings love stories about Cossacks and young women—well, at least Zissel doesn't understand them! But those worthless fairy tales Zoshka tells her— they're full of Babayaga the witch, and monsters and death! Sometimes she's so scared she goes around checking the windows to make sure they're locked before she goes to bed at night! I wish we had the money to send her to a private kindergarten."

"How much does it cost?" Father asks.

"Too much!" says Mama.

They talk for a long time, and I fall asleep listening to them.

Not long after that, Mama takes me to a private kindergarten in the neighborhood.

"Now you won't have to be bored at home any more," she tells me.

I know she doesn't want me peeling potatoes with Zoshka, and listening to Zoshka's songs and stories all day long. And she doesn't like it when I play with the children in Kleparov, either.

"Those are silly stories and silly games," she tells me. "You need to *learn* something! Education is very important!"

So she takes me to a kindergarten where we play with clay and we learn to sew and do other handicrafts. The kindergarten teachers take us on trips, and they have a summer camp for us. They give us lunch there, too. Now, I'm never bored anymore. I like going to kindergarten and I especially love the teachers!

But, today, when Mama came to take me home, she said, "Sonya, take everything out of your locker and come home with me. We don't have enough money for you to continue here. It's just too expensive."

I left without saying goodbye to anybody, because I felt so ashamed and so sad.

One Sunday Zoshka takes me to visit Michalova, and her son, Kazhik, comes in by himself. He's walking with a limp. He staggers around the apartment, talking loudly and saying crazy things. He's drinking vodka straight from a bottle. It scares me to see him. I've never seen anybody act like that before.

"Look at you!" screams Michalova. "It's the middle of the day, and you're already drunk!"

It scares me even more to hear Michalova yell at him—nobody yells like that in our house! And Kazhik yells right back at her!

"You stupid bitch," he yells. And he says some other words that I don't understand.

"Put the bottle down and stop drinking!" Michalova screams at him, again and again, and "Stop talking like a maniac!"

"No, *you* stop talking like an old woman," he shouts, taking another gulp from the bottle. "Stupid bitch."

I start to shake. He's screaming and cursing at his own mother! What if he hits her? Maybe he's going to yell at me, too, or try to hit me! Terrified, I grab a handful of Zoshka's skirt and hide behind her, so that he can't see me.

Michalova goes over to Kazhik, takes his arm, and talks to him quietly in a very sweet tone of voice. "Look, Kazhik, it isn't doing you

29

any good to drink any more of that. You've already had enough. Why don't you give me the bottle? I'll put it away for you. You can have it back, later."

I peek out from behind Zoshka's skirt and see Kazhik swat at Michalova's hand. She walks away in a hurry.

When I glance at her face, she looks scared, too.

Michalova keeps on trying to talk to Kazhik, but he answers by shouting and cursing at her. By that time, I'm shaking very hard.

Finally, Kazhik slams the bottle down on the kitchen table and it breaks. Shattered glass falls on the floor, but nobody pays any attention. Waving the jagged end of the bottle in the air, Kazhik runs after his mother, screaming words I don't understand. He catches up with her and cuts her forehead with the broken bottle, and she screams, "You lousy good-for-nothing!" And she says something else, too—some words I don't understand.

When I see the blood gushing from her head I feel like I can't breathe, and I almost fall down. Zoshka sits me in a chair and gives me a glass of water to drink while she takes care of Michalova's wound. Meanwhile, Kazhik runs out of the apartment, still screaming and cursing. Zoshka wraps Michalova's head in strips of white cloth, and Michalova sits in a chair, sobbing, for a long time.

Later, Zoshka has to carry me all the way home. I'm trembling from head to toe, still worried that Kazhik might come back. Zoshka puts me straight to bed, and I stay there until the next morning. I'm thinking that I never want to go back to Michalova's again!

There are twenty-two apartments in our building, and all the families are Jewish. Some have children close to my age or a little older, but most of them have grown-up children. We all play together in the courtyard, but I don't have any close friends among them.

Our family lives on the first floor, so I can easily run out to play in the courtyard whenever I hear children's voices outside. Our front door faces the Teppers, and I try to go in and out very fast, so I can stay away from Ulek, who always bothers me. He has a sister my age who I like to play with, but I never go into their apartment because I'm afraid of Ulek. He's a big bully!

When I was little, Mama used to take me to visit the neighbors because she's friends with everybody. But now I go by myself. I've been in most of the apartments in our building at some time or other.

The oldest couple in the building is the Druckers. Mr. Drucker looks younger than his wife does, but he's completely bald. He buys the most fashionable hats to cover his head, and he also wears very stylish suits. One of his legs is shorter than the other, and he has a special shoe with a very thick sole. Even so, he walks with a limp. Mr. and Mrs. Drucker live in a tiny, one-room apartment off the courtyard. They have no children, and they're both very kind to me.

Sometimes I go to the Lempels on the third floor to play with their daughter, Adela. Adela

31

is a teenager, but you wouldn't know it to look at her. She's retarded and all she says are nonsense words. Mrs. Lempel is the only one who can understand what she means. Adela has a very big head and she's also very fat. She's tall like her father and her older brother. She walks around half-naked, even in winter, and she pees on the floor. Mrs. Lempel cuts her hair very short and it stands out from her head like porcupine quills, so she looks very strange.

Mama says the only place Adela could live in, other than her own home, is an institution. But Mrs. Lempel won't let anyone send her away, so she takes care of Adela herself. Adela has so many problems that Mrs. Lempel never takes her out of the building. Mr. Lempel built her a special bed—one she can't fall out of when she rolls over in her sleep. Mrs. Lempel is always very nice to me when I visit—which isn't too often—but sometimes on a rainy day when I have nothing to do and I'm feeling bored, I go upstairs to play with Adela. It's better than staying at home and fighting with Rosa.

Mr. Goldberg lives upstairs with his family. He has a son and a daughter. They're a lot older than I am and I never play with them. Mr. Lanzberg is a lawyer, and he lives upstairs with his sister. Neither Mr. Lanzberg nor his sister have ever been married, and neither of them has any children.

In a corner of our courtyard there's a middle-aged couple named Jijo, and Jijova (meaning "Jijo's wife"). Mama says they're Serbians. Jijo is very dark-skinned and also very short. The top of his head is completely bald, but he has a

32

lot of black hair all around his face. And he has a thick, black moustache that reaches from ear to ear, curling up at the ends. Whenever he smiles, it looks as if his moustache is standing up and smiling, too! And he smiles all the time. He looks like a magical character from a fairy tale.

His wife, Jijova, speaks very fast, and her Polish is even worse than Father's. It's hard to understand her, but she's always very nice to me, and we're good friends. Mama is also friendly with Jijo and Jijova, but I go there to visit on my own.

Jijo and Jijova live in a tiny one-room hut made of wood and covered with mud. They're even poorer than we are. They were living here before my family moved into the building, and Mama thinks they built their house by themselves.

Their room has a table and chairs, and a bed piled high with quilts and pillows. The walls are completely covered with paintings of Jesus: Jesus carrying the Cross, Jesus with his disciples, Jesus nailed to the Cross, and Mary holding the infant Jesus. I like to look at the pictures and ask about them. Jijova is always happy to tell me the stories of Jesus. I like those stories very much.

Jijo and Jijova always seem happy to see me. Jijo pats me on the head and he smiles from ear to ear whenever he sees me coming. Sometimes Jijova is sewing when I come to visit and she hands me the needle and asks me to help her. She knows I can thread a needle because I've told her that Mama taught me to darn old socks on a darning "mushroom."

"How wonderful you come just now," says Jijova, as I walk in the door. "I sit here and try to thread this needle a whole hour!"

Jijova is a wonderful cook, and she always gives me something to taste when I come to visit. She also lets me peel potatoes with her, which makes me feel very important and grown up.

Jijo and Jijova have no children of their own, and they take in the babies of unmarried women. They raise the babies until they're a few years old. I like to play with the babies. Mama says that Jijo and Jijova get paid by the Church to raise them.

Jijo has a horse and cart—the kind called a "ladder wagon." He earns money by carrying heavy loads for people. Jijo keeps the horse in a small stable next to their hut. On a small piece of land next to the stable, Jijova plants corn to feed the horse, and also sunflowers and beets, and other vegetables.

Mama is good friends with Jijo and Jijova, and sometimes she gives them free bread and rolls for the babies. I know that Jijo sometimes helps Mama transport the heavy loaves of bread on his ladder wagon. But they seem more like friends than business partners.

The apartments in our building don't have their own toilets—instead, we have a communal toilet on each floor. Piotrova ("Piotr's wife"), a Gentile woman, cleans the stairway and the toilets in our apartment building.

Piotrova lives in a small apartment very near our building, with her husband, Piotr, and their two children. They're from the Ukraine. Her daughter is my age and we sometimes play together. She speaks Polish, but we also speak Ukrainian to each other when we play. Piotrova's younger son plays with the children in our building, too.

My parents each have brothers and sisters, and some of them have children. But they live far away and it's expensive to travel, so we see them mainly at weddings and funerals. Both of Mama's sisters—Devorah and Nechama—went to live in Palestine when I was little.

Mama's uncle, Abraham Freiheiter, introduced my mother to my father, and Mama has a close relationship with him. Uncle Abraham owns a large bakery. He lives with his family in a beautiful neighborhood in Lvov. They're very rich. He had four sons and two daughters with his first wife, Malka, but she got sick and died when she was very young. Uncle Abraham got married again, and his new wife is much younger than he is. Father and Mama went to their wedding. I almost never see them, but Mama walks across town to visit them sometimes. She always comes home with a big package of goodies for us.

Mama's family is from Rava Russka, a small town on the Ukrainian border. It's a long bus ride from Lvov. Mama says it's a very pretty town, with a lot of Jews. Mama's brother, Michael, lives there with his wife. He has a shop where he sells kitchenwares.

35

Michael is younger than my mother. He's religious, so he wears a small *tallit* (a prayer shawl) under his shirt, with the fringe sticking out, and he has a long black beard. Like most of the Jews in Poland, he wears a white shirt and a black suit. Michael and his wife, Sarah, can't have children, and it makes them very sad. So Sarah invites me to come and visit them. Mama says okay, because I'm not in school yet, and I'm very bored at home.

So Sarah takes me home with her, by bus, to Rava Russka.

I love riding the bus and looking at all the trees. I tell Aunt Sarah, "This looks just like the forest that Heidi went to!"

Sarah takes me for a walk around the town, and we visit the huge outdoor market—it's just as big as the one Mama takes me to! Then we go to Uncle Michael's shop and I look at all the pots and pans, and dishes and bowls. He's got more pots and pans than I've ever seen.

Sarah takes me to visit Mama's family. Aunt Toby is a young widow with two sons. They're very poor and they live in a small, dark, gloomy house that smells of mildew. It's nothing like Sarah and Michael's house, which is big and beautiful. In Sarah and Michael's house, the walls are covered with family portraits. Sarah tells me about each one of them.

I like being in Rava Russka, but tonight, I can't fall asleep. I've never been away from home before. The portraits on the walls look scary in the dark. I'm afraid that the people will come down off the walls and do terrible things to me during the middle of the night! I cry for

Mama and I can't sleep at all. So the next morning, Aunt Sarah takes me back home.

School Days

It's the happiest day of my life. Over the summer I turned seven, and I'm starting school today! Finally, finally, I'm going to learn how to read. Then I'll read all the fairy tales in the whole world, and I'll read them over and over again, as many times as I like!

On the first day of school, Zoshka takes me by the hand and we walk very, very slowly to the Lenartovich School. It's far from our street. I wave to Mama, and she waves back to me. She's still going around to the grocery shops in our neighborhood with her baskets of bread.

The next day, Mama walks me to school. "I'll finish selling the bread later," she tells me.

At first, either Zoshka or Mama walks me to school every day. Then, in the middle of the second week, I decide, "I can walk there by myself, now. I'm all grown up!"

It's a good thing I speak Polish so well. That's the language we study in. And the kids in the playground ask me to join in their games at recess. They don't ask the other Jewish children, whose Polish sounds more like Yiddish. Everybody tells me that I speak Polish with a Ukrainian accent. I even look like the Ukrainian kids in my school, with my dark eyes and dark hair.

And I can speak Ukrainian with them, too. The Ukrainians speak their own language, which is just like Russian. And sometimes, the Gentile kids invite me home after school to play with them. It's easy to make friends in school!

But even though I look Ukrainian, everybody knows I'm Jewish. After all, Sonya Hebenstreit is a Jewish name. And some of the Polish children call me *"Zhydouvka!"*—"dirty Jew"— and speak to me in a nasty tone of voice. Mama says, "Don't pay any attention to them. Just ignore them and study." But I've never been treated like this before, and I'm very hurt by it.

We Jews are in a "special" status at school. They take us out of the regular classes and give us religious lessons once or twice a week, while the Gentile children are studying their Bible— The New Testament.

There's a scout organization that all the children belong to—all except the Jewish children. The scouts have uniforms with the scouting emblem on them, which Jews are not permitted to wear. And when the scouts go on trips, we Jews are forbidden to go with them. I would love to be a scout, to wear the uniform and join in the special activities, but Mama says, "Never mind. There are other things for you to do. It's not so important."

But even Jews are allowed to wear the school uniform and the matching beret. The girls' uniform is a plain, dark apron that we wear over our own clothing. It ties in the back. I'm very proud to wear my uniform. I love the way it looks on me, and it makes me feel like one of the "regular" kids in school.

40

I've never really thought about being a Jew before, but now I'm thinking about it a lot.

My parents aren't religious, but they keep the Jewish traditions and celebrate the holidays, and Father and Mama never work on Saturdays.

Shabbat and holidays are the only times we all sit down and eat together. On regular days, we all eat separately, whenever we're hungry. But on *Shabbat*, Mama clears the kitchen table and spreads a white tablecloth over it. She has special candlesticks that she uses on *Shabbat* and holidays.

On ordinary days, Zoshka prepares the meals. But every Thursday, Mama goes to the outdoor market to buy the special foods for our *Shabbat* dinner. Then she comes home and she cooks our *Shabbat* meal herself. Sometimes she buys fish, sometimes a chicken or a goose, and sometimes beef. She always buys fresh celery and other vegetables to make soup. We have fish or chicken or meat every *Shabbat* and on holidays, but we never eat meat during the middle of the week.

We have a sign in the kitchen, written in Polish, which says, "Where there are seven cooks, there is nothing to eat!" So on Fridays and holidays, Mama takes over the kitchen and she prepares all of the traditional foods.

Every week, Mama makes *lokschen*—the wonderful noodles for the chicken soup. It's a lot of work. First, she kneads the dough and rolls it, which takes a long time. Then she lets the dough stand while she prepares the chicken or the fish. If we're having beef, she

41

salts it on a special platter, to make it kosher. She lets the meat stand for a few hours until all of the blood drips out. Then she washes the blood off the meat before she cooks it.

She doesn't let me help her with the cooking, but I like to watch. What seems like hard work for Zoshka and Mama looks like good fun to me.

On Passover, Mama always buys a goose to make a special dish for our feast—the *seder*. This dish is filled with bits of goose meat and pieces of skin, and it's one of the most delicious dishes I can think of. I could eat it every day! Mama also buys beets for Passover, to make the holiday *borscht* that symbolizes the blood spilled during the Egyptian plagues.

Father goes to synagogue every Saturday morning and on holidays. He takes his Bible, his *kippa*, his *tallit* and *tefelli* —the skullcap, prayer shawl and prayer bands—and carries them under his arm. He only puts them on when he gets inside the synagogue.

Once I went to synagogue with Father on a Saturday. The synagogue was just a small room with no special decorations. I couldn't help noticing how different it was from the fancy, beautiful churches I had seen. It wasn't any fun there because the men don't do anything but pray, so I never wanted to go back.

On Saturdays, Mama sits down at the kitchen table to do the bookkeeping. How much money did she spend, and what did she spend it on? Who owes us money? When will they pay us? She locks the front door, so that none of the neighbors will walk in and see her. Jews are not supposed to write on Saturdays.

42

Hanuka comes around Christmastime. On *Hanuka*, Rosa and I sing the special holiday songs and Father gives us *Hanuka gelt*—a small amount of money. We light candles every night in the *Menora*—the special *Hanuka* candelabra. Mama puts the *Menora* on the windowsill until all the candles burn out. It's very pretty.

Passover is in the spring, and we always have the special Passover feast in our own apartment with just our family. Father sits at the head of the table, dressed in his best clothes and wearing the *kippa* on his head. He looks like a king. He reads to us from the *Haggada*, the story of Passover, in Hebrew. At Passover, Rosa and I ask the "four questions," in Hebrew. That's the children's part in the Passover ceremony. Father and Mama help us a lot, because we don't know Hebrew. We also act out the ten plagues and sing the traditional Passover song—"*Dayenu*." It's fun, even though we don't understand the words.

After I start going to school, I learn more about the holidays from the lessons in religion that we have every week.

When I go to school, I bring a sandwich for a snack every day. I take thick slices of bread, spread with a delicious filling. My favorite is *gribenes,* a paste made from chopped goose meat fried with onions. Eating a sandwich like that is like eating a whole meal.

In school, there's a group of Gentile orphans who come from the orphanage on the other side of Lvov. They wear uniforms that are different from ours, and they never bring food

43

with them to school. Two of the orphan boys are in my class. I can't help but notice how they stare at my sandwiches. I can see how hungry they are. One day I asked them, "Do you want a sandwich?" Of course they nodded, "Yes." So now, I bring three sandwiches to school every day—one for each of us.

I can't think of anything worse than being an orphan!

Mr. and Mrs. Drucker are the only elderly couple in the building. Mrs. Drucker likes to talk to me, and she invites me into her apartment whenever she sees me. Nowadays, if I run into her after school, she says, "Let me look at you." She likes to guess what kind of day I had at school.

"Today you had a good day," she says. "You got good marks on your test."

"How did you know?" I ask her.

"It's written on your forehead," she answers me. "But only I know how to read it!"

If I have a bad day at school, I avoid going near the door of their apartment all afternoon. But the next time I see her, Mrs. Drucker tells me, "Yesterday you had a bad day."

She's always right, and I'm amazed. How can she read my forehead?

One Sunday, Mama says, "Let's go to an art exhibit. There's something special—paintings by Jan Matejko. He's one of the most famous Polish artists of our time. Now that you're in school, you should learn about culture."

The exhibit has Matejko's World War One paintings. They're huge pictures with dozens of
44

scenes from the war. The paintings are full of horses and soldiers in uniform, waving their swords. They're very violent, with wounded soldiers and lots of blood. Even the horses are wounded, and one horse is falling on top of the wounded soldiers and crushing them. You can see every detail in the faces of the horses, and they look terrified.

The paintings are arranged in a circle, surrounding the viewers. That makes me feel as if I'm really there.

"Mama, it feels like we're inside the battlefield. It's exciting but also very scary."

"You have the most overactive imagination of anybody I know!" Mama says. "Who knows? Maybe you'll grow up to be a writer?"

I think about that, but I'd rather read books and listen to stories than write. I want to read everything!

It's my second year in school, and now I can read all by myself! By the time I get home from school in the afternoon, Mama is home, too.

"Come Sonya, she says one afternoon. "I have a nice surprise for you."

Together we walk to a private library in our neighborhood, a few short blocks from home. The librarian is a Jewish man, and the library is only for Jews.

"Do you like to read?" the librarian asks me.

"Oh, I love books!" I answer.

Mama smiles proudly.

"What do you like best?" he asks me.

"Fairy tales!"

And the librarian takes me to the special section that has short stories. I've never seen so many books of short stories before. There's no library at school.

"Oh, I want to read everything you have here!" I tell him.

"That sounds like a very good idea to me," he answers in a serious tone of voice.

"You can borrow three books at a time. When you return them, you can have another three."

"How many times a week can I come here?"

"As often as you like."

"Oh, Mama, this is wonderful!" I say, on the way home.

"I'm glad you're so happy," she tells me.

"But remember, it costs a lot of money to be a member of the library, so make good use of it."

"I will!" I promise.

And I do. I go there to exchange books at least once a week—sometimes twice. I take out three books at a time, and I usually start reading one of them while I'm walking home.

Whenever I go there, the librarian asks me about what I've read, and he helps me select new books. I'm reading the Grimm Brothers stories and Hans Christian Andersen, and Polish fairy tales, too. Some of them are stories that Zoshka has already told me, but I'm happy to read them to myself, even if I know them already.

Now that I know how to read, I'm never bored or lonely anymore, even if Zoshka is busy. At home, I spend a lot of time reading. I'm going to read everything in the library!

46

My favorite story is "The Singing Bird, the Talking Tree and the Golden Spring." It always makes me feel hopeful about life. The story begins with an old man sitting at the side of a road:

Many people passed him by, but nobody paid any attention to him, except for one ragged young man. When the youth saw the old man, he stopped and asked, "Is there anything I can do to help you?"

"You're very kind," said the old man. "Please help me pick up my heavy bundle."
When the youth had done this, the old man said, "Thank you. Now I can manage on my own. But I will give you a ball. You would do well to follow this ball wherever it may lead you."
The old man disappeared, and the ball started to sing:

Round and round, hold your ground,
The ball of life swirls round and round!

When the youth held the ball up to his ears, he heard voices coming from it. They told him the ball would lead him to the greatest wonder of the world: the Golden Spring. He must simply follow the directions of the Singing Bird and the Talking Tree, and pay no attention to the many temptations along the way.

Round and round, hold your ground,
The ball of life swirls round and round!

47

*The young man passed a tavern where peo-
ple were laughing, singing, and dancing merrily.*

"Come join us!" they called to him.

"The beer is free and there's plenty of it!"

*The young man was hot and thirsty. He
would have liked very much to drink. But the
Singing Bird sang to him,*

> *"Don't be tempted, don't give in.
> Hold your ground and you will win!"*

*So he walked by the tavern without stopping
there.*

> *Round and round, hold your ground,
> The ball of life swirls round and round!*

*Later that day, the youth passed a beautiful
young woman who was singing a song of love.*

*"Come, listen to my song," she said, "and
rest awhile with me." The youth was tired, and
he would have liked to sit down, but the Talking
Tree told him, "Keep walking! You will hear her
beautiful voice and her enchanting song, but
don't turn around!"*

*So he walked past the young woman with-
out stopping.*

*On and on he went, passing many exciting
scenes and many chances for adventure. But
every time he was tempted, the Singing Bird
and the Talking Tree put him back on the path to
the Golden Spring. Finally, the youth arrived at
the enchanted land. There, he saw piles upon
piles of stones that were able to talk. They told
him they had once been human beings and had
committed suicide because they had lost all*

48

hope. They were supposed to follow the directions of the Singing Bird and the Talking Tree, but they had allowed themselves to be tempted by other voices. The youth, unlike the speaking stones, had followed the path shown to him by the Singing Bird and the Talking Tree. He had managed to ignore all of the temptations along the way and to overcome all of the difficulties. As he gazed upon the beautiful waters of the golden spring, a voice spoke to him, saying, "The golden spring contains a magical treasure. If you splash its waters on the lifeless stones, they will come back to life." The youth did this and to his delight, the stones immediately started to cry out, "We're alive! We're alive!" And all of their troubles were over.

Round and round, hold your ground,
The ball of life swirls round and round!

No matter how many times I read it, this story always fills me with happiness and hope. It always has the same happy ending, even though the problems the youth has on his way to the enchanted land are sometimes different from one version to another. Sometimes the youth meets beautiful women, other times witches. Sometimes he's tempted to get drunk, other times to steal from people, but he never pays attention to these things. The singing bird and the talking tree are his guides. I never get tired of reading it, especially at night. Afterward, I feel happy enough to go to sleep and dream sweet dreams all night long.

But there are many stories with sad endings, too. At the library, I take out a book of Andersen's stories and I read "The Little Match Girl." It's about a little girl from a very poor family in Denmark. The girl is too poor to go to school. Instead, she walks around the streets, selling matches. One New Year's Eve, when everybody in the streets is rushing off to New Year's Eve parties, the little match girl is walking around, trying to sell her matches. At home, it's very cold, and her father is in a mean and nasty mood, because he has no money for food. He tells her not to come home until she's sold all of the matches. But everybody is rushing off to their parties, and nobody even looks at her. She sits down to rest and she lights one of the matches to warm her hands. In the flames, she sees her grandmother's face and she remembers how kind her grandmother was to her. When the flame goes out, she decides to light another match, and then another one. Each time, she sees her grandmother's face and it makes her feel better. Finally, she lights all of the matches at once, and she smiles to see her grandmother beckoning to her. The next morning, on the first day of the New Year, they find her frozen body in the street, with the smile still on her face.

I shiver when I read that story, and I look for a different version—one that ends happily. I know there can be different versions of stories, but I never find a version of "The Little Match Girl" with a happy ending.

All the kids at school have memory scrapbooks, and I want one, too.

"I'll buy one for your birthday," says Mama, and she buys me a memory scrapbook when I turn nine, on June 16th.

All summer long, I go around the neighborhood, asking my friends from school to sign my memory book.

When we go back to school, all of my classmates sign it, and they ask me to sign theirs. Even the principal of my school signs it and draws pretty designs all around what she writes:

If you want to be something in life,
You must study
So that you won't get lost
In the crowd.
Education is the key to power!

Now I really feel like I belong!

Rosa is in school now, too. And she's still just as annoying as ever! When Mama buys our notebooks, she tells us not to waste paper because notebooks are very expensive. So I always make sure to cover the whole side of every page of my notebook. But Rosa writes one or two words and goes on to the next page. She makes me furious! Will she ever learn to do anything right?

Mama says now that I know how to read Polish, it's time I started learning German.
"The Germans have the greatest culture and civilization in Europe," she tells me. "You should be able to read their language, so you can take out books from the library in German. You should start reading great literature while you're still young," she says. "Your father and I

51

never had a chance to get an education, but we're going to give you every opportunity to get ahead in life."

So she hires a private tutor to teach me German at home. He's an older man who lives in our neighborhood. He tells me that German sounds a lot like Yiddish, but Yiddish is written in Hebrew letters. We don't study the letters, just the words. And he's right—it sounds a lot like Yiddish, so it's easy.

I'm in third grade now, and our class is putting on a play for Polish Independence Day—the 3rd of May. My teacher tells us, "Everyone will be in the play, and you'll all wear costumes on stage."

The children are excited. We all want to wear costumes!

And we learn a special song for the play. It's by a famous Polish poet. It goes like this:

"Who are you, my little one?"
"I'm proud to be a Polish son!"
"And what's that eagle on your chest?"
"It's the sign that we're the best!"
"What place do you call your home?"
"Poland is the land I roam."
"What does Poland mean to you?"
"For Poland, anything I'd do!"
"Would you protect her if you could?"
"With my body and my blood!"
"And are you ready for a war?"
"I'll defend Poland with my sword!"
"What are you willing to give in strife?"
"For Poland, I'd give up my life!"

I learn the song with the rest of the children and I sing it at home and at school. I feel very patriotic, and I feel that I really belong here. I'll never forget the words.

Our teacher tells us, "I've given everybody in the class something to say. The children with a good memory and the ones who speak well in front of the class will get big parts. The others will get smaller parts. But you each have to know your part by heart, so you'll have to work hard and memorize it!"

She knows I'm a good student, so she gives me an important role: I'm going to be a soldier in the Polish cavalry.

I go home to practice my lines, and I tell Zoshka all about it. I read her my lines and I practice them at home every day, until I know them by heart. I sing her the Polish patriot's song, too.

On the day of the play, I get dressed up in my costume, a Polish cavalry uniform. All the pupils, the teachers, and the principal go into the auditorium where the play is going to be performed. Many parents are in the audience, too, but not mine. Father is at home, sleeping, of course. I don't know where Mama is.

The play is about to begin, and I'm standing close to the stage. Just then, one of the Gentile children in my class, whose father is with him, points me out to his father. The man runs up to me and shouts, "Just a minute! You're a Jew! You can't be allowed to dirty the uniform of a Polish soldier!" He tries to block my way, so that I can't go up to the stage.

When I hear him say that I'm "dirtying" the uniform of a Polish officer, I start to sob hys-

53

terically. I don't know what to do. My teacher sees what is happening and rushes over to my side. Without saying a word, she stands between this man and me and pushes me up onto the stage. With tears streaming down my face, I stand in front of the whole school and recite the lines that I've studied so carefully and with so much enthusiasm.

After the play, I go home and tell Mama what happened. I'm still crying.

"Sonya," she says, trying to calm me down, "You shouldn't pay so much attention to nasty people who say ugly things about Jews. This is the way things are at school, and it's the same way everywhere. You have to learn to live with it," she tells me.

But how can I learn to live with people calling me "*Zhydouvka!*" and telling me that I'm dirty? In our home, we each take a bath every Friday, before *Shabbat*. Why do they say Jews are dirty? I'm not dirty!

Back at school, my teacher doesn't say anything about what happened. I sit in class very quietly, and I don't say anything about it, either. I don't even raise my hand in class for the rest of the week.

I'd like to forget all about what happened, but somebody in the audience took a photograph of me standing on stage and reciting my part. Somebody—I don't know who it was—gave the photo to my parents, and Mama sent a copy to her sisters Devorah and Nechama in the Holy Land. She also put a copy in our family photo album. So now I have to see it and remember what happened every time I open the album!

54

Sonia in a Polish Cavalry Costume

We have a radio detektor* on the wall in the kitchen. Mama listens to it more and more all the time, and I sit next to her, trying to understand what they're talking about. They talk a lot about Germany and Czechoslovakia and the Sudetenland. I know those places are in Europe somewhere, but I'm not sure where. They seem very far away. I don't understand what they're talking about, but I hear them

---

* **An Early Radio**
In 1939, news traveled slowly. Information was relayed via telegraph, not by satellite or telephone or through the Internet. And mail went by train or boat, not airplane.

Many families in Lvov had a "radio-detektor"—an early version of a radio, with a crystal set inside a cone. In order to tune into the radio station, one took a metal stick and pressed the crystal.

talking about the same places every time Mama turns on the radio detektor.

I also hear Mama talking about the war with Father, and with her friends. She's furious with England and France and she calls them "prostitutes." She says they "sold" Czechoslovakia. I don't understand what she's talking about, but I can see that she's very angry. I ask her about the news, and she tells me, "There's a war in Europe, and it's getting bigger and worse day by day. If the war comes to Poland, it could be very bad for the Jews."

The Russian Occupation[*]

Lvov is in the southeastern corner of Poland, on the Ukrainian border. That area of Poland— known as "Galicia"—changed hands many times throughout history. On August 23rd, 1939, according to the Molotov-Ribbentrop Pact, Western Poland was taken over by the Germans, and Eastern Poland was partitioned to the Russians. That September, the Russian army entered Eastern Poland. Tens of thousands of Jews fled from the German army into Lvov, doubling the Jewish population of Lvov.

---

[*] Lvov: 1939
On September 17, 1939, the Russians entered Lvov.
At that time, the Jewish population of Lvov was 110,000.
This was about one third of the population of the city's 340,000 residents. The Jews represented a cross-section of Poland: a few were wealthy, but most were poverty-stricken because of the Great Depression.

Map of Molotov Ribbentrop Pact

Zoshka is shaking me very hard.

"Sonya, Rosa, wake up, wake up! The war has begun!" Her voice is very nervous and upset.

But Rosa and I jump out of bed, yelling, "Hooray! Finally, we're going to see some action!"

"This is nothing to be happy about!" Zoshka yells at us.

But summer vacation is long and boring, with nothing to do at home. A war sounds like something exciting.

Zoshka is mad at us all day long, and we try to keep out of her way. That day she slaps us very hard whenever we annoy her.

58

A few days later, the sound of sirens wakes us up. Mama must be out working. Father isn't home, either.

Zoshka rushes into the back room and grabs Rosa and me.

"Hurry!" she shouts at us. "We have to get out of here."

"Okay," I say, sleepily. "I'll get dressed in a minute."

"No!" she screams. "Come in your pajamas. There's no time to get dressed!"

She pulls the blankets off us, forces us out of bed, and drags us behind her, walking as fast as she can.

We meet the other neighbors in the court-yard. Everyone is running around the corner to the bomb shelter in the basement.

Nobody speaks as we sit there, wondering what's going to happen next. Suddenly, there's an explosion. It sounds like it's just outside the door. The walls begin to shake and the ceiling lamp sways. All the babies are crying and I'm too scared to move. Nobody knows what's going to happen now. It seems like hours are pass-ing, and we sit there in silence, afraid to make any noise. Maybe the soldiers are right outside the door? The only sounds I hear are the babies crying and their mothers shushing them. We sit there for what feels like a whole day. Finally, someone knocks on the door to tell us that the air raid is over. We can go home now. Everyone says we were lucky that nobody got hurt.

Sitting in the crowded shelter, looking at the fear on our neighbors' faces, Rosa and I had learned very quickly why Zoshka and the other adults were so terrified of the war. Walking back home, Rosa and I agree, "It's better to be bored all summer than to be in a war!"

But just two weeks later, the war is over. We hear on the radio detektor that the Polish army—a cavalry on horseback—has surrendered to the German army, with its huge tanks. The Germans and the Russians have split Poland in two. Our area belongs to the Russians now. Mama says that's too bad because the Germans have the best culture. "Their art, their music and their theater are the best in Europe," she tells me.

I go out into the street with Mama to watch the Russian soldiers march by. Mama holds my hand as the soldiers file past us through our neighborhood. I'm amazed when I see their faces.

"Mama, look! They don't have blond hair and fair skin, or broad shoulders. And look how short they are!"

The Russians don't look anything like what I was expecting. Mama says that some of them are from the Mongolian or Eastern regions of the Soviet Union, so they have dark skin and slanted eyes.

None of the grown-ups seem to be afraid of the Russian soldiers, so I'm not scared, either. The soldiers just march by us, without saying or doing anything.

I'm happy to go back to school. I love to study and I like to play with the children I meet there. Not much is different in school, except that now we study Russian a few times a week.

Russian is easy for me; it's just like Ukrainian, and I learn it quickly.

And now there are no more religious lessons. In fact, the Russians don't let us talk about God at all.

"God is a lie!" they tell us.

I don't mind, but I can see that the Gentile kids don't like hearing that.

In some ways, I like the Russians. Mama says they never call Jews *"Zhyd"*—dirty Jew. They're very fair to us, she tells me.

It's a cold, snowy winter evening, and Zoshka tells me that tonight I have to sleep in her bed in the kitchen, because Mama is "sick." This is something that has never happened before. Mama never gets sick! I squirm around in Zoshka's bed, feeling miserable. I can't fall asleep, and Mama is groaning loudly. I'm worried.

"Is it scarletina?" I ask Zoshka.

"Oh, no!" she says, smiling, "Nothing like that. Everything is going to be all right."

Suddenly, in the middle of the night, in comes a woman who I recognize from the neighborhood. She's the midwife, and she carries a big bag of equipment into Mama's room. What's she doing here? She's the one who helps women who are having babies. But she also comes sometimes when people are sick, especially babies.

Zoshka comes into the kitchen and heats a great big vat of water on the stove.

"What's happening to Mama?" I ask, feeling very frightened.

61

"Oh, everything's fine," Zoshka says. "Go to sleep!"

But the moans coming from the other room are getting louder and louder. Then Mama starts to scream and I'm really worried. I know Zoshka is lying to me. Mama *isn't* all right! I don't even try to sleep.

After what seems like a very long time, I hear a baby cry, and right after that, Zoshka comes into the kitchen saying, "Sonya, you have a little brother!"

"What?" I ask. "How can that be? Where did he come from?" I didn't see any baby arrive!

"A stork brought him through the window," Zoshka tells me.

I know she's lying. She can't fool me!

"How did a stork get in through the window?" I ask, "The windows are frozen shut and iced over. Nobody could open a window tonight!"

"Never you mind, Sonya. Just go to sleep now," says Zoshka. She shakes her head, but she doesn't try to argue with me.

And amazingly enough, I do have a new baby brother! I can hear him crying. I can't fall asleep, so, in the middle of the night, I go into the bedroom to see him. He's wrapped from head to toe in a blanket, with his arms pinned close to his sides. Mama is holding him and beaming with joy.

I think of my baby sister Malka, and I'm thrilled to have a new baby in the family. Now it's not just me and stupid Rosa any more!

But the baby has no name. Mama and Father can't agree on what to call him.

"We have to have a name by next week, before the *brit,*" Mama tells me.

One of the names I've read in a story is Emmanuel. I don't know the meaning of the name but I love the sound of it.

"Maybe we could name him Emmanuel?" I ask Mama.

"That's an idea," she says.

All week long, I hear Father and Mama talking about the baby's name. They still can't agree on any other name for him, and the *brit* is coming up in a few days. The *mohel* will come to the house, and ten men from the synagogue, and we'll have to have a name for the baby in order to have the ceremony.

Finally, Mama says they've decided to call him Emmanuel. I've named my baby brother!

"That means you'll always have a very special connection to each other," Mama tells me.

I can feel she's right, even though he's only a week old.

In our house, things don't seem very different because of the Russians.

As always, Mama goes to visit Uncle Abraham Freiheiter. He lives on the other side of Lvov in a wealthy neighborhood, and he always owned his own bakery. But Mama says the Russians took over his bakery and made it into a "cooperative." That means the Russian government became the owner, and Uncle Abraham is now just a baker—like Father! He gets paid for his work, and the Russian government takes all the profits.

It's different for us, because my father and mother were just hired workers before the Russians came. They still have their old jobs and they bring home about the same amount of money as before. But Mama says that Uncle Abraham and his family are very hurt by the Russian occupation. Even so, I notice she doesn't say, "Too bad it wasn't the Germans." I never hear her say that anymore.

More and more, I can see how much the Polish people hate the Russians. They have this awful system of standing in long lines in the middle of the night to buy anything that's for sale, whether or not they need it.

The Polish people make fun of the Russians, especially when they say that a special cargo train will be coming to Lvov, "full of wonderful surprises." After seeing a few of those "special" cargo trains, the Polish people say, "Three boxcars full of beautiful words, three boxcars full of nothing, and three boxcars of the plague!"

Near our school there's a small army base, where I go with the other kids after school to watch the Russian soldiers drill. Yesterday, as I was walking home from school with a group of children, a Russian officer saw us looking at him and came over to the fence to talk to us. He had a lot of colorful medals on his chest, and he looked very important. In Russian, he asked us, "Children, do you study Russian in school?

"*Da!*" we answered. "Sure we do!"

"And do they teach you about the great Lenin?"

"Yes," we answered, all together.

"Do you like the Red Army?" he asked us.

"Of course!" we said. It's fun to watch the soldiers doing their drills at the army base.

Then he asked us, "Would you like to have a present from the Red Army?"

Naturally, we all said, "*Da!*"

The officer reached his hand into his pocket and pulled out a fistful of tiny red stars—the symbol of the Soviet Union. Each one was about the size of a thumbnail.

"This is your present," he said, reaching through the iron bars of the fence to hand each of us a star. But when he got to me, I hesitated to take the star, thinking that I ought to tell him the truth about myself.

"I'm a Jew," I told him. "Maybe you don't want to give me a present."

"But are you a good student?" he asked me.

I nodded my head.

The soldier looked at me and smiled. He stuck his hand through the bars of the fence, and handed me a red star.

"Little girl, in the Soviet Union, everyone is equal: the Russians, the Ukrainians, the Polish—everyone, even the Jews!"

This was the nicest gift that anyone could have given me. As I took the little red star from him, I swelled with pride. I had never heard such words of unconditional acceptance from a Gentile before. I thanked him, "*Spaseba,*" and I put the star on top of my school beret and walked home with my head held high, thinking that everybody who saw me would know that I was a worthwhile human being.

"Zoshka, look!" I ran into the apartment and told her what had happened.

Zoshka sewed the red star onto my school beret, so I could wear it to school.

I wake up this morning, thinking it's going to be a wonderful day. I eat my breakfast cheerfully and run out of the house to meet the other kids and walk with them to school. Nobody else has sewn the red star onto their berets—only me!

I walk into the classroom, smiling from ear to ear. But when I get to my desk at the front of the room, my teacher, Miss Honsova, looks at me angrily. I see her point to my beret, and her face turns just as red as the little star.

She stands up and, in a loud voice, she announces to the class, "Today, you Jews are sitting on your high horse. But soon there will come a day when we will knock you down from that horse!"

I can hear some of the kids giggling, and whispering *"Zhydouvka!"* behind my back.

I sit at my desk in shock and shame all day long, and I don't raise my hand even once. I'm thinking that later, when I go home, I'd better ask Zoshka to take the little red star off my beret.

Since Emmanuel was born, it feels like food and other things are harder to get. Mama does strange things that she never did before.

"Mama, why are you getting up in the middle of the night?" I ask her. It's dark and very cold outside.

"I'm going to stand on line to buy vodka," she tells me. "Go back to sleep."

"Vodka!?!" But we don't drink vodka. Why are you going to buy vodka?" I ask her.

"It's a good trade item," she says. "I can sell it and get a lot of money to buy other things we need. I'll take it to my friend Lucia and trade it for food from her garden. Then she can sell it at the market. That's the way people do things, nowadays," she tells me.

I remember another time Mama stood on line all night to buy shoes, which she also traded for food. She calls it bartering. "That's the way things are," she tells me.

One day, Mama tells me a strange story.

"Sonya," she says. "I want to tell you what happened to me last night. I was walking home in the middle of the night, carrying a big bundle of things I had bought. I was all alone when I passed under the Peltevna Bridge."

The Peltevna Bridge is the one we go under to get to the outdoor market on Starozakonna Street.

"The snow was very high, and I could hear it crunching loudly beneath my feet. I thought I was all alone, but just then, I heard loud footsteps behind me, and I was very scared."

"What did you do, Mama?" I asked.

"I was afraid to turn around because I thought maybe it was a thief. So I said to myself *Shema Israel!* That's the prayer for help," she told me. "And just then a strong gust of wind blew and I heard the sounds of shrieking. And as suddenly as it began, the wind stopped and the shrieks stopped, and the footsteps behind me were gone."

So Mama teaches me the prayer: "*Shema Israel!*" It's in the Hebrew language.

"Remember to say it if you're ever in trouble," she tells me.

Under the Russian occupation, I'm allowed to join the "Pioneers"—the Russian youth group. It's like the Polish scout group that Jews weren't allowed to join. All the Pioneers wear red ties, and I'm very proud to wear mine. It makes me feel good to be in the Pioneers. I like the Russians.

Pioneer meetings are held in a great castle. Before the Russian occupation, it was owned by a royal Polish family. The Russians "nationalized" it, the same way they took over Uncle Abraham's bakery.

I was never inside a castle before the Russian occupation, and I'm very impressed with the huge rooms, the expensive furniture and the magnificent paintings hanging on the walls. The Russians tell us that all of the things the wealthy people used to own are now owned by "the people"—meaning people like us. I like that!

Today there's a puppet show at the castle. It's a children's version of a play by Pushkin, called "The Pope and the Peasant." At the beginning, we see the peasant working hard to support the Pope. The Pope is kind to the peasant and they seem to be good friends. But as the play goes on, the Pope begins to demand more and more from the peasant. The peasant has to work harder and harder, and he's very tired. He has no time to pay attention to his wife. Finally, the peasant sees that the Pope is
68

looking at his wife and talking to her in a very strange way. It's as if he's courting her! The peasant becomes angry with the Pope and threatens to beat him. At the end of the play, they tell us that this was how the peasant uprising against the church began. I don't know anything about that, but they say we're going to study it in our history lessons.

The Russians are very anti-religious and they're constantly saying there's no such thing as God. All of the churches are closed and boarded up, or converted into community halls, like the mansions and the castles of the aristocracy. The Polish Gentiles are angry, but there's nothing they can do. Zoshka and her family hate the Russians, and so do Jijo and Jijova.

Father can't go to synagogue to pray on Saturdays and holidays any more. He prays at home and we still celebrate the holidays at home, but it feels like something has changed.

I go to the library more and more, nowadays. I love reading stories, and I take out all of the fairy tale books I can find. I read the Grimm Brothers, Andersen, and Polish fairy tales, too. I know there can be different versions of the same story, so I read as many different versions as I can find. I'm looking for stories with sad endings that change to happy endings, but I haven't found one, yet. I'll keep looking until I do.

I especially like the story of Hansel and Gretel. They're just kids like me, but they're able to trick the witch! I wish I had a sister or a brother who was my friend, instead of Rosa, who I'm always fighting with. When Emmanuel gets older, we'll be best friends, like Hansel and Gretel.

I found a Polish version of Hansel and Gretel. It's called Yash and Malgosha in Polish. It goes like this:

Once there were two children who lived with their parents in the middle of a forest. The boy was called Yash and the girl, Malgosha. Their mother got sick and died, so the children were left alone at home every day while their father went to work.

One day, their father brought home a new wife who was very mean to the children. One night, when Yash and Malgosha went to bed, they heard their stepmother say to their father "You work from early morning to late at night. Do something with the children, so they won't be a burden to us any longer."

When the children heard this, they were very angry. But they knew their father would do whatever their stepmother told him to do. So Yash snuck out of the house in the middle of the night, and filled his pockets with pebbles. The next morning, their father said, "Children, you're coming with me to the woods today." As they walked behind their father, Yash dropped the pebbles on the ground so that he and Malgosha could find their way home again. The father left them in the woods, saying, "I'll come back for you this evening." But he never came back, and the children found their way home by following the trail of the pebbles. Their father and stepmother were very surprised to see them. That night, they heard their stepmother complaining

70

about the children again. But, this time, she locked all the doors and the windows before she went to bed, for she suspected that Yash had found a way to mark the way home, and she didn't want him to do it again.

In the morning, their father said, "You two will come to the forest with me this morning." So, instead of eating his bread for breakfast, Yash took the bread and put it in his pocket. He crumbled it up into crumbs, and dropped the breadcrumbs along the way, so that he and Malgosha could find their way home. Again, their father left them in the middle of the forest, saying, "I'll come back for you this evening." But he didn't come back.

Breadcrumbs are not like pebbles, and the birds ate them up, so the children couldn't find their way home. They wandered around the forest, hungry and tired. Finally, they found a beautiful little house made entirely of candy. While they were tasting the candy, Babayaga the witch came out of the house and smiled at them. "Children," she said, "I see you like my candies. If you want to stay with me, you can have all the candy you want." So they went inside and ate and went to sleep. But Yash was suspicious. In the middle of the night, he got up and walked around the house, and found a cage with a little boy in it. The next day, he spied on Babayaga, and saw that she was heating up an oven. Babayaga spoke in her sleep, saying, "Soon, I'm going to have a feast!"

The children thought of running away, but they were lost in the forest, so they stayed. After they had been there for a few weeks, they had gotten very fat. One day, Babayaga invited them

71

to a feast. She heated up the oven, and Yash feared that she was planning to cook and eat them! So, as Babayaga was putting sticks of wood on the fire, Yash got behind her and pushed her into the oven. Then the children ran away. When Yash and Malgosha got home, their father was thrilled to see them. "Your evil step-mother is dead," he said. And they lived happily ever after.

I'm very disappointed in the father because he let the stepmother tell him what to do, and because he did something terrible to his own children. And the story makes me afraid of forests. They seem like evil, unfriendly places where terrible things happen to children, like in the story of Little Red Riding Hood.

Now that I can read to myself, I notice that I've been spending less and less time with Zoshka. We never sit together and peel potatoes anymore, and she hasn't told me stories for a long time. She also speaks nastily to me, which is something she never did before. And she slaps me much more than used to. When I tell Mama, she says there's nothing she can do about it. But I'm furious.

Mama and Father seem to listen to the radio detektor a lot more, nowadays. I hear the name "Hitler" a lot, but I don't really know who he is. I want to understand what's happening, and I ask Mama a lot of questions. I notice that she doesn't like to answer them when Zoshka is around. But one day when we're alone, Mama tells me that many Jews in Poland are becoming Communists.

"A lot of Jews like the way the Russians treat us better than the Poles or the Ukrainians who are always calling us *'Zhyd'!*" says Mama.

There are rumors that the German army is going to push the Russians out of Lvov. Mama says, "That could be a terrible thing for the Jews."

Nowadays, I often hear Mama talking to Father, and to the neighbor women, about leaving Lvov. The Russians are offering the Jewish families of Lvov free emigration to the Soviet Union. That means we can go there and become citizens if we want to, says Mama. In our neighborhood, everybody is talking about moving to Russia. A few of our neighbors—mainly the families with older children—are packing up and leaving already.

Mama and Father talk about emigrating all of the time now. Our problem is that we have no bank account and no gold, and Emmanuel is still a baby—he's just beginning to walk.

"What would we do in Russia, with no jobs, no home, no relatives, and no money—and with a baby? Where would we sleep in the frigid Russian winter? How would we carry our belongings?" I hear them ask each other over and over. But there's no answer.

I think about the Little Match Girl, freezing to death in the snow, and I'm scared.

There's a strange young man wandering around our neighborhood. He says he's from Warsaw, and he talks Yiddish with the accent of the Jews from Warsaw. But he's telling an incredible story, and a lot of people think he's either crazy or else a con-man.

73

He's dressed in an elegant beige suit, and he says that he comes from a wealthy family. Wherever he goes, groups of Jews gather around him to listen to his story. His clothing is fine, but he has a strange, dazed look in his eyes. He says that the Germans have been forcing Jews to leave their homes in Warsaw and relocating them in crowded apartments in the center of the city. He said that Jews have been disappearing, and that nobody knows where they are. He says that the Jews of Warsaw are no longer allowed to walk on the sidewalks— they have to walk in the streets. And the religious Jews in Warsaw have been forced to cut off their beards and do menial labor, like cleaning the streets.

Nobody knows whether to believe him or not, since his story is so bizarre and he seems emotionally disturbed. Mrs. Tepper and some of the other neighbors think he might be an escaped criminal—or maybe a con-man—who just wants the Jewish community to take him in and support him in Lvov. My parents talk about him a lot. I think they believe his story, because they've started packing up our clothing in huge bags.

We start hearing a lot more about Hitler on the radio detektor. He says that the Germans are winning the war and they're going to take over all of Europe. He says the Jews are the enemies of civilization and that Germany will get rid of all the Jews. But Mama tells me, "War talk is always worded in extreme language. Hitler's speaking empty words. I can't believe that the great German people, with the highest culture in Europe, really stand behind Hitler's slogans and speeches. It's impossible!"

It's summer again, and I've just turned eleven. There are a lot of rumors going around, saying that the German army is going to enter Lvov and throw the Russian soldiers out. One day, I see Russian soldiers leaving Lvov. They leave in such a hurry that they leave their food storage sheds unguarded. The next morning, Father comes home from work, saying that people are breaking down the doors of a Russian government storage building, and carrying away bags of food and supplies.

"There's nobody to stop the looting," he tells Mama. He and Mama talk about it for a few minutes, and then he goes out with a big sack. He goes back to the Russian government storage building and brings home a huge sack filled with sugar cubes.

Mama is afraid that the Russians might return and find stolen merchandise in our home, so she hides the sugar in a big armchair with a wooden-box style bottom. When you raise the seat of the chair, there's an empty space beneath it.

My parents are still talking about leaving Lvov before the Germans come, but how will we bring all of our belongings with us? They still haven't decided what to do.

The German Occupation[*]

It's before dawn on a summer morning, and Father hasn't come home from work yet. We're awakened by a siren and the loud sound of airplanes flying overhead. Mama grabs Emmanuel

---

[*] **Lvov: June, 1941**
June 22nd: about 10,000 Jews left Lvov with the Russian army.
June 29th: the German army entered Lvov.
July 8: the Germans ordered the Jews to wear identifying armbands.
Early July, 1941: hundreds of bodies of political prisoners—mostly Ukrainians—were found buried beneath the Brygidki prison in Lvov. The Germans spread a rumor—later proved untrue—that the Jews had collaborated with the Russians in their murder. German soldiers and Ukrainian nationalists began to murder Jews on the streets.
By August 3rd, four thousand Jews had been murdered. Everything took days—sometimes weeks—to reach the news media. And rumor was also considered a reasonable way of spreading news.
    One of the rumors was that the Germans, under Hitler, were treating the Jews with unprecedented cruelty. It was hard for people to believe the stories, because until that time, the Germans had been considered the most cultured civilization in Europe. Many people discounted the stories of cruelty against the Jews as unfounded rumors. There was no reliable news agency where people could check the facts.

in her arms and runs with him to the bomb shelter around the corner from us. Zoshka hurries there with me and Rosa as fast as she can. As we run, we can hear the sound of gunfire and an ear-piercing "boom" knocks me off my feet. I fly backwards through the air, but I'm not hurt. I can hear Zoshka scream, and one of the neighbors grabs me and drags me into the bomb shelter. We all sit here, shivering and tense, until the bombers pass. Nobody says a word; the only sound comes from the babies, crying. I remember the last time we sat here. It was when the Russian army entered Lvov. Back then, Rosa and I thought a war would be exciting and fun.

When we come out of the bomb shelter, we see a huge pit in the ground at the bottom of the steep incline on Lokietka Street, where Rosa and I always go sledding in winter. I walk home in a daze, wondering what will happen next.

Day after day, there are sirens and we hear planes crossing the skies over the city. Then the German soldiers come to Lvov and ride through our neighborhood. Many are on motorcycles, and they bounce wildly over the cobblestones of the narrow side streets. They parade through the city, announcing their presence and their authority, and kicking up great clouds of dust. They're nothing like the Russian soldiers. Just looking at their faces, with their cold and distant expressions, makes me shudder. We don't see them again for a few days and everybody wonders what's going to happen to us.

Mama says the German occupation is going to be very different from the Russian occupation.

For the next few weeks, we hear about terrible pogroms in Lvov. Mama says the Germans are spreading a false rumor, saying that the Jews had collaborated with the Russians during the Russian occupation. The Germans have found hundreds of bodies buried beneath the Brygidki prison in Lvov, and they're saying those prisoners were murdered by Jews. They're telling the Ukrainians in Lvov to organize "revenge strikes" against the Jews. Mama says that a lot of Jewish men have been rounded up and beaten—or even killed—by the Germans. Father doesn't go to work, and Mama tells Rosa and me to stay close to home.

The hero in a fairy tale is not always brave—at least not at first. In fact, she is often frightened and unsure of herself. And the reader, like the hero, has no way of knowing if the hero will survive....

We're listening to the radio detektor, when the Germans announce a new law: all Jews over the age of fourteen must wear a white armband with a blue Star of David on it. Rosa is nine and I'm eleven, so we don't need to wear the armband.

There's a Jewish woman walking around the streets of our neighborhood, selling the armbands. Some families can't afford to buy ready-made armbands, so they make their own. Mama tells me and Rosa not to walk around the streets any more, not even in our

79

own neighborhood. It's too dangerous, she tells us.

Then, for a while, things are quiet again. The neighbors stand in the courtyard talking about the situation, and I listen carefully. Some of them think our lives may continue to be the way they were under the Russian occupation. Mama tells me there have always been pogroms in Poland—and everywhere in Europe and Russia.

"This is nothing new," she says. "Polish Jews have suffered from anti-Semitism many times before. You know how the children call you 'Zhydouvka' sometimes, in school," she reminds me. "After a while, they'll stop bothering us," she says. "There's a large Jewish community in Lvov because—most of the time—it's a safe place for Jews to live. It's better here than in other European countries. Maybe things will return to normal soon. We can't lose hope."

And things do return to normal. As soon as my parents see things quiet down again, they go back to work. We need the money and the bread.

But the quiet days don't last long. Later in July, there's another pogrom in Lvov. It's led by the Ukrainians, and the neighbors are saying that many Jews have been killed. Mama doesn't let me and Rosa out of the apartment at all, these days.

Zoshka is still living with us, in spite of all the nasty rumors that the Germans are spreading about the Jews. She's been with us for seven years now, and I've always felt that she's part
80

of our family. But she's Ukrainian, and Mama says the Ukrainians are very angry with the Jews. They think that Jews killed the prisoners at Brygidki Prison.

It seems like there's a new law every day now. The Germans say that no Gentile is allowed to work for a Jew. They say that Jews are an inferior race, and nobody from an "Aryan" ethnic group is supposed to have any dealings with Jews in business, or socially, or in any other way.

It's only the middle of summer, but I wish desperately that I could go back to school because the atmosphere is so tense at home. Mama and Zoshka aren't fighting, but they hardly talk to each other at all anymore.

Mama doesn't say anything to Zoshka about leaving, but she expects that Zoshka will say goodbye to us very soon, and take all her things with her. There's so much tension in the house that I wish she would go right now!

I hate being at home all summer. There's nothing to do except fight with Rosa. So I go out whenever Mama lets me. But I don't go far from home anymore.

One day, as I'm coming home from a walk, I see all the neighbors standing in a circle in our courtyard. Naturally, I'm curious to see what it is they're crowding around.

I'm short for my age, so I decide to crawl through the crowd between the legs of the neighbors. There, in the center of the circle, is a man. I'm so close to the ground that I can only see him from the shoes, upward. I don't see his face at first. But I hear the neighbors

81

calling him Mr. Lanzberg. I can't believe this is really our neighbor, Mr. Lanzberg, the lawyer who lives on the second floor. He always goes to work wearing shiny, polished shoes and a black suit with a tie. But this man has rumpled pants and dirty shoes. Looking up, I see his suit jacket is missing, and his white shirt is filthy and caked with blood. It's a big shock when I see his face. He doesn't look anything like Mr. Lanzberg! His face is black and blue, his eyes are red and swollen, and one arm is hanging loose from his shoulder. He can hardly stand, so the neighbors bring a stool for him to sit on and give him water to drink. Someone wipes his face. When he's finally able to speak, he tells us what happened.

On his way to work that morning, gangs of Ukrainians attacked all the "Jewish-looking" men on the streets. Anyone who had darker hair and skin than the ordinary Poles, or who was dressed in the black suits that the Jews generally wore, was rounded up and taken to the Brygidki jail, on the other side of Lvov. Mr. Lanzberg managed to run away, but he had been badly beaten.

The neighbors help Mr. Lanzberg upstairs to his apartment, and everyone tells me to go home and stay there. "This is no time for a child to be walking around the streets!"

Later that day, other neighbors come home with the same story. Jacob Zinger, a young man, comes home all black and blue from the beatings he had received. When his mother sees him, she runs to him screaming, "Jacob, my son, what have they done to you?" He has dried blood all over his body.

Another neighbor—a woman—went out in the morning to clean houses. She also came home badly beaten, with bruises all over her head and face and body.

I ask Mama, "How could anybody do that to a woman?"

If Mama had been caught while she was out selling bread, would they have beaten her, too?

It feels like an enormous but invisible force has split yesterday from today, like a giant, unseen axe crashing through the air. And I wonder what horrible things are coming next.

Mama says the newspapers are full of anti-Semitic articles. My parents are horrified when they read what's written about the Jews. On the radio detektor, we hear announcements calling on the "Aryan citizens of Lvov" to gather together and take revenge on the Jews. "No law will hold you guilty of committing a crime, no matter what you do to a Jew!" they say. "Aryans should go Jew-hunting."

Mama shudders when she hears these things, and she and Zoshka keep their distance from each other. Zoshka is Ukrainian and most of her family lives in Lvov. I wonder if Michalova's son, Kazhik, is one of the men who goes around attacking the Jews.

It's been a long, miserable summer. I'm anxious to return to school, and I've gotten all of my school supplies together and packed them in my backpack, which is standing near my bed ready to go back to school with me. One morning, after Mama goes out to work, I get up and tell Zoshka that I'm going to school.

"What are you talking about? There's no school!" Zoshka yells at me, in an angry tone of voice. "It's summer!" She's been yelling at me a lot lately, but Mama never says anything to her.

I argue with her. "There's nothing for me to do at home, so I'm going!" I insist.

But Zoshka also insists, "There's a war going on! The Germans have taken over the city of Lvov. There won't be any school! Not even in September!" And she slaps me very hard.

I'm furious, so I grab my backpack and go. Who is she to tell me that I can't go to school? And how dare she slap me so hard? She's just a servant in our home!

As I pass the small military base near the school, I notice it's empty. Maybe the German army isn't going to use it?

The schoolyard is empty, too. Instead of the sounds of children playing, stillness hangs in the air. I have no idea what time it is. "Maybe I came too early," I think, still feeling hopeful.

I walk up to the school building, looking at the sign that says, "Lenartovich School," and I climb up the steps that lead to the huge front door. It's closed. The door is locked and bolted. Everything is quiet and there's nobody else in sight. So I sit down on the steps of the school building to wait. I stay there for a very long time, but nobody comes—no children, no adults, no teachers—nobody!

Sadly, I get up, thinking to myself, "Okay, I'll come back tomorrow. Maybe the school will be open then," and I start to walk home, very, very slowly. I'm in no hurry to get home. There's nothing to do there but fight with Rosa.

And I don't want to be around Zoshka anymore!

The bakery where Father works, which was
taken over by the Russians during the Russian
occupation, is now under the control of the
Germans, like all Jewish businesses. Father
still works there, but instead of money he
brings home a few loaves of bread a day. But
the Germans won't let Mama work there any
more. Besides, it's too dangerous for her to
walk around the streets, even in our neighborhood.

With Mama and Zoshka together at home
all day long, there are all sorts of arguments
and angry words. The neighbors keep asking
Mama, "Why do you keep Zoshka? You don't
need her anymore. You're not working."

Mama says, "But she's been with us for
seven years. She's like one of the family."

Maybe that was true before, but now it's
different. Zoshka, who was always like a friend
to me, is changing. She slaps me, sometimes
very hard, if I do anything to annoy her. She
sometimes used to slap me when I was little,
but now she slaps me all of the time, and very
hard! Mama doesn't say anything to Zoshka,
but when she turns her back I can see her
shoulders shaking.

This morning, Zoshka started to slap me
very hard, and she's been slapping me all day
long. Her hand is big and heavy because she's
a very fat woman. Finally, I can't stand it anymore.

"Stop it!" I scream at her. "You can't keep
hitting me. All of a sudden you're acting as if

you're the boss around here. But you're not. This is our house. If you feel so superior to us because we're Jews, maybe you shouldn't stay here anymore!"

When Mama hears this, she turns her back to us and looks away. What can she say? She knows it's true, but what can she do? If the Germans stay in Lvov, then Zoshka will have to leave us, according to the new law.

Mama used to say, "Maybe things will get better. The Germans are a very cultured people." But she hasn't said that in a long time.

Nobody is surprised when Zoshka tells my parents, "I'm Ukrainian and I have special rights under German law. The Germans say I can't work for Jews anymore." Since she's been so mean to me, it comes as a relief when she finally goes. It's as if my friend the storyteller never existed!

Mama says, "It's just as well. Zoshka is a very large woman and a big eater, and we don't have enough to feed her, anymore."

As the situation gets worse, we hardly have enough to feed ourselves.

Mama says, "Zoshka has plenty of problems and very little money, so she does whatever the Germans tell her to do. She's working for them in order to support herself. When this blows over, who knows? Maybe she'll come back to us."

Meanwhile, she's living in her brother, Michael's, apartment, near our neighborhood. She has a job as a cook at the German military base near my school. Once in a while, she still comes to visit. She brings us soup and scraps of food from the base where she works as a cook. But things are changing every day. The Germans are making it harder and harder for us. Bringing food to a Jewish family is getting very dangerous, so Zoshka doesn't come very often.

After all the years she's been with us, I don't want to believe that she's anti-Semitic, like the other Ukrainians. But her behavior has become so strange since the German occupation began that I'm beginning to think she is.

With Zoshka gone and Mama home, everything is different at home. For the first time I can remember, Mama stays home and takes care of the house and my baby brother, Emmanuel, all day long. Now Father is the only one supporting our family. And he doesn't earn money anymore. Instead, he brings home loaves of bread and bags of coal. The bread isn't enough to feed us, so Mama sells some of our household goods to get money for food and other things we need.

One afternoon, Mama brings home a Ukrainian farmer with a huge basket of green tomatoes. I see that the tomatoes aren't ripe, so I ask her, "What can we do with all those tomatoes? We can't eat them like that!"

"No, we won't eat them," says Mama, "but I can make preserves from them. We still have some sugar cubes."

So, Mama pays the Ukrainian farmer in sugar cubes, and she uses the remaining sugar cubes to make a huge amount of tomato jelly. I help her cook it in a big pot. It takes hours and hours. This is the first time she's ever let me

87

help her in the kitchen, and I feel very grown up!

Things are changing so fast, it's hard to keep up with the new laws. Almost every day, there's a new poster on the walls of the apartment buildings or on the notice boards in our neighborhood. One says, "All Jewish shop owners must close their shops. All of their stock must be handed over to the German government." A few days later, a new poster says, "All Jews must continue working at their regular places of work, and also at jobs that the German government is going to create for them." Every poster ends with the warning: *"Anyone who breaks this law will be severely punished!"*

Another poster says, "No Jew may own or wear watches or jewelry of any kind, except a wedding ring." My family has no wealth—we don't even have a bank account. But Mama has a gold ring that she always wears, along with her wedding ring. When she hears about the new law saying that Jews are not allowed to wear jewelry, Mama takes off the ring and hides it in the apartment.

"Maybe we'll need it, later," she says.

Mama also has a beautiful set of six wine glasses with real gold trim. One day, a group of Jews comes to the door, collecting "expensive items," to give to the Germans, saying, "Maybe if we give the Germans some silver and gold, they'll leave us alone." She gives them the wine glasses, saying she hopes they're right.

I have nothing to do at home, so I play with Emmanuel. Mama teaches me how to change his diapers and take care of him. I sing him nursery rhymes. Mama says I'm a big help. And I hardly ever fight with Rosa anymore.

The latest rumor is that all the leaders of the Jewish community have been rounded up and taken to jail by the Germans. These men are the heads of all of the Jewish organizations in Lvov—not only religious leaders, but secular community leaders, too.

Mama and Father talk about it, but what can they do? Like every other family, we're busy trying to take care of our own problems. We hardly have enough money for food. Then, one day in August, two young Jewish men knock on our door, asking our family to make a "contribution" in order to free the Jewish leaders. They ask for anything we can spare—money, gold, any object of value. So, Mama takes her expensive gold ring from the place where she had hidden it and gives it to them, in exchange for a receipt that describes it. The men say, "Keep the receipt. Who knows what will happen? Maybe good times will come again, and you'll get the ring back."

The next morning, the neighbors say there's good news: the Germans have freed the Jewish leaders! Mama is happy that she gave her ring. Perhaps, after all, there's hope for a better future!

That afternoon, she lets me go out for a walk. I go over to Lokietka Street. It's one block away from our street—Kressova. On one side, Lokietka Street has tall apartment buildings with balconies on the upper floors. On the other side, there's a slope where all the neighborhood children go sliding in the snow in winter. In summer, this open field is always covered with weeds.

As I approach Lokietka Street, all along the open side of the street, people are standing and holding their heads in their hands, looking upward at the balconies. Nobody says a word; their mouths are hanging open in shock. I follow the direction of their eyes to see what they're staring at. Overhead, I see some figures dressed in the traditional black suits of the Jews of Lvov, with their collars open and their ties loosened. They're all hanging by the neck. At first, it looks like huge puppets are suspended from the balconies. But, when I see their green and bloated faces, I realize they're real men—and they're dead! Someone whispers, "These are the Jewish leaders!"

I can't bear the sight, and I run home to tell Mama. She doesn't say a word. Like everyone else, she's in a state of shock.

The neighbors gather in the courtyard and talk in hushed whispers.

"What can we do?" they ask each other.

"There's nothing we can do," Mama says. "The Germans are in complete control of Lvov."

Now the Germans have organized another group of Jewish leaders called the *Judenrat*. But Mama says that the members of the *Judenrat* can't make real decisions. They can only decide between the choices that the Germans give them—and they're all bad for the Jews. I don't understand a lot of what is going on, but I hear my parents talking in hushed voices at night, when they think I'm asleep.

When the weather turns colder, Father is given permission to bring home a bag of coals from work every day, in addition to a loaf of bread. The coals are the remains of the wood fire used to bake the bread. They're very important to us, because we heat our apartment by burning wood in the stove in the salon, and we need wood for the cooking stove, too. But as the weeks go by, the loaves of bread get smaller and smaller. So Father begins to steal an extra loaf or two of bread every day, hiding the loaves in his sack of coal. Mama wipes the charcoal dust off the loaves of bread very carefully, and she trades the extra loaves for vegetables, or fruit, or milk, or butter, the basic foods that our family needs. Sometimes, she walks the great distance across Lvov to the home of our wealthy relatives, the Freiheiters, who still send her home with a big package of food for us.

Nowadays, there are so many changes in our lives that I don't even think about going back to school any more. I can't, anyway, because one of the new German laws forbids Jews from attending the public schools. And I can't take out books any more, because the library has been closed down. Whenever I think about school, I miss it very badly.

One afternoon, Chesha, a Gentile girl from my class, knocks on our apartment door when I'm at home alone. When I open the door, I'm surprised and delighted to see one of my schoolmates.

"Come on in," I say, happy to see her.

But she just stands in the doorway, refusing to enter, and I realize this isn't going to be a friendly visit.

91

"Sonya," she says, "I came because I'm going to school and I need more notebooks to write in. There are no notebooks for us to buy any more. The other kids told me that you have new notebooks that you bought for school. Since you won't be going to school, maybe you can give them to me?" she says.

I'm furious! How dare she come and ask me to give away what's mine, so that she can go to school, while I have to stay home, doing nothing and missing the studies that I long for?!

During the summer, I had written my name on the cover of each of my notebooks in the anticipation of returning to school. It hurts me and makes me even angrier because I know she's right—I'll probably never use those notebooks. But I'm certainly not going to give them to her!

"I can't give you my notebooks," I tell her, as calmly as I can. "While you're in school, I'm studying on my own," I say, even though it isn't true. I close the door in her face.

Now I realize that while I'm going through the most nightmarish period of my life, their lives are continuing pretty much as usual. And not one of my Gentile classmates comes to visit me, just to pay a friendly visit.

Another change I notice is a lot of new foreign words in our everyday speech. They're mostly long words, with strange sounds that are difficult to pronounce. I used to love learning new words, but these words frighten me. We're told that every Jewish family has to be "productive." The "*productivization*" of the Jews will make us acceptable to the Germans. Whoever is not productive will be taken to a place near Lublin. They'll be "deported." "*Deportation*" is the most frightening of the new words. Several of our neighbors have been "deported" and we have no idea where they are.

All at once, our building and our whole neighborhood is changing so fast that I hardly recognize it anymore. People that I've known all my life are gone, and strangers are living in their apartments now. The few non-Jewish families in our building—like Piotrova's—have moved away and Jewish families from other neighborhoods have moved into the apartments that they left empty.

One day, I see a new poster on the notice board, saying, "Every Jewish family must contribute a volunteer worker to the German war effort. Any family who fails to give one worker to the German war effort will not be allowed to live in Lvov." As frightened as my parents are of going to work for the Germans, they're even more frightened of what might happen to us if we don't obey the law: *deportation*. Father still goes to work, but he and Mama often talk about reporting to the Germans to do "volunteer work."

One morning, Father is not feeling well. He leaves the house, dressed in his work clothes and a warm jacket, since it's late autumn and the temperature is just a little above freezing. But he doesn't go to work, and he doesn't go to the German work headquarters, either. Instead, he goes to the local Jewish clinic to ask for a doctor's note releasing him from the obligation to work, since he has pains in his legs.

93

Father leaves home in the morning, but that evening, he still hasn't come back.

"Could he have gone to work?" Mama wonders. "But if he did, why didn't he come home to tell me?"

Since the summer, there's been no Jewish organization that can help us. We don't know if the Germans have taken Father to a work camp, or to jail, or even worse.

Mama is worried. As the hours pass, she goes from one neighbor to another, but nobody knows anything more than we know. Mama says it's good that at least nobody has heard about any more pogroms in Lvov.

The next morning, Mama leaves me in charge of Emmanuel, with Rosa, at home. She goes to look for Father. "Maybe they remember him at the clinic?" she says, "Or maybe he went to work and left me a message?"

But when she comes back, she says that nobody saw him yesterday.

With Father gone, Mama is doing her best to take care of us children. But Emmanuel is still nursing, and he wants to be held and fed all day long. When Mama has to go out to buy food for us, she leaves me to take care of Emmanuel. She comes home every few hours to nurse him, and then she goes out again. It makes me feel important and gives me something to do with my time. Mama says she doesn't know what she would do without me.

Mama still goes to her Gentile friend, Lucia, in Kleparov. Lucia is not exactly a widow, but her husband was taken to serve in the Russian army during the Russian occupation and Lucia has never heard from him—not even once! She doesn't even know if he's still alive. So, she supports herself by growing vegetables in her garden. Mama goes to Lucia's house with money or goods to trade for food from the garden. She brings back vegetables from Lucia's garden to trade for other foods and goods that we need. I used to love to go with her, but now I have to stay home to take care of Emmanuel while she goes.

Mama has a lot of friends and business contacts from all the years that she's been selling bread and rolls to the local shops and to our neighbors. So, now, instead of bread, she fills her baskets with carrots or parsley or dill—tied in bunches, with string—and she takes them around to her old customers, the ones who haven't been deported.

One evening, we hear a knock on the door. Mama answers it and, at first she thinks it's a beggar looking for food.

Then, "Sroulik!" she screams.

It's Father!

"You're alive! Thank God! You're alive!"

Mama and Father hug each other and I can see they're both crying.

It's true—Father's alive, but he looks terrible. He'd been gone for a few weeks, and he looks like a different person. His legs are so swollen that he can hardly walk. His face is skinny and his eyes are shriveled up. He's a very short man, and now he's bent over and he can't straighten up.

Mama makes him something to eat and she heats up a vat of water for a bath. Father's clothes are filthy and torn, and they stink from animal manure because he's been working in stables.

It takes Father a long time before he can talk. He tells us that the Germans took him, with a group of Jewish workers, into the countryside, to a village called Sokolniki. They spent all day, every day, working in the fields, in stables, and digging ditches. They weren't told what the ditches were for, but Father thought they were going to be used as trenches for the German army. At night the men slept either in the ditches they had dug or in the stables where they worked.

Like the other men, Father was given a tiny amount of food to eat, and he had slept in the clothes he worked in.

When Father tells Mama about the beatings the workers got from the German soldiers, I put my hands over my ears. I'm too terrified to listen. The men were not allowed to get in touch with their families, even though they weren't very far from Lvov, and Father was worried all of the time, because he knew that we had no idea if he was dead or alive.

I don't know how Father escaped, or how long the Germans would have kept him, if he hadn't run away. From the way he looks, I think he might have died if he hadn't run away. But, somehow, he escaped from the Germans and had enough energy to walk home in the middle of the freezing night.

It's late autumn now, and the weather is turning cold. The Germans have just announced a new law: "No Jew may appear in public wearing a fur coat, a fur collar, a muff, fur cuffs, or any other fur decorations." Everything made of fur has to be taken to a special collection center on a certain day.

Rich people have muffs made of fur, but our family has muffs made of heavy wool, lined with fabric and stuffed with cotton. My muff has a pocket inside, where I can keep money or other small things.

We don't have fur coats, but Mama has a fur muff and a coat with a fox collar. She removes the fur from the muff and the coat, and, on the collection day, she takes her fur pieces to the collection center. After that, all the Jews walk around with coats that have replacement collars and cuffs made of cloth, and we all wear muffs made of fabric instead of fur.

With Father home, our family is better off. Even though he's sick, Father works every day. He has terrible pains in his back from the beatings he received, and he can't stand because of the pains in his legs, so he sits and makes rolls in our kitchen.

Mama says that Father is not just a baker—he's really an artist. I understand what she means. The rolls he makes are shaped like miniature pieces of sculpture, and he decorates them with poppy seed or sesame seed, in pretty designs.

We're lucky to have a large supply of flour at home. With Father home, Mama goes out bartering every day. She's trading our household goods, one by one, for the foods we need. While Mama goes out to barter, Father bakes rolls. As soon as he bakes one tray, Mama takes them out to sell in the street. Food is so

97

scarce and bread is so much in demand, that Mama has no trouble selling the rolls in our neighborhood.

At first, it's a great relief to have Father home, but now that winter is almost over, it's becoming a problem. My parents talk about the situation more and more. If we don't send somebody to work for the German war effort, the Germans might deport our whole family. Nobody knows where the deported families go.

One afternoon, Uncle Abraham Freiheiter comes to visit. He's Mama's favorite relative because he introduced her to Father. And she says he's very generous. Whenever Mama goes to visit him, he gives her food and other things to bring home.

Uncle Abraham lives on the other side of Lvov, so I've only met him a few times. His three grown-up sons are with him: Eli, Herschel, and Leibel. They're all very sad, because Shlomit, Uncle Abraham's daughter, was taken to do "volunteer" work by the Germans, only a week after her wedding, and she never came back! Nobody knows where she is. Mama is shocked when she hears this. She had been to Shlomit's wedding, and told me about it. She said that Shlomit had married for love, and that she and her husband had had a very small wedding in somebody's apartment, instead of in a large wedding hall, because Jews aren't allowed to rent wedding halls anymore.

Uncle Abraham has come to ask if their family can move in with us for a few days. The Germans have said that his family has to leave their apartment. The Germans are taking over

98

all of the apartments where the Jews live in that area of Lvov. Now all the Jews have to move into our area, which the Germans have started calling "the Jewish section." Of course our apartment is too small for Uncle Abraham's family: he has three grown-up sons, and his second wife, Minna, and their little boy, Mendel. But they want to stay with us while they look for a larger apartment where Uncle Abraham thinks he can set up a bakery and continue working.

Of course, Father and Mama agree to take them in. So the next day, Uncle Abraham brings his family, but they keep most of their things in the apartment that belongs to Shlomit's husband, since our place is too small. It's much too crowded for them to stay with us, but it doesn't take them long to find a larger apartment and move into it. Uncle Abraham sets up a small bakery in his new apartment. I don't see them again, because Uncle Abraham is busy with his bakery and his sons are all working for the Germans. But Mama keeps going to them for help, and they keep giving her packages of food.

Our few Gentile neighbors are moving away. Piotrova, the cleaning woman, no longer cleans our toilets, and I never see her daughter anymore. I guess their family has moved away. And Jijo comes by to say that he and Jijova are moving, too. They've been given a bigger apartment on the other side of Zamarstynovska Street. Jijo gives Mama their new address before they leave, and he wishes us well.

As winter wears on, we're more and more worried about what might happen to us if the Germans find out that Father escaped from his labor group, and that we aren't contributing a "volunteer" worker to the German war effort. At first, we hoped that Father would get better and go back to his "volunteer" work, but his health has gotten worse and worse, instead.

I can hear my parents talking about this every day. On the first day of spring, March 21st, they finally decide that Mama must "volunteer." So, that morning, Mama leaves home to "volunteer" for the Germans.

That morning, we're all very busy. Father sits in the kitchen baking rolls, as usual. When the rolls are ready, Rosa and I carefully arrange about ten rolls on a tray, and we go out to sell them in the neighborhood. While we're walking around selling the rolls, my father is baking another batch. The streets are full of hungry people who willingly give us a few *groschen* for each roll.

We go back and forth from home to the street all morning, and we hope to sell rolls all day long. But that afternoon, a teenage Gentile boy walks up to me, grabs all the rolls, pushes me hard and runs away. Rosa and I scream, "Stop, thief! Somebody stop him! He stole our rolls!"

I look around for somebody to help us, and I see a man walking on the other side of the street. I recognize him as one of the Ukrainian police—a group of men who wear civilian clothing, but who the Germans have authorized to act as an underground police force in our neighborhood, since they've forbidden the Poles to have their own police. I run up to him without thinking.

"Please, can you help us?" I ask him. "That boy took all our rolls and ran away with them!"

I point to the boy, who I can still see. He's walking down the street, eating a roll.

The man looks at me angrily and says, "Get off this street! You're a Jew. You have no right to sell rolls or anything else, for that matter! You're lucky I'm not taking you to jail!"

At that moment I realize that the Germans are not our only enemies: the Ukrainians can be just as mean.

Rosa and I go home to tell father what happened. We're both crying. Father tries to comfort us. He says, "Don't worry, I can bake more rolls."

But Rosa and I are afraid to go out selling rolls again.

Emmanuel is still nursing, and he's been crying for Mama all day long. I cook cereal and feed him, but he's too little to understand what's happening and he keeps asking, "Mama, Mama, where is Mama?"

I feed him and change his diaper. I'm proud of myself and I can't wait for Mama to return, so I can tell her how well I've managed to take care of Emmanuel while she's been gone all day. This is the longest she's ever been away from Emmanuel, and we all feel how hard it is for him.

Towards evening, we can see people returning to our neighborhood from the "volunteer" work projects. Rosa and I are waiting for Mama impatiently, telling each other, "She'll be here soon. She'll be the next person we see!"

101

But, when she still isn't home, Rosa and I decide to go to the bridge and wait for her there. Since Emmanuel is crying for Mama, we decide to take him with us. I have to carry him, since he's too weak to walk.

We walk to the Peltevna Bridge, where the main sewer of Lvov is located. The Peltevna Bridge is very tall. Trains pass over it every day on their way back and forth from Kiev in the Ukraine. There, at the opening of the bridge, we stand and wait for Mama, as hundreds of "volunteer" workers pass by us.

The women of Lvov all wear similar headscarves, and Mama left home this morning with a burgundy-colored flowered wool scarf. I get excited every time I see a woman wearing a scarf that color. But Mama doesn't come. We wait for a long time, and many women pass us by. After a long time, the crowds are beginning to thin out.

"What are you children doing here?" one woman asks us.

"We're waiting for Mama," we answer.

She tells us, "This is a very dangerous place for children to be. You should go home before it gets any darker. Your mother is probably on her way home. Maybe she passed through here already and you didn't see her and she's at home, worrying about you right now!"

So we turn around and walk back to our neighborhood, hoping to find Mama waiting for us at home. But, when we get home, Mama isn't there. Father doesn't say anything.
Emmanuel is crying. "Mama! Milk!" is all he can say.

He's hungry and he wants to nurse. I put my finger in his mouth to soothe him, but I'm crying, too. We spend the long, miserable evening hours waiting for Mama to come home, and I go to bed still crying.

In my dream, Mama comes home, wearing her burgundy-flowered headscarf and smiling. She brings us fruit and candies, and I tuck a piece of candy into my fist and put it under my pillow. In the morning, when I wake up, I'm still clutching the "candy" in my fist. But when I open my hand, it's empty and I realize it was only a dream. There's no candy in my hand. And much worse, Mama has not come home.

I'm bored staying home all day, but I need to take care of Emmanuel because Father is too weak to lift him and Rosa is too young to care for him properly. The thought of selling rolls on the street frightens me, but Father says this is the end of the flour, so I agree to take the last tray of rolls outside to sell. After selling it, I'll use the money to buy cheap food because we have nothing to eat at home.

Out on the street, I'm very nervous. I'm afraid somebody will steal the rolls from me, and even more afraid that the underground policeman will see me and take me to the Germans. But, luckily, nothing bad happens. I sell all of the rolls and use the money to buy food, and then go home as quickly as I can.

A day or two after that, a young woman— someone I've seen in our neighborhood—comes to our door.

"I know where your mother is," she tells us. "She's in the Rey School, where the Germans have locked her up along with a whole group of women."

This young woman says she was with Mama on the day that Mama went to "volunteer" for the German work project. She, too, had "volunteered" that day. In the evening, when the women had finished working, the German soldiers surrounded them and led them into the Rey School, not far from our neighborhood in Lvov. They locked them in that building, which was guarded by German soldiers.

"I jumped out of a second story window from the bathroom during the middle of the night, with a few other girls," this young woman told us. "I don't know what you should do," she said. "It's very dangerous to go near the Rey School. The German guards have guns and I'm sure they won't let you go inside to see your mother. Or, even worse, they might take you, too."

Once again, we're in a situation where there's nothing we can do. But at least we know that Mama is somewhere near home. We hope she'll find a way to escape and come home, like Father did.

In a fairy tale, the hero is often confused about who to believe, and who to trust. Many things people say turn out to be lies or distortions of the truth.

A few days later, Zoshka comes to the door with a container of soup and acts very friendly.

All winter she's been coming, although not very often, to bring us scraps of food from the kitchen where she cooks for the German soldiers. When we tell her that Mama is gone, she begins to cry. She takes me and Rosa in her arms and hugs us, and promises to ask around for information about where Mama is and when she might come home again. Zoshka acts as if she's really concerned, and she comes back to the house with soup for us again the next day.

This time, she brings her brother's wife, Michalova, with her. Michalova says, "We could help you, if you like."

I ask, "What do you mean?"

"We could take packages of old clothes and other things and sell them for you.

Then you wouldn't have to walk around the streets, and maybe get into trouble."

Father agrees, and we give them a big bundle of things to sell. But, when they come back the next day, they have only a few *zlotys* for us.

"That's all you got for all those clothes and blankets?" asks Father.

Zoshka looks down and doesn't say anything, but Michalova says, "What do you want? How can I sell your dirty second-hand clothes and blankets for more money than this?"

We don't complain, knowing how the Germans have organized the Ukrainians to fight against the Jews. But after they leave, Father says we won't give them anything else to sell for us.

Then Michalova's daughter, Olga, comes to see us. I haven't seen Olga for a very long time. Olga tells us that yesterday she was in the village of Skalat, not far from Tarnopol, where they have family. She was buying vegetables from a gardener. She says she saw Mama there, working with a group of women in the fields. We're very happy to hear that Mama is alive.

"But what can we do?" we ask Olga, "And when will she come home?"

"First of all," says Olga, "your mother needs warm clothes. And she needs a bra very badly."

Of course she does! She's been wearing the same clothes for a whole week. And of course, she needs a clean bra. Her breasts must be leaking milk. So we take a sweater, a warm skirt, some underwear, and heavy socks, and we make a package for Mama.

"I'll take the bundle to her," Olga promises us. "I'm going back there in a few days."

"But when is she coming home?" we want to know.

"I'll try to find out," Olga promises us, and she leaves.

When she comes back a few days later, she tells us, "The Germans want five hundred *zlotys* to let her go."

We're shocked. "Five hundred *zlotys*!? How can we pay that much? We have no money anymore."

We don't know what to do, but we know we have to come up with five hundred *zlotys,* somehow. I think of going to Uncle Abraham, but I don't know where they've moved to, and Father doesn't know, either.

Father looks around our apartment and decides, "We'll sell our curtains and our rugs."

But it isn't easy to find people to buy these things. We can only sell our household goods to the Poles, since the Jews, like us, have no more money. But even that isn't easy. Mrs. Tepper tells us about an underground group of Polish businessmen who trade goods for other goods and money on the black market. They wander around the neighborhood on foot and some of our neighbors know who they are. It takes a few days, but we finally find people who are willing to pay cash for our carpets and curtains.

The next time Olga comes to the house, Zoshka is with her. We have the money, and we give it to Olga.

"You'll soon see your mother again," she promises us.

I want very badly to go with Olga on her trip to the village. "Please can't you take me?" I beg her. "I can't wait until Mama comes home."

"Oh, no," says Olga. "It's much too dangerous for Jews to travel."

It's true; Jews are no longer allowed outside the Jewish district.

"You'll be much better off waiting for your mother at home," she says. And Zoshka agrees. "You don't want to go near the Germans if you can possibly avoid them," she warns me.

Father says they're right. "And anyway, I need you to take care of Emmanuel," he reminds me. So I stay home and look after Emmanuel, hoping to see Mama very soon.

Every day we expect to see Mama, but she never comes. A week passes, and then Zoshka comes to bring us food. She's shaking with anger. "I could wring that liar's neck!" she screams. "Olga never saw your mother! She didn't even go to Skalat!"

107

Zoshka tells us it was just a story Olga made up to get money from us. Olga had taken Mama's clothing and the five hundred *zlotys* and run away with it! What can we say or do? We're shocked and miserable.

I want to believe that Zoshka was caught in the middle—that she hadn't meant to trick us or harm us. After all, she's been bringing us food and trying to help us all along, even though it's getting more and more dangerous. I tell myself that Zoshka really cares about us, and wants to help us, but I can't help but wonder if that's really true. It hurts me very badly to think that Zoshka doesn't care about me, after she had been like a second mother to me during the years she lived with us. But, since her family knows what she's been doing for us, and since many Ukrainians have become as anti-Semitic as the Germans, maybe they forced her—or convinced her—to trick us.

With both Zoshka and Mama gone, I'm lonelier than ever before. Father hardly talks at all, and Rosa and I just get on each other's nerves. But at the same time, my responsibilities keep me very busy.

Like every Jewish family, our family has food coupons. Each family is entitled to receive one loaf of bread and a container of jam every week. Mama has always gone to the one small bakery where the coupons are accepted, to bring home the weekly ration for our family. Now I go, instead. But no matter what time of day I go, there's always a long line of people waiting to get their bread and jam. Everyone pushes and shoves, arguing, "I was in front of you!" "No, I was in front of you!"

We're each given a heavy loaf of bread, which is never baked enough, so it's always wet in the middle, and a very small container of watery jam, made from beets. This is supposed to last our family for a whole week. Yet, as small as the portions are, everybody depends on them and everybody pushes and shoves to get inside first.

Father still has some money that we can use to buy food, although it's running out. One day, I decide to take the money and go to my mother's friend Lucia to buy vegetables from her garden. Father says not to be gone too long because Emmanuel needs me. "And be careful!" We're not supposed to go outside the Jewish district.

When I tell Lucia that Mama went to work for the Germans and never came home, she's sympathetic. "I know what that's like," she tells me. "My husband was taken into the Russian army and I've never heard from him again. But can't anybody help you find her and bring her home?" she asks me.

"But how?" I ask.

"I don't know," she answers. Lucia doesn't have any ideas. After a few minutes, I can feel that the subject disturbs her, and that she only wants to sell me her vegetables. Lucia has been friendly with Mama for a long time, and I was hoping that she would offer to help us in some way, but I've begun to see that Gentiles can be very cool and distant. So I pay Lucia for the food, understanding that there's nothing more I can expect from her.

It's late spring, and Father says we're running out of money. We have very little to eat and we go to bed hungry every night. Emmanuel needs milk every day, and it's hard for us to get it for him.

One day, Father gives me a little money and tells me to ask the neighbors what we can buy to eat. So I ask Mrs. Tepper and she tells me there's a family that has enough money to eat potatoes every day. They sell the potato peelings to whoever wants to buy them. So I go to them and buy a kilo of potato peels to make *latkes* (potato pancakes). But without oil or an egg, the *latkes* don't taste right. Father says that's okay. It doesn't have to taste good. It keeps our bellies from grinding so we can fall asleep, and that's all that matters, now. So I buy potato peelings every day.

We've run out of flour, so I buy chicken feed, made from grains and seeds, because it's very cheap. Father says he'll try to make *pletzek*—flat bread—from the chicken feed. *Pletzek* was always my favorite kind of bread. Since Father is a professional baker, I believe he can take almost anything and bake it into delicious rolls. But even he can't make chicken feed into flour! He makes dough from the chicken feed and shapes it into *pletzek*, and bakes it. But it comes out of the oven looking very strange. And when we swallow it, the sharp particles stick in our throats and hurt us. I give Emmanuel a piece to suck on, but he screams and kicks and cries even harder than before. We should have spit it out immediately, but we're

110

so hungry that we swallow it. It only makes the pain in our bellies even more terrible. I can feel the sharp pieces of grain and seed churning inside me and scraping the inside of my belly all day long. Rosa is crying, too. But Father's groans are the worst. He's getting weaker every day, and he can hardly walk any more.

Rosa and Emmanuel and I are always hungry and father is very weak and in a lot of pain. There's nothing to do at home and nothing to eat in the apartment, so Rosa and I take Emmanuel outside and we walk around the streets, looking for food or information on where we can get more food coupons.

At home, Father is in so much pain he can hardly move. He has terrible stomach cramps all of the time. His legs are so swollen that he can't stand on them, and they've become stiff. His eyes seem to be getting smaller and sinking into his head.

One morning, he crawls out of our apartment and into the street. Mrs. Tepper comes in to tell me that he's sitting on the corner, holding out his hand and begging for food. I'm so ashamed that I just want to disappear. Instead, I go outside and try to help Father come in. But we have no food, and we're all hungry.

Out on the streets, there are lots of people like Father, sitting and begging for food. And there are dead bodies, too. If somebody gets sick, there's nothing they can do. The Germans have taken all the doctors away.

I say a silent prayer for my family: "Please, God, if we have to die, let us all die together! Don't leave me an orphan, without my father and my mother. If we have to die, please let us all fall asleep, together, and never wake up again." Being an orphan is the most terrifying thing I can imagine.

The next day, Father goes out to the street to beg for bread again. This time he faints and one of the neighbors drags him home.

"Oh, no! This can't be my father," I think, when I see his shrunken body. He looks like a stranger to me. His body is the size of a child's. The next day, Father can't move at all. He can't even crawl. And he can't see us anymore—he's blind! His swollen legs are black and pus is coming out of them. The sight of the pus frightens me more than blood. That afternoon, he sits in our apartment and calls out, "Bread, bread." A neighbor girl, a small child, comes into the apartment with a crust of bread in her mouth. She's chewing on the bread, but she takes it out of her mouth and hands it to Father. But Father is too weak to take it. He keels over on the floor.

Rosa and I scream and run to him, "Father, please don't leave us. If you die, we want to die, too."

Our next-door neighbor, Mrs. Tepper, hears us screaming and comes into our apartment.

She looks at Father and says, "Children, your father can't hear you anymore. He's dead." Rosa and I are crying and screaming, "No, no! How can we live without our parents? If Father is dead, we want to die, too!"

But Mrs. Tepper says, "Stop talking about killing yourselves! You don't know what you're saying! It's not as if you're the only orphans in Lvov. Every family has lost somebody. Everybody is hungry or sick. You need to be strong now. You need to take care of each other, and Emmanuel. One day, maybe soon, this terrible war will be over! You need to do anything and everything that you can, in order to live!"

Mrs. Tepper orders the furniture cart to come and pick up father's body. Rosa and I hold onto each other, crying, until the cart comes along. This cart is pulled by two men, since Jews are no longer allowed to own horses. Rosa and I watch the men load Father on the cart with the other dead bodies. They cover his body with a black cloth. We have to give them Father's ration card, in order for them to take his body away.

The men with the cart take Father to be buried in a common grave, I don't know where. Rosa and I are too tired and upset to follow the cart and anyway, what use is it? Mrs. Tepper says, "Save all your strength and ingenuity to take care of yourselves and Emmanuel."

As I watch the wagon roll away, I'm furious with Father for abandoning us. How can he leave us alone? And how will we survive without him? How will I take care of Rosa and Emmanuel, and find food for all of us, with no father and no mother?

One minute I'm sad, and the next minute I'm angry. I, too, want to escape from this nightmare that we're living in. But there's no way out—only death. I ask myself why God, who is supposed to be so good, has done this to us? What terrible thing have we done to deserve this?

We're orphans! Rosa, Emmanuel, and I are all alone! Father is dead and Mama has been

113

gone for months. Like her friend Lucia's husband, she may never come back, and we may never find out where she is or what happened to her. When I think back on the orphans who I used to know in school, it terrifies me. I'm an orphan now—the most horrible thing I could ever imagine while I was growing up has happened to me!

I'm an orphan—like some of the heroes in fairy tales. I'm like a character in a story. It's as if I'm trapped inside a horror story—a story so strange, so far-fetched, and so nightmarish that it can only be a fairy tale.

A fairy tale hero is not aware of her own bravery in the face of danger. She is locked in a life-or-death struggle, with a strong will to survive and no thought of giving up. . .

Most of my time is taken up searching for food, and it's not easy. It's like Mrs. Tepper said, I need all my strength and ingenuity since we have no money and food is so scarce. As I walk around the streets, searching for food, I have no time to think about anything else.

The streets are full of hungry people. Many of them are children. Some of them have swollen stomachs and skinny legs, like sticks. They sit on the street begging for bread. Some of them die of hunger or of typhus. I see the furniture cart every day, collecting the dead bodies and taking them away.

People walk around the streets without talking to each other or even looking at each other. One by one, our neighbors and people I've known all of my life have disappeared. Mr. and

Mrs. Drucker were the first to disappear. Mrs. Drucker was the one who always used to "read my forehead" and tell me what kind of day I had at school. I'm not sure when they disappeared, but I haven't seen them for a few days. I knock on their door, but there's no answer. One of the neighbors says maybe they went to live with relatives outside Lvov. But Mrs. Tepper says they hadn't said a word about leaving to anybody, so she suspects that the Germans took them away. But when? We didn't hear any loudspeakers or see any German soldiers. It's very strange.

And then, one by one, all of the people in the Tepper family, whose front door faces ours, disappear. The Teppers have two adult sons who don't live with them, but who come to visit, and their son Ulek, who is a year or two older than me, and a daughter about my age. Ulek is tall for his age, and he's very strong. He's always been a terrible bully. He used to go around the neighborhood daring the other boys to fight with him. He even bullied the girls. All the years we were growing up, he used to pull my hair and punch me whenever there was no grown-up around, so I'm still frightened of him. Especially now, with Mama and Father gone.

Ulek always had friends among the Polish boys who lived in the crowded apartment buildings near our neighborhood. And even though the Polish and Ukrainians are getting more and more anti-Semitic, Ulek still has friends among them.

Now Ulek lives alone with his mother. Mama always used to tell me that Mrs. Tepper was stingy and she never shared anything or

115

gave anything away. Now, whenever I go into their apartment, I can see that she keeps all of their belongings stored in cupboards that she locks with a key. And I hear some of the other neighbors gossiping and saying that Ulek is taking some of those things to sell. Ulek always has money. The neighbors say he's like a criminal. Only criminals have money when everybody else is poor, they say. Ulek still dresses in nice clothes and he takes food to share with his friends, the Polish boys who live near our neighborhood and wander around threatening and hitting the neighborhood children. Ulek doesn't threaten or hurt the Jewish children in our neighborhood, but it's awful to see that he's still friendly with those mean young bullies, and shares his food with them, while the Jewish families in our building are starving.

One day, Mrs. Tepper and her daughter are taken away in a round-up. All the neighbors are talking about it.

Of course, I can still hear Ulek going in and out of the apartment every day, and I try to avoid him, like I always have. When I go out to look for food, I sometimes see him, at a distance, walking around the neighborhood with his Polish buddies. The neighbors say he's sold everything in the Tepper's apartment, in order to buy food. But now I notice that Ulek isn't wearing fine clothes any more, and he looks a lot thinner.

One day, there's a knock on the door. When I open the door, it's Ulek. I see that he isn't wearing shoes.

"Please, Sonya," he says, "do you think I could have a pair of your father's shoes? I have no shoes of my own anymore."

"Of course," I answer quickly. I'm still afraid of him. I run to get Father's shoes and give them to Ulek as fast as I can. I don't want to have any quarrels with him!

He says, "I have no money today, but tomorrow I'll come and pay you for the shoes."

"It's okay," I answer "you don't need to pay me." I'm hoping that he doesn't force himself into our apartment and try to take something from us.

"Oh, but I want to pay you," he insists. "I'll come back with the money tomorrow."

Rosa and I are very surprised. This isn't the same Ulek we've grown up with! I try to remember the last time I spoke to him, but I can't. The only thing I remember is all the times Zoshka told me, "When you grow up, the two of you are going to get married", and how much I always hated hearing that.

That evening, Ulek comes back, bringing bread for me and Rosa and Emmanuel. Again, he promises to pay us for the shoes. He looks weak and very tired. He doesn't act like a bully any more.

The following day, Ulek comes in with the money. He doesn't stay long, and I can see that he looks sick. A few days later, we realize that we haven't seen or heard Ulek coming and going, which is unusual, since the doors of our apartments face each other. So Rosa and I go and knock on the door of the Tepper's apartment. In a weak voice, Ulek says, "Come in." When we go inside, we see Ulek sitting on a

117

chair, slumped over the kitchen table. I run upstairs to get Mrs. Lempel. She says, "He's burning up with fever. I'm sure he has typhus." A few other neighbors come in and somebody takes him away. I think they've taken him to the Jewish clinic, but I'm not sure.

Now all of the Teppers are gone, and a new family has moved into their apartment. Rosa and I knock on their door and an older woman answers. She smiles warmly and invites us to come in. Mrs. Spiro tells us all about her family. Her husband and her two sons were taken by the Germans in an "*Aktzia*"—a round-up. Now she lives with her grandson, Joseph, and her two daughters-in-law. I tell her about our family, and how hard it is to find food every day.

Rosa and I call Mrs. Spiro "Grandma" because she's old enough to be our grandmother. She's also very kind to us, and treats us as if she really is a relative. It's wonderful to have a kind adult to talk to. And "Grandma" brings us a cup of soup for Emmanuel every day!

The Spiros are a wealthy family. They used to live on Academitska Street, a large street in the center of Lvov, where the people are much wealthier than in our neighborhood. Now, all the Jews in that neighborhood are being forced to leave their apartments and to move into our neighborhood. Their apartments are being given to Aryans.

Mrs. Spiro tells us that her husband and her two sons are doctors. Her two daughters-in-law work in the medical profession, too. One is a laboratory assistant. She's very pretty, and she goes to work wearing a lot of make-up. I've almost never seen women wearing make-up and I'm very impressed with the way she looks. Mrs. Spiro's grandson, Joseph, is an intern in the Jewish "hospital." He's twenty years old, and like Mrs. Spiro, he's very kind to us. Mrs. Spiro explains that the "hospital" he works in is really just a clinic that's been set up in the old Jewish "Gymnasium" (i.e., high school).

"That must be the place where Ulek went," I tell Rosa.

"I'm hungry, I'm hungry, I'm hungry!" All I can think about is food and how to get it. Hunger pains make my stomach growl day and night. Not having anything to eat makes me feel dizzy and weak. I've lost my sense of time. I don't wash, or change my clothes, or comb my hair. And I'm not even frightened of all the terrifying things that are happening around us because I'm too hungry to think about them. All days are the same, all hours are the same. They're all an agony of hunger!

A hunger monster, an invisible but powerful creature, has invaded my body. No matter what I do, I can't escape from it. Even when I eat, I'm never satisfied. The hunger monster sucks the food out of my belly into its own body, leaving me forever empty inside.

I can feel the hunger monster moving around inside me, and growing day by day. Its arms and legs scratch at my insides, with their long, pointed claws. The monster is hungry: "Food, I want food!" it screams. And it claws at my guts, making me double over in pain. Some days I can hardly get out of bed, it hurts so

119

much. And I feel weak and light-headed. I know if I don't feed the monster, it will kill me. But sometimes I feel too weak to get up and search for food. And I have nobody to help me. Rosa's just a little girl, and she's always been much weaker than I am. And Emmanuel is a baby. I'm supposed to take care of them!

Mrs. Spiro tells us about a place where Jewish children can go for free handouts of food. It's the Jewish Council on Starozakonna (Old Testament) Street, near the "hospital" where her grandson, Joseph, works. I know the neighborhood—it's where the outdoor market used to be. Of course, there's no market there any more.

It's a long walk from our neighborhood, and it's very hard for Rosa and me to go there with Emmanuel. He's too weak to walk, so we have to carry him all the way. I want to go there by myself, but Rosa begs me not to leave her alone—she's afraid there will be a round-up. And we can't leave Emmanuel alone. So, the three of us go there together, and Rosa and I take turns carrying Emmanuel. It takes us a long time because we have to put him down many times along the way. There are a lot of children waiting outside the building. Rosa stands on the side of the street with Emmanuel, while I go up to the window to wait in line. It takes a very long time for me to reach the window. I tell the clerk about our family. He says, "They'll give you half a kilo of jam, but you'll have to bring a container for it." He gives me a slip of paper with our names on it, and the address of the place to go for the jam.

"You can only go there once," he says.

120

We have to go all the way home to get a container for the jam. But the thought of getting something to eat gives us a bit of energy.

When we finally get to the address written on the slip of paper, I can see it had once been a synagogue. There's Hebrew writing on the building. It was partially torn down by the Germans, and it's standing in ruins. I look at the remains of the building with sadness. But then I think, "Maybe amongst the ruins, there is still a bit of holiness left here, a bit of strength that will keep us alive. From this holy place, where all of the prayers of the religious Jews are collected, maybe a miracle will come."

I remember the prayer Mama once taught me, in Hebrew: *Shema Israel!* and I say it to myself. I leave Rosa and Emmanuel standing in the street outside, and go inside the very dark room. It's so dark inside that I can hardly see. I'm lost in a daydream, thinking about all the power collected in this holy place. Suddenly, I hear a man's voice asking me,

"What are you looking for, little girl?"

I walk up to the man, and hand him the slip of paper and the container for the jam. He takes the jar and fills it. I thank him and leave as fast as I can.

Outside in the street, I show the jar of jam to Rosa and Emmanuel. We're so hungry that we can't wait to get home to taste it. So we open it and stick our fingers inside and lick them off. The jam is made of beets. We dip our fingers and lick them off, dip and lick, dip and lick, all the way home until we start feeling nauseous. When we get home, I take a spoon

121

and we take turns scraping the jar clean. But, as soon as we finish it, we're hungry again.

Every day, when Mrs. Spiro brings a cup of soup for Emmanuel, I taste it to make sure it isn't too hot. I always swallow a lot of the soup myself, because I'm so hungry. But today, Emmanuel doesn't even want his soup. I think he's sick. He's been whimpering and crying all day long. I ask him what hurts, but he doesn't answer. He's stopped saying the few words he used to know. His arms and legs are very thin, and he has sores all over his body. His hair is clumped together, and it's dirty and full of lice. His eyes look huge in his skinny face.

I ask "Grandma" what to do. That evening, she sends her grandson, Joseph, to look at Emmanuel. Joseph says, "You could bring the baby to the "hospital" where I work tomorrow." The "hospital" is on Jakuba Hermana (Jacob Herman) Street, a long walk from our apartment, but we decide to go there with Emmanuel, even though it's very far for us to carry him.

So the next morning, Rosa and I take turns carrying Emmanuel to the Jewish "hospital." We're so hungry and weak that we can't hold Emmanuel for more than a minute or two at a time. Halfway there, we just can't lift him anymore, so we make him walk between us, holding our hands. We walk very slowly. Even so, we have to stop and rest many times. It takes us a very long time to get there.

On the way, we see two young blond women wearing nurses' uniforms. It's obvious they're German. As they get near us, I think of stopping them on the street and asking them for help. After all, they're nurses and it's their profession to help people. In Polish, nurses are called "sisters of mercy." But as they pass us, I can hear them talking to each other and giggling. They don't even notice us, and I think they probably wouldn't agree to help Jewish children, anyway, so I don't talk to them at all.

When we finally get to the hospital, all three of us are exhausted from the long walk. Inside the hospital, we find Joseph Spiro, and he takes us to the on-duty doctor. The doctor looks at Emmanuel and asks, "What do you think we can do for him? He isn't sick-he's simply hungry. Look how swollen his stomach is! We haven't got any food for him here in the hospital. You'll have to take him home."

When I hear that, I start to cry. I can't imagine walking all the way home with him again. But Joseph takes the doctor aside and whispers something in his ear. The doctor tells me, "Wait here. I'm going to talk to the director."

We wait a while beside Emmanuel. When the doctor comes back, he says, "Okay, you can leave the baby here. If you find something for him to eat, bring it to him tomorrow. You may visit him twice a week."

We thank the doctor very gratefully and we watch as he puts Emmanuel into a bed. Poor Emmanuel! He's too young to understand what's happening and why we're leaving him in the hospital by himself. He holds out his arms to us and whimpers as we leave. I try to explain to him that we'll come back in the morning, but I don't think he understands. Finally, Rosa and

123

I leave Emmanuel in the hospital and go home, planning to come back the following day with food for him.

Back at our apartment, I'm very sad. I can't help feeling how lonely and silent the apartment is, with Mama and Father gone—and now Emmanuel. I ask myself if I've done everything I can for Emmanuel. Since I had named him, we were supposed to have a special relationship all our lives. I was waiting for him to grow up and be my best friend. If only I had given him a little more food, maybe he wouldn't have gotten so sick! I feel very guilty about leaving him in the hospital all by himself.

Later that day, Mrs. Spiro's daughters-in-law come to our door, looking for "Grandma," but we haven't seen her. They knock on the door of every neighbor in the building, asking for Mrs. Spiro, but nobody has seen her. Somebody says that the Germans had been driving around our neighborhood, rounding up people from the streets that day. It must have been while Rosa and I were at the "hospital." Mrs. Spiro must have been taken away in an "Aktzia."

That evening, Rosa and I have nothing to eat. The next morning we go to the soup kitchen where Jewish children can get a free cup of soup several times a week. We each save some of our soup to bring to Emmanuel.

Carrying the soup, Rosa and I slowly walk the long way to the hospital. We're very sad that we have so little food to bring him. To our surprise, when we arrive at the hospital, the gate is standing wide open, and so is the large front door. When we enter the building, there

124

isn't a single person in sight. All of the beds are empty, including Emmanuel's. We search upstairs and down, but we don't find anybody at all. The building is completely empty! We don't know what to do. There's nobody there to give us any information. We keep going upstairs and downstairs, looking in all of the rooms for a long time. Finally we decide to go home, since there's nothing more we can do.

"Maybe the Germans came into the hospital and took everybody away," I think. But there's no way for us to find out.

We still have the coupons to get a free loaf of bread at the small bakery once a week. That's the place where everybody stands in line, pushing and shoving and shouting at each other. Today, the shopkeeper is angry with the people who are making so much noise. He comes out into the street and yells, "Quiet down! You're giving me a headache!" and goes back inside, angrily. I'm standing near the door, almost inside, when he comes out again. Like all of the small shops in Lvov, the bakery has a metal door that rolls up during the day and rolls down at night to be locked so that thieves can't break the window and get in. The shopkeeper puts his hand on the metal roll-up door and threatens the crowd, saying, "If you don't stop screaming, I'll close the shop right now!"

But nobody listens to him.

Suddenly, he shoves a few of us inside and lowers the metal roll-down door so that nobody can get in or out. I'm very pleased that I've gotten inside! He gives each of us a very heavy loaf of bread that hasn't been completely baked, and tells us not to come back again.

"I'm sick of you people!" she shouts at us. "This is the last time I'm giving out free bread!"

As I carry the bread home, I realize that the loaf won't last a whole week. In fact, Rosa and I finish it the same day. And the next time I go back there, the shop is closed.

A few weeks later, I see a relative of Zoshka's on the street, someone I'd met at Michalova's apartment. Her name is Stanislava, but I call her by her nickname, Stacha. She's married to Kazhik, Michalova's son. I've always liked Stacha, and she's always been very nice to me.

Stacha says hello and asks about my family. When I tell her that Rosa and I are all alone now, she asks, "What's going to become of you? How are you going to live?"

I shrug my shoulders and she says, "Sonya, you need to get a job. That way, you can eat and bring home food for Rosa every day."

"But how can I get a job?" I ask her.

Stacha invites me to come and work for her as a servant. She and Kazhik are now living in a large apartment on Halitska Street with their son, Yurek, who is nine years old. I remember Yurek from the times I'd gone to Zoshka's family on Sundays, although it's been a few years since I've him. Even though he was several years younger than me, we had liked each other and been friendly on the occasions when we met.

Stacha's family has moved to a neighborhood that I've never been to, so she explains how to get there and gives me money to take the tram. She says, "It's easy to find, because on Halitska Street there's a big outdoor market."

I'm very willing to work, but I'm scared about going to their apartment because I remember the time when Kazhik had come home drunk. But Stacha says, "Kazhik goes to work every day. He'll be at work by the time you arrive and you'll leave before he comes home."

So I agree to try it out. After all, we have no money and I don't know how we're going to survive.

I go home and tell Rosa about it.

"But first, I need to fix myself up," I tell her.

Around the time father died, the water in our building had stopped running regularly. There are hours—even days—when there's no running water at all. Rosa and I haven't washed ourselves for a long time. We're filthy and our scalps itch day and night. Our heads are full of lice, and we don't know how to get rid of them. Sometimes we sit for hours at a time, picking the lice out of each other's hair and squashing them. It feels like sweet revenge to kill the awful bugs that torment us. I especially love to hear the popping sound they make when we squeeze them. But we never seem to get rid of them all!

Rosa and I walk over to Lokietka Street to look for the Jewish barber who had always cut our hair when we were little. He's still there, in his small shop, and of course he remembers our family—especially Mama, who was always friends with everyone in the neighborhood. It doesn't surprise him when we tell him that Mama is missing and Father has died.

"Our heads are full of lice and we need haircuts," I tell him.

He's sympathetic and very kind.

"I can't cut your hair inside the shop," he says, "because your heads are crawling with lice. But, let's go outside and I'll give you haircuts in the street."

So, he carries the barber stool outside, sets it down on the sidewalk in front of his shop, and carefully checks Rosa and me for lice. Every time he drags the fine-toothed comb through our hair, it comes out full of lice. His scissors are full of lice, too, by the time he finishes cutting our hair. But he's pleasant and kind, and he doesn't charge us for the haircuts.

The following morning, I get all dressed up in the one clean summer dress I have left. It's made of a flowered pink fabric, and has a matching decorative apron. It's a very pretty dress, and one that I would have worn only on special occasions, under normal circumstances. But nothing is normal in our lives anymore, so I put on my most beautiful dress to go to work, cleaning Stacha's apartment!

Her apartment is a long way off, and Stacha gave me money to take the tram. So I walk over to Zamarstynovska Street, where the electric tramline runs. I stand next to the tram after it stops, and wait for all the other passengers to get on. After the tram starts to roll away, I jump on the steps and hold on tightly to the metal railing. That way I can ride without paying for a ticket. I've seen many children do that. I'll save the tram fare to buy food.

I ride like that all the way to Halitska Street. When I get off the tram, I'm in a neighborhood where I've never been before, on a street I've never heard of. I can see that it's a very wealthy area. There's an outdoor market-the Halitski Market-covered by a clear glass rooftop. This is nothing like the outdoor market on Starozakonna Street where I used to go with Mama. It's clean and quiet, and the stalls are far away from each other, so that people have a lot of space to walk around. The market has a huge variety of fresh fruits and vegetables piled high on the stalls. I haven't seen that much food in months—maybe years! I feel as if I had gotten on the tram in one world and gotten off in another. Just looking at the plenty that surrounds me makes me feel better than I've felt for a long time. I feel as if I've moved up a station or two in life. I've got a job and Rosa and I are going to have food every day now!

Stacha's apartment is very large and luxurious, with wooden parquet floors that have designs in them. I've never seen anything like them before. Under the German occupation, the Ukrainians have gotten better jobs and now they're moving into bigger and finer apartments—apartments that had belonged to Jewish families who the Germans had deported or forced to move. Even though it's very large, there are only three people living in their apartment—Kazhik, Stacha, and Yurek. Kazhik is out working when I get there, and Stacha is waiting for me.

Stacha greets me kindly, and she asks, "Would you like a cup of coffee before you begin to work?"

I'm very pleased to sit and drink coffee with her. Everything feels no *normal* here! Things

129

haven't been this way in my life for a very long time.

When we finish our coffee, Stacha explains the tasks that need to be done, and she tells me that she's going to work alongside of me. Together, we get down on our hands and knees, rub the wooden floors with oil, and polish them with clean towels. At first, Stacha says she doesn't think I'll know how to do some of the chores, but I soon show her that I've learned all about housekeeping from Zoshka! I'm very proud that I remember how to clean and straighten up the salon the way Zoshka did. I carry the carpet outside and shake it hard. I hit it very hard with a stick to shake out the dust. Then I clean the kitchen and wash the dishes.

Stacha says, "You're a wonderful little worker! Even though you're so small, you can do everything."

I'm very proud and happy. But the best part of working for Stacha is the food. She gives me delicious soup and thick slices of bread to eat at lunch. I eat quickly and thank Stacha happily.

"What else do you have for me to do today?" I ask her.

"Oh, you've worked hard enough for one day!" she says. "Now it's time for you to go home." She gives me a container of hot soup and a few very thick slices of bread, generously spread with butter, for Rosa. Food is my payment for the work I'm doing. These days, food is the payment that everybody wants. The families in our neighborhood are selling all of their clothing and household goods just in order to

130

get food. And I have a job! I can't believe how lucky I am.

Every day I come to work with enthusiasm and the energy that comes from having enough to eat. I save the money that Stacha gives me for the tram by hopping on while it's moving, and I use the money to buy more food. Rosa and I eat every day, and we're both feeling a lot better.

Every afternoon when I come home, Rosa is standing near the tram stop on Zamarstynovska Street, waiting to eat the bread and butter as we walk home, and to sit down and eat the soup when we get to our apartment. After everything we've been through, we're finally living with a feeling of hope. We're merry in the evenings, now, and I'm amazed that Rosa and I are talking to each other without fighting. We've actually become friends!

It's wonderful to go to Stacha's apartment every day and be surrounded by beautiful things in a wealthy neighborhood.

But one day, Yurek comes home from school while I'm still there. I haven't seen him in a few years.

"Look how big Yurek is!" I say.

I remember when he was just learning to walk. But now he's almost as tall as I am— since I'm very short for my age, and he's tall for his. I can see that Yurek has changed in other ways, too. He's no longer shy and he looks me over carefully, as if he's searching for something. And he's not at all friendly like he used to be. Right after we say hello, he grabs a slice of bread and butter and goes out to play. I don't know why, but I feel troubled about him.

131

Another day, Kazhik comes home early from work, while I'm still at their apartment. He isn't drunk, but I'm afraid of him anyway. And I notice that Stacha is very quiet and she stands far away from Kazhik. I think she's afraid of him, too. Kazhik isn't nice to me, and I leave in a hurry soon after he gets home. That day, Stacha doesn't give me anything to take home for Rosa. When I leave their apartment, I hear Kazhik yelling at Stacha, and I think I hear him mention my name, and the ugly word *"Zhydouvka."* After that, I make sure to leave earlier in the afternoon.

Yurek's behavior worries me, too. Sometimes he comes home while I'm still there, and when he looks at me, I can see anger in his eyes. He mutters under his breath, *"Zhydouvka!"* and Stacha doesn't say anything.

One day, Yurek comes in and yells at me: *"Zhydouvka,* get out of here!" Stacha tries to quiet him, but he turns on her and says, "Throw her out of here. I don't want a dirty Jew in my house. I'll tell my friends she's working here and they'll come and beat her up!"

I can see that Stacha is shaken by Yurek's words, and she's very frightened of the neighbors. I have to hide from them as I come and go. Jews are not supposed to go out of the ghetto, and the Germans have started building a fence around our neighborhood. Aryans are not allowed to help Jews in any way—certainly not by giving us jobs with food for payment! So I have to come and go very quietly, hoping that the neighbors don't notice. If a neighbor comes to Stacha's door while I'm there, I have to hide in one of the many rooms of the large apartment.

It's also hard for Rosa to stay at home alone all day. She's frightened of the round-ups and she's lonely at home without any company. Every morning, she begs me, "Please come home as soon as you can."

Then, one day when I get to work, Stacha says, "I'm sorry, but I can't keep you here anymore, because some of the neighbors have seen you and they're angry with me for helping a Jew." But she lets me work for a few hours and when I'm ready to go home, she fills up the soup jug and gives me extra slices of bread and a small cabbage to take home for Rosa.

With a heavy heart, I get off the tram at Zamarstynovska Street, and I'm surprised that Rosa isn't waiting for me. Maybe I'm home earlier than usual, I think.

I walk home slowly and sadly, not knowing what we're going to do next for food. When I get home, the apartment is very quiet.

"Rosa, where are you?" I call into the empty apartment. I look all around, but she isn't here.

I'm getting hungry, so I taste some of the soup that I've brought for Rosa. Then I put the cabbage in a pot of water and look for wood to light the stove. We haven't cooked anything for a long time, and there's no wood left.

Meanwhile, I'm getting more and more worried about Rosa. It's not like her to stay away from home. She must be hungry, not having eaten anything all day long. A little while later, when she still doesn't show up, I go to one of the neighbors and ask if she's seen Rosa.

133

"Sonya," she tells me sadly, "There was a round-up this morning, and the soldiers took all of the children off the streets. After that, they came into the building and took more children from their apartments."

"Oh, no! It can't be!" I scream. "Rosa, come back! Don't leave me alone," I wail.

I'm beside myself. Rosa is gone, and I don't know when I'll see her again. I sit and cry until it's dark outside. Later, I'm hungry, and I finish the soup and the bread that I had brought home for Rosa, feeling guilty about eating food that's meant for her. After that, I'm still hungry, so I eat the whole cabbage. I don't know when I'll have anything to eat again, except for a cup of soup from the public soup kitchen.

What's happening to me? My whole world has gone crazy! In the past few months, I've lost every member of my family. On June 16th, I turned twelve, but I didn't even notice the date. Father must have died around that time, I think. And now Rosa and Emmanuel are gone, and I'm all alone. Where is Mama? Will I ever see her again? Where are Rosa and Emmanuel? Will I ever see them again? Everything is topsy-turvy. Nothing makes sense any more. In all the years we were growing up together, Rosa and I had fought every day, sometimes bitterly. And now, in the past few months, she's become my closest friend. Day and night, I had thought about feeding her, about coming home to her, about helping her to survive. And now that she's gone, I miss her terribly! What's going to happen to me? Will the Germans come and take me away in a round-up, too? And where do they take all these people?

I'm hungry all of the time, and I have questions that I can't answer. Nobody can answer them. If only I had somebody to talk to!

One day, Zoshka shows up at our apartment! I haven't seen her for such a long time that I'm very surprised. I wasn't expecting to see her ever again. I'm so happy she's here! All I remember is growing up with her, and the wonderful stories and rhymes she used to tell me. I've forgotten about the way she began to yell at me and to slap me very hard. I've forgotten about the bundle that she and Michalova had taken from us. I hug her and she hugs me back.

"Where is Rosa? Where is Emmanuel?" she asks.

"There's nobody left but me," I tell her, "and, tomorrow or the next day, the Germans will probably take me, too."

"Don't talk that way, child!" she says. "You must go on. Your mother and the children will return some day."

She has soup for me. "Eat this, and I'll come again tomorrow," she says. "Or maybe you should come to the kitchen at the base where I work. The soldiers make it very hard for me to cross into this neighborhood. They stand at the bridge on Peltevna Street and check everybody who passes. If you come to me at the base, I'll give you soup. It will be easier for you to cross through the bridge than it is for me."

But I've seen the soldiers at the Peltevna Bridge. They call Peltevna "the bridge of death" now. I'm afraid to cross it.

Zoshka says, "Those awful soldiers make it terrible for everyone! They search us and ask questions and check everything we're carrying. But they'll get what's coming to them, one day!"

After Zoshka leaves, I wonder what to do. I'm too frightened to go to the base where she works, even though I'm terribly hungry. What if the soldiers catch me?

The next day, I walk over to the base and I see a lot of German soldiers wandering around. I'm very hungry and I want to go to Zoshka, but in the end, I'm too frightened to go any nearer. And Zoshka doesn't come back to the ghetto. The Germans are building a fence all around our neighborhood, and they check everybody who crosses it. When will I see Zoshka again?

The Ghetto

In a fairy tale, the hero sometimes turns to people who have been friendly in the past. But often, these people prove to be false friends....

I haven't seen Zoshka for a long time, and I wonder if she'll ever come by again. It's very dangerous, I know. Even though I know she's tricked my family before, I think I'll go see Zoshka's sister-in-law, Michalova. After all, I've known her almost all my life. Maybe she'll help me now? Who else do I have to turn to?

When I tell Michalova all that has happened, and how hungry and lonely and frightened I am, she says, "I'll look for a safe place to send you. I have relatives in Tarnopol. They live in a small house. Maybe they could take you to live with them for a while, and you could work for them, like you worked for Stacha."

That gives me some hope, and I wait a few days for Michalova to come and let me know about the family in Tarnopol. But the long days pass slowly and Michalova never comes. So one day, I decide to go back to her apartment, which isn't very far from our neighborhood.

When Michalova answers the door, I can see she's surprised to see me. And when I ask her about the family in Tarnopol, she looks at me as if I'm crazy. Then she answers, "No, I'm sorry, they can't take you."

Now I realize that Michalova never really planned to send me to her relatives in Tarnopol. She just told me a story in order to get rid of me. She isn't going to do anything to help me!

I know I should leave, but when I see a plate full of *pierogi* on her kitchen table, Michalova notices me eyeing the food.

"Why don't you sit down and have some *pirogei*?" she invites me.

I'm so hungry that I sit down and eat, in spite of the pain in my heart.

When I finish, she says, "When you come here, it's very dangerous for me. If the Germans see you, my whole family will get into trouble."

She doesn't mention the connection that our families had for many years, or the bundle of our clothes that she had taken to sell, giving us just a few *zlotys* in return.

"But at least it's possible to live well under German rule, "she tells me. "The Russians were bad for everybody, but the Germans are only bad for the Jews."

When I hear her say that, I know I'll never come back here again.

There's a soup kitchen where I can go once a week for a free cup of soup. I eat there every time it's open. I meet people there, and it's a good place to find out about all sorts of things.

But there are some very strange things going on there.

Once I saw a young man who had come from a different city, with an unusual accent. He had very dark eyes and a sad face. Somebody said he came from Warsaw. He took all of the little children and sat them down along the length of one wall and taught them a song in Yiddish! I couldn't believe what I was seeing. Why was this man teaching starving children a song? I stood apart from the other children, unwilling to participate, but I wasn't able to ignore them. The scene fascinated and repelled me, at the same time. While our lives are one big tragedy, this man is teaching starving children a song in Yiddish! Nothing makes sense any more.

This morning, when I got to the soup kitchen, one of the young women who was dishing out bowls of soup—a very pretty girl—was acting very nervous and distracted. She looked at me and said, "Please, can you help me? I have so much work to do here that I can't leave, not even for a minute, and I have to get a very important message to my mother."

I didn't know what to say. Why had she picked me to help her? And what was the message? I was curious, so I agreed to do it.

"Run as fast as you can," she said, giving me the address, "and tell my mother that the Germans are coming! She needs to prepare immediately for a search. After the search, she needs to hide somewhere else—not in the apartment."

I understood that the danger was great, and that I needed to get there as soon as I could, so

139

I did my best to run quickly. When I knocked on the door, an older woman opened it and let me into a very large room that was crowded with people sitting or lying on the floor, with bundles piled up all around them. I know it was a private apartment, but it looked more like a train station! It was hard to look at these people because they all looked like they were starving, and they all seemed to be staring at me! I delivered the message and the woman thanked me very warmly.

I left as soon as I could, but the image of the strange room is still with me. Who were those people? And what were they doing there? Would they have time to clear out before the Germans arrived? And what would the Germans do with them if they didn't get out in time? But, back at the soup kitchen, the pretty young girl isn't there, and nobody knows where she went.

One sunny day, when I'm walking on Lokietka Street, I see a boy about my age holding a paper cup full of candies and selling them. I have a little money, so I buy a piece of candy from him and I ask him, "Where did you get the candies?"

He says, "That's none of your business," and walks away.

Food is so scarce that people keep secrets from each other. I guess they're afraid that there won't be enough for everybody.

I have nothing to do, so I decide to follow the boy, pretending that I'm wandering aimlessly. I see him walk down Zamarstynovska Street, which is the longest street in our area of

Lvov. It's the street where the tramline runs, so it's always full of people.

I follow him for a long way, without his noticing me. Finally, he passes a train station, and comes to a house that looks like it's been hit by a bomb. There's a low brick wall around the house, and the boy climbs over it. I watch him walk through one of the holes in the wall of the house and go down some steps. It isn't long before he comes out again, holding a paper cone. I hide in the rubble, watching him walk back in the direction of our neighborhood.

When he's out of sight, I go through the broken wall and down the steps, looking for the entrance. A woman opens a window and asks, "What are you looking for, young lady?" It's obvious to me from the way she looks and talks that she's Jewish.

"Do you have any candy for sale?" I ask her.

She puts her finger to her lips and hisses, "Sh! Don't let anybody hear you!"

Then she motions for me to come closer, and asks, "Do you have any money?"

I show her the few *zlotys* in my hand and she tells me to wait. There's a delicious aroma coming from the open window, and I peek inside to see the big cooking pots where the candies are boiling. Very soon, the woman comes back to the window and hands me a paper cone full of candies. I give her the few zlotys I have.

"Just don't tell anybody where you got them!" she makes me promise.

I'm delighted. I immediately take one of the colorful candies and put it in my mouth. The candies are round and flat with a thin layer of yellow coating the outer rim. Inside, they have

141

a star design in red and green. The yellow coating has the flavor and aroma of lemon. I try hard to stop myself from eating them all. But I realize that I can sell the candies to get money for real, nourishing food, and I walk back towards our neighborhood, selling candies to children all along the way.

I've sold everything on my way back home, so I turn around and go right back to the woman again. And once again, I can't resist taking several candies for myself, although I'm arguing with myself all the time that I need the money to buy food. But the candies are so delicious I just can't control myself. I even try closing my eyes so I won't be tempted by the sight of the candies, but that doesn't help much.

For the next few days I go back to the candy-seller every day, using the money I earn to buy food. I suppose that during all the years I saw Mama selling bread and trading on the market, I somehow learned how to barter.

But very soon, it seems like all the kids on the street have found out the secret of the "candy store." After a few days, I notice other children standing on Lokietka Street trying to sell candies. The next time I go to the ruined house, it's empty. Like so many other people, the candy-maker has disappeared.

Walking around the streets, I notice that most people are dressed very poorly, and they look very thin and weak. Nobody seems to look anybody in the face anymore. We all just pass each other by and go our separate ways.

Of all the families in our building that I've known during the years I was growing up, only two are left now: the Gottliebs and the Lempels. Mr. Gottlieb and Mr. Lempel both have professions that are useful to the Germans, so nobody bothers them.

I haven't seen the Freiheiters since before Mama left. They must be living somewhere near here, but I don't know how to find them. I've looked around our apartment for their new address, but I can't find it.

I feel very sad and lonely, and I long for somebody to talk to. I miss Rosa! I've been having conversations with myself, but they don't help me much because, after all, I'm just a kid, so what do I know about anything? I think about my childhood heroes, Ivasyk, who saved himself from the witches by jumping from tree to tree, and Yash and Malgosha, who tricked Babayaga—the evil witch—and escaped from her. They were all children, like me, and they were able to help themselves because they were so clever! I wonder how they thought up the solutions to their problems? I think about them all the time. If only I could talk to them!

"You mustn't lose hope!"

This is the coldest winter I can ever remember. Maybe it's because I'm always hungry, or because I'm alone in the apartment and there's no more coal or wood to heat it. I spend most of my time searching for food.

At home, all alone, I start looking around our apartment for small things to sell. Some of Rosa's clothes are left, and I don't know when—or if—she'll be back again, so one by one, I sell them or trade them for food. I'm hungry and I

143

need the food. But, every time I trade something of Rosa's I feel guilty. What if she comes back? What will she wear? What would Mama say if she ever found out what I did? Would Yash have sold Malgosha's clothing? I have nobody to talk to, and I'm not at all sure if I'm doing the right thing. I remember how after Father died, Mrs. Tepper told me and Rosa that we should do anything and everything that was necessary to keep ourselves alive, and that someday Mama would come back. I can't lose hope.

One day, I see a boy selling cigarettes on Lokietka Street. I see a lot of people smoking and it looks easy to sell cigarettes. I notice that on almost every street, there are boys selling cigarettes. So I decide to try it, too. When I have a little money, I go up to the boy on Lokietka Street, and ask him to sell me a pack of cigarettes. Then I open the pack and sell each cigarette separately. I don't make a lot of money that way, but it's an easy job because so many people want to buy cigarettes.

My parents never smoked, and I've never known anybody who was a smoker. So I can't understand why, when people are so hungry, they're willing to spend their money on cigarettes. I would have thought they would prefer to buy food. So I ask somebody who I see smoking, "Why do you smoke?"

He answers, "It makes me feel good, as good as if I had eaten."

That makes me very curious, so I decide to try smoking a cigarette. I've never done that— or even thought about it—before. When I've

144

sold all but one of the cigarettes that day, I take the one cigarette that's left back to our apartment. I take a match and light the cigarette, and I take a deep breath—and I regret it immediately! It makes me feel dizzy and nauseous and I almost throw up. I'll never try to smoke again!

For every family that leaves our building, new neighbors move into the empty apartments, and our building is becoming crowded with strangers. Next to our courtyard, there's a tiny building with just two apartments. Piotrova, the Polish woman who used to clean our apartment building and the toilets, had lived in one of those apartments with her family. Now, a new family has moved into the small building.

They're a young couple with a child who looks a little older than my brother, Emmanuel. The other neighbors call them "the Serbs" because they have dark skin and they speak a foreign language, I guess Serbian. It's hard to talk to them because they only speak a few words of Yiddish, even though they're Jewish.

But the strangest thing about them is that they obviously have a great deal of money. While the rest of us are struggling to find food every day, they're eating like kings and queens! The other neighbors gossip about them, saying, "Instead of eating bread, they eat chocolate." That makes me so curious that I go to visit them in their apartment, and sure enough, they offer me a piece of chocolate!

They haven't been living here for a very long time when something very strange happens. A

145

private car drives up to our building. We almost never see private cars on our street, so everybody notices. There are a few men in the car. They force their way into the apartment and take the husband away. I hear the neighbors talking about it, but I don't really understand what they're saying. Somebody thinks the Serbian man was dealing on the black market and was caught doing something illegal. But that doesn't make sense—it wasn't the Germans who took him away. Nobody knows who it was.

Since then, the wife has been walking around the neighborhood, carrying her son in her arms and crying. She tries to talk to the neighbors, but we have no common language, except for a few words of Yiddish, so it's hard to understand what she's trying to say. But it's obvious that she's miserable and very frightened.

A few days later, another private car drives up to our building—*another car!*—and again, some men get out and force their way into the apartment. But, unlike her husband, the woman doesn't go quietly or willingly. She screams and she cries, and in her broken Yiddish, she begs the neighbors to help her. But what can we do? The men force her and the little boy into the car and they drive off. Nobody knows who it was who took them away, or where they were taken.

On my way home one day, I hear a voice over the loudspeaker announcing: "*Aktzia!* Everybody out into the streets!" I don't think I can make it back home in time, even though I'm near our apartment. When I get to Jijo and Jijova's abandoned hut in the courtyard of our building, I hear the motors of the German police cars getting very close. To get to our apartment, I have to cross the large courtyard outside our building, and I know I won't be able to reach our apartment before the Germans arrive, so I look around and decide to hide in the dried-up corn stalks that are still standing in the small field outside Jijo and Jijova's old hut. As I'm crawling through the stalks of corn, I see other children hiding there, too. Everyone is totally silent.

Next to the field of corn is a small storage hut where the families in our building used to keep charcoal for heating our homes in winter. On top of the hut, on the flat wooden roof, a few Polish boys are sitting and looking into the cornfield where we children are trying to hide. They're laughing and joking, and pointing to us children, saying, "There's a dirty little Jew!" and "Look, there's another one!"

I'm lying face down, too frightened to look up, but I can see the boots of German soldiers pass close by me. A soldier reaches down and grabs one child by the hair, pulling him up, and then another and another. There are terrible screams from the Jewish children, and laughter from the teenage Polish boys. My heart is beating so fast, it feels like it's going to explode!

I can't remember what happened next, but somehow the Germans overlooked me. I must have fainted from the weakness, the hunger, and the fear.

When I wake up, still lying in the cornfield, it's dark. My clothing is wet, and I'm ashamed of myself for having peed in my pants at the age of twelve!

What's going to happen to me? What's happening to my world? The streets are full of strangers—even our own building is full of strangers, and I have nobody to talk to. Where are all of the people who have disappeared? Will I ever see them again?

I think about Jijo and Jijova. I know they would help me, if only I could find them!

Months earlier, Jijo and Jijova had left their little hut. Jijo had come to say goodbye to Mama, and given her their new address, but I don't know where they're living now. If I knew, I would go to them for help. I'm sure they would help me!

One evening, as I'm walking around the streets, I meet a young woman who I recognize from the neighborhood. We start talking, and I ask her about Jijo and Jijova.

"They're living in a large apartment and running a restaurant on Poddembem Street," she tells me. That's not far from our apartment. This restaurant had belonged to a Jewish man whose family was forced to give it up, under the new German laws. The restaurant had been given to "Aryans"—Jijo and Jijova. The young woman tells me that Jijo had once mentioned my name to her and told her that, if she ever saw me, she should tell me to come to his restaurant.

I knew I could count on them!

But it's hard to go out of the neighborhood now, because they're building a fence and it's guarded by German soldiers.

I'm afraid to try going out of the ghetto. I think maybe I should try to go through the gate, along with all of the other Jews who work outside the ghetto and have work passes. I'm too young to have a work pass, and I wouldn't know what to do if the Germans stopped me. I think about it day and night. What would Ivasyk do? Or Yash? Or the young man from the golden spring?

"Put a kerchief on your head and wear an old coat!"

The following morning, I stand in line at the ghetto gate with the other workers, shaking with fear, since I don't have a work pass. If the police stop me, I don't know what will happen. All of a sudden I hear music and can't believe what I see. There's a small orchestra playing! All of the workers who pass through the gate have to march in tune to the music. I'm very short for my age, and I'm worried that the soldiers will notice that I'm too young to be a worker, so I stand on tiptoe and dance to the rhythm of the music as I pass through the gate with the other workers. It's very crowded and they let me through without questioning me. I guess nobody noticed me.

As soon as I get through the gate, I walk as quickly as I can to the address where Jijo and Jijova's restaurant is located.

Jijo is happy to see me. He and his moustache smile from ear to ear. But Jijova is so busy and

149

so pressured that she hardly speaks to me at all. Jijova is managing the kitchen, and it's very crowded with Polish workers. Jijo is the head-waiter, and they have a few other waiters as well.

When I tell them what happened to my family, they give me food to eat and a simple job. Jijova points to a pile of potatoes and tells me I can peel them for her. But my hands aren't used to peeling potatoes, and I work very slowly. The potato peels are thick. And, after a while, my fingers start to hurt. Jijova sees that I'm working slowly and comes over to see what I'm doing. When she sees how thick the peels are, she says I'm wasting a lot of food, and she tells me to stop peeling these potatoes. Instead, she shows me a pot of boiled potatoes. It'll be easier for me to peel them, she says. But, the boiled potatoes are so hot that they burn my fingers. I blow on my fingers to cool them off, but it doesn't help. Meanwhile, I can see how busy Jijova is and how much work she has to do, so I try harder.

Somehow, the morning passes and the customers start arriving for lunch. There's stuffed cabbage and soup with grits. The potatoes are served with fried onions. I sit and eat a large lunch and I feel full and satisfied. I clean up after the customers have eaten and left. This is the first time in a long time that I've had enough to eat.

I was hoping that Jijo and Jijova would invite me to stay with them—I remember how they used to take in babies—but they don't invite me. They give me thick slices of bread and butter to take home, and tell me to come back the next day. I'm disappointed that they haven't asked me to stay with them, but I don't say anything.

Day after day, I go back. There's soup with vegetables, plenty of potatoes, thick slices of bread, and even meat. Now that I eat every day, I feel stronger—and a lot happier! And I have somebody to talk to. Jijova is too busy to talk, and her Polish is still very limited. But Jijo has time to talk to me.

But working for them is a problem, both for them and for me. First of all, it's forbidden for Jews to leave the Jewish neighborhood, which makes it very dangerous for me to come and go. And for them, helping a Jew is illegal. If the Germans find out, they'll be severely punished.

One day, a German officer comes into the restaurant and sees me. Of course, he suspects that I'm Jewish. When he asks Jijo where I'm from, Jijo pretends not to know. He shrugs his shoulders.

"She said she was hungry and asked me for a job," he tells the officer.

But we know the officer will be back.

Jijo is very warm and kind to me, and I can feel that he truly wants to protect me. But Jijova is working under a lot of pressure and she often gets angry with me. I overhear her telling her husband that it's too dangerous to keep me there. And I understand that since she's telling him this in Polish, she *wants* me to overhear her! She clearly isn't interested in risking anything in order to help me. After all the happy hours I spent in their tiny house during the years they were our neighbors, I expected her

151

to care about me, but I can easily see it's not that way at all.

Since Jijova manages the kitchen, she does most of the cooking. She even bakes cakes. She's always very busy and pressured. But Jijo has a much easier job. He manages the dining room, which means that he takes the money from the customers. He only waits on customers when it's very busy. A lot of the time, he stands at the counter and looks at the customers, nibbling on cakes. And he always winks at me, and invites me to share a piece of cake with him.

One day, Jijova is busier and more irritable than usual. She sees Jijo and me eating cake, while she's working hard in the kitchen. She starts to yell at Jijo, "All the time, you stand around eating cake. You getting fatter and fatter and I working hard. You don't even ask if I need help! What you think, the little girl help me a lot? No, hardly at all! Enough of this!"

Jijo tries to calm her down, and apologizes to me, but I understand that I'm no longer welcome there, and I leave that afternoon with a big package of bread and leftover meats, knowing that I'll never go back.

Once again, I'm on my own, looking for food every day. I may never see Jijo and Jijova again, and I may never get over the feeling that they've sent me away like a stranger.

Now the Germans have passed another law: Jews are only allowed to leave the Jewish quarter with a permit. The only ones allowed to go in and out of the ghetto are people with professions that are useful to the Germans, like our neighbors, Mr. Lempel and Mr. Gottlieb.

It feels like the round-ups and deportations are becoming more and more frequent. We have no idea what happens to the people who are taken away in round-ups. Do they beat everybody, and make them dig ditches and sleep outdoors in their clothes, like my father? Seeing how cruel the Germans are to us, and how much they hate us, I can only imagine that it must be terrible to be taken away in a round-up.

We always used to know when there was going to be a round-up because we heard the sounds of the sirens. But now the Germans have stopped putting on the sirens, so we can't hear them coming from far away, anymore. We can only hear the motors of the cars when they get close.

When the German soldiers drive their cars around the streets, they shout over a loud-speaker: "*Raus!* Everybody into the street!" They take any children who are playing outdoors and the adults who are unfortunate enough to be running errands at the time—in short, anybody who is on the street. It's horribly frightening, with people pleading for mercy, and the Germans screaming at them, "*Schnell!* Move faster!"

But no matter how dangerous it is to be in the streets, staying at home is worse because it means certain death by slow starvation. So, I spend most of my time walking around the streets, looking for food. So far, I've been very lucky to escape being taken away in a round-up.

There's almost nothing left in our apartment to trade for food. It's a very cold winter and I don't know who I can turn to, and I'm lonely at home. Sometimes I don't know which is the worst: the cold, the hunger, the fear, or the loneliness.

Piotrova's family moved out of our neighborhood around the same time that Zoshka left, soon after the German invasion. Looking around the apartment for something to sell, I come across some papers. Piotrova's new address is there, so I decide to visit her. She's in an apartment that used to belong to a Jewish family. It's outside the Jewish neighborhood, of course, but not far from our street. It's near the Lenartovich elementary school where I used to study.

It's a few days before Christmas when I go to Piotrova. I tell her what happened to my family and she immediately says, "You'll stay with us for the holiday!"

This was much more than I expected, and of course, I'm thrilled to have a warm place to stay and food to eat.

Their new apartment isn't very large, but their family is happy, and I feel welcome and wanted. I sleep in the bed with Piotrova's daughter, a girl my own age, who was a playmate throughout my childhood. The hours pass very quickly. Their apartment is heated and it feels wonderful. We're decorating the apartment and the Christmas tree with colored paper streamers and cutouts in the shapes of hearts and stars. We also sing Christmas carols, which I've learned over the years from lis-

154

tening to the groups of children who roam the streets singing them at the Christmas season. I feel very comfortable staying with Piotrova's family. Nobody asks me any questions, and their cheerfulness and good mood is contagious.

While we're playing and decorating the Christmas tree, Piotrova spends all day cooking, and the apartment is filled with delicious aromas. She makes the special Ukrainian holiday dish called *kutya*. This is a grain, like wheat, soaked in honey with raisins and spices. She also bakes a lot of cakes—every one a different size and shape. When we sit down to have our Christmas dinner, the table is so crowded with things to eat that there's barely enough room for the plates! Some of us have to sit on the bed because there aren't enough chairs, but nobody minds. This is the first time in a long time that I've sat at a table full of food with a family, and I feel wonderful. There's lots of talking, and laughter, and we sing more Christmas carols after dinner.

But, when Christmas day is over, Piotrova makes a big package of food for me and sends me home. Once again, I'm in my cold, empty house, with my daily search for food, and my never-ending loneliness. At the age of twelve, I'm all alone in the world with nobody that I can depend on. I know that if I'm going to survive, it will have to be through my own efforts.

One afternoon, I go to visit the Lempel family, one of the last of our original neighbors to remain in the building. Their daughter is Adela, the mentally retarded girl. Mr. Lempel works

155

for the Germans, so they're still allowed to live here. On my way downstairs to go back to our apartment, I hear the sound of motors and people screaming, and I realize that this is another round-up. In recent round-ups, the Germans have started coming into apartments and taking people, so I have to find a safe place to hide. I remember when I ran into the cornfield near our courtyard, but I can't get there now. And, anyway, it's almost winter and the cornstalks are completely bare. I have to think of something fast, because I can hear the motors of the cars, so they must be getting very close. I look up the stairwell, and I think I might go up to the area under the roof where the women used to hang the clean laundry to dry. I'll have to move very fast, since the motors have stopped and the Germans are screaming for people to come out and give themselves up. "*Raus! Schnell!*" they yell, and my heart is beating wildly.

The stairs are old and made of wood. With every step, they creak loudly, and I'm afraid the Germans will hear me, so I decide, instead, to run into one of the toilets on the floor above where the Lempels live. I lock myself in the toilet and try to keep from peeing in my pants, in spite of my panic.

What will I say if they find me here? I decide to tell them that I had a terrible stomachache, and so I couldn't come out of the toilet when they yelled "*Raus!*"

I can hear the Germans entering our building and screaming, "*Raus! Schnell!* Everybody out!" They beat on the doors of the apartments with their guns. Then, I hear the Mrs. Lempel

156

screaming, and begging for mercy and telling them that her husband works for the Germans. But they ignore her. They probably don't understand Polish, anyway. From where I'm hiding in the toilet, I hear them dragging Adela down the steps, and she's babbling in her weird, wailing voice. I wonder if this is the first time that Adela has ever been out of the Lempel's apartment.

After that, I hear the cars pull away and then there's silence—a terrible, frightening silence. I'm certain that the Germans are gone, but I stay in the toilet for a long time. Then, I'm afraid they might blow up the apartment building, because I hear they've done that to other buildings, so I decide to come out. Slowly, I step out of the toilet and peek between the slats of the staircase. Below me, in the courtyard, I can see Mr. Gottlieb. He's looking at the building and holding his head in his hands. I make my way downstairs very slowly and stand near him, whispering his name. When he looks at me, I can see tears streaming down his cheeks. He doesn't say anything to me, and silently, I go into my apartment.

After a round-up, there's always a period of quiet in the ghetto, and new neighbors move into the empty apartments. The Germans are forcing all of the Jews into our area. So, in the next few days, new families come to fill the empty apartments. Now, only Mr. Gottlieb remains of all the neighbors I've grown up with.

One day a pretty young woman moves into one of the tiny, one-room apartments in our courtyard—the one where Piotrova's family used to live.

I meet Genia in the courtyard and she invites me into her apartment. "Tell me about your family," she says.

"They're all gone," I begin. She asks a lot of questions, and slowly but surely, I tell her everything. When I finish, she hugs me and holds me close for a long time.

"Don't give up hope," she tells me. "We don't know where they take everybody, but maybe they'll come home soon."

I ask her about selling Rosa's clothing, and she says, "You need food. What good will it do Rosa if she comes home and you're too weak to help her? You need to take care of yourself right now."

That makes me feel a lot better.

Genia tells me about herself, too.

"My husband was taken to the Janowska Camp on the other side of Lvov. It's a work camp where the Germans take Jewish men to do forced labor. I don't know when I'll see him again," she says. "Nobody knows. But we mustn't give up hope. We have to believe that the end of the war is coming soon, and that our families will come home very soon," she tells me.

Genia used to be a teacher, and she's warm and kind to me. It's wonderful to have a friend, and I visit with her every day. Every word of hers is sincere and true.

"You need to be very careful what you say to strangers," she warns me. "It's very easy nowadays for people to take advantage of a child who is left all alone."

"Oh, Genia," I say, "I wish I could be your daughter!"

She hugs me and says, "You're a wonderful girl, and any mother would be proud of you. When your mama comes back, she's going to tell you that you did exactly the right thing," she assures me.

"But what if she doesn't come back?" I ask her. "What if I'm an orphan after the war? Sometimes I think it would be better to die."

"Oh, no!" she says. "Don't give up hope yet. You're much too young to die. Even if your father is dead and your mother never comes back, maybe another family will adopt you. Anybody would be happy to have you for a daughter!"

Then, one afternoon, when Genia and I are talking in my apartment, we hear shouts outside and people screaming. Then comes the noise of engines and the sound of boots stamping on the cobblestones. Suddenly, the door of our apartment is thrown open. I don't look at the door, but run into the other room and hide behind the large stove. Meanwhile, I hear Genia screaming, "No, no!"

Luckily, the soldiers don't come into the salon. I wait behind the stove for a long time until all the noise is gone. When I come out, Genia is gone.

Alone again, with no adult to turn to, my loneliness is sometimes as frightening as my hunger. With countless long hours to fill and nobody to talk to, I begin to roam the streets, pretending that some of the imaginary companions from my beloved fairy tales are walking beside me.

There's no point in talking to myself because, after all, what do I know? I'm
only a child. So I ask Ivasyk and Yash, "What would *you* do in my place?"

"Always keep your eyes and ears open"
"Look all around you, everywhere you go."
"Run fast when you think you're in danger"
"Don't give up!" and *"Don't lose hope!"*

The Germans are building a fence around our neighborhood. It runs along Zamarstynovska Street. One side of the boulevard is inside the Jewish ghetto, and the middle of the wide street—where the tramline runs—is on the Aryan side. At Zamarstynovska, a steep embankment crosses over the street to carry the train line that runs from the Ukraine to Przemysl. Under the embankment is an opening for traffic to pass through. The border of the Jewish ghetto is marked by the corner where the train line meets Zamarstynovska Street. I don't know where the other borders of the ghetto are. This corner—between the embankment and Zamarstynovska Street—is always busy. There are always people walking, riding bicycles, driving private cars, or riding in carts pulled by horses or *"fiacres"*—the taxis for the wealthy, pulled by horses. The electric trams run all day long. The train passes overhead a few times a day—I sometimes hear it in the middle of the night, too.

One day, a rich-looking gentleman knocks on our apartment door and asks if he can come in. Mr. Weinberg is a tall, distinguished-looking man with a moustache. He makes a very good impression on me. He says that he's a fabric merchant, and I believe him. Mr. Weinberg tells me that his family used to live in a prosperous non-Jewish neighborhood of Lvov. But now, the Germans are forcing them to move into one of the empty apartments in our neighborhood. Mr. Weinberg asks me if he and his family could share our apartment with me. In exchange, he promises to give me good meals every day. This sounds like a fine offer. Living with a wealthy family, I would be certain to eat every day. I would have company, too. And, just as important, Mr. Weinberg says he'll bring logs of firewood and keep the wood-burning stove going to heat the apartment. So, of course I agree to have the Weinbergs move in with me.

Mr. Weinberg invites me to come to the small apartment on Zhrudlana Street where his family moved after the Germans forced them to leave their apartment. Zhrudlana Street is near our neighborhood, but outside the fence that the Germans have built.

When I go to their apartment, I meet their daughter, Lilly, who is 18 years old, and their eleven-year-old son, Henrik. Both of them are tall, like their father. Mrs. Weinberg is very pleasant to me. She smiles and says, "I was just making breakfast for the family. Why don't you sit down and join us?"

What a breakfast—just like the breakfasts I used to have at home before the Germans came! There's fresh-baked bread with butter,

161

eggs, sardines in tomato sauce, and real coffee with a delicious aroma, served with milk and sugar. I can't remember the last time I had such a wonderful breakfast! It reminds me of my own family and I start to feel a terrible longing for them.

Over breakfast, we talk about the move. The Weinbergs want to move into my apartment with their two children and their uncle, whose wife has been taken away by the Germans, and his daughter, Lusha, who is a year or two older than Lilly. I think that's too many people, but I don't say anything. After all, when Mama and Father and Zoshka and Rosa and Emmanuel and I lived in our apartment, we managed fine.

The next day, the Weinbergs arrive with one wagonload of their belongings. That's all they're allowed to take from their previous apartment. The wagon is piled high with rolls of colorful fabric, since Mr. Weinberg made his fortune selling fabric. He unloads the rolls of fabric and stacks them in every corner of our apartment. Mr. Weinberg plans to sell the fabric in order to buy food and firewood.

The Weinbergs also bring a double-decker bed—something I've never seen before. Mrs. Weinberg says we need to save space, since there will be seven of us living in the apartment.

The Weinbergs have a very comfortable daily routine: Mr. Weinberg and the uncle go out to work every day, trying to sell the fabrics. Mrs. Weinberg stays home and cooks. Both Lilly and Lusha work for the Germans, serving coffee in an officers' club. They work mostly in the evenings, and they put on fancy dresses and a lot of make-up when they go to work. I love to watch them when they put on their make-up. They're very friendly, and they put make-up on me whenever I ask them to. Except for lipstick, Mama had never worn make-up, so rouge and mascara are new to me, and getting dressed up is like a game.

When Lusha's at home, she likes to sing. She sings the songs that are popular in the ghetto. They're very sad songs, but I like to listen to them, anyway. One of the songs goes like this:

Every bird has its nest,
Where she can rest her head
And have her festive meal.
Only we have no nest,
No place to rest,
No place to sleep
Safely in the night.

Almost every night, the girls bring home special treats from their jobs: sometimes candy, or smoked fish, or strawberry jelly. I've been living mostly on bread and potatoes, and I haven't had foods like these for a long time.

But I soon notice there's a problem between the two girls. They don't talk and laugh with each other so much anymore. I sometimes overhear Lilly telling Mrs. Weinberg that Lusha is doing "terrible things" with the German officers. She doesn't say exactly what, but Mrs. Weinberg looks shocked. She doesn't say anything to Lusha, but I can feel the tension between them.

163

The Weinbergs really are wealthy, and we have good hot meals every day. After dinner, we sit around the stove in the salon. It's nice and warm, now. Since it's winter, it's hard to take a bath, so we sometimes put a big bowl of water on a chair (a *taboret*) in the kitchen and take off our shirts and wash ourselves under the arms. I haven't washed myself since I worked for Stacha, and it feels very nice to be clean.

One evening, Mr. Weinberg says, "Now it's time for the louse promenade." At first, I don't understand what he's talking about, but I soon find out. He takes off his shirt and runs his fingers along the seams, which is where the lice mostly go. Everybody has lice, since we no longer take regular baths or launder our clothing. We're constantly scratching ourselves, and it's very uncomfortable. The lice collect along the seams, but especially under the arms. One by one, Mr. Weinberg takes each louse out of the stitches of his shirt and throws it into the fire. His son and daughter and I take off our shirts and do the same. Only Mrs. Weinberg is too shy to take off her shirt in front of us. The "louse promenade" has become an evening ritual with us, and I think it's fun.

Although it's wonderful to have hot meals every day, and a fire, and company, this is a terrible time in all of our lives, and I can feel the distress of the Weinberg family very strongly. Mr. Weinberg has ulcers and whenever he has an attack, he moans and groans and staggers all over the apartment, clutching his stomach for hours on end. Sometimes, he screams at his daughter, Lilly, and criticizes her harshly. He yells, "Your cousin Lusha

164

brings home all sorts of delicacies from the officers' club-like cigarettes and bread. But you only come home to eat—you never bring anything. You're a burden on the household!"

This makes Mrs. Weinberg very nervous and miserable, but she never answers him back.

There are no doctors to turn to and of course, the Jewish "hospital" is gone, so Mr. Weinberg can't get the medicine he needs for his condition. When he's feeling well, he's very pleasant to me, but whenever he has an attack of ulcers, he becomes mean and nasty. He even throws dishes and breaks them. Once he screamed at me, yelling, "You're a burden to our family! Why should I give you my family's last crust of bread?"

When he says that, I crouch in a corner, thinking to myself, "You don't need to give me anything to eat." But I'm too frightened to say anything to him. Mrs. Weinberg tries to console me, but she's very pressured and distressed by her husband's illness. When Mr. Weinberg yells at me, Mrs. Weinberg just puts her arm around me and takes me out of the room without a word.

Mrs. Weinberg tells me that her husband's ulcer attacks come from eating certain foods. But in the ghetto, it's impossible to get the foods he needs. It's hard enough to get any food. We buy whatever is available every day. So Mr. Weinberg's condition is getting worse and worse, and there's nothing we can do for him.

I still go out every day, partly out of boredom, and partly to get away from the tension in

165

the house. Even when Mr. Weinberg is feeling well, Mrs. Weinberg is always sad and nervous. One day, Mrs. Weinberg asks me if I want to try to go out of the ghetto to buy food. It's dangerous, but we know that a lot of children are doing it, so I begin to watch them, to learn what to do.

I walk past the Peltevna Bridge where Rosa and Emmanuel and I had waited for Mama to come home. Everybody calls it "the bridge of death" now. It's the place where the Germans march the Jewish workers out of the ghetto to work every day, and return them every evening. It's called the Bridge of Death because if somebody who is not supposed to be in the work brigade tries to escape from the ghetto via that bridge, the German guards, armed with rifles, shoot at them. You need to run very fast to get across the opening under the bridge without being noticed. And you need to be lucky enough to get across when the guards are all looking in a different direction.

I notice that some children get across the bridge by jumping onto the back of a wagon that's crossing. They hide in the wagon until they're out of sight of the guards. Some of the guards are German, but there are some Jewish guards, too. The Jewish guards look the other way when they see children doing this, and it's like a game.

I have to watch what the other children are doing for a long time before I work up the courage to do it myself. I keep telling myself, "The next time a wagon comes by, I'm going to jump on it." But I'm too scared the first day.

I go back the next day and stand watching, again, for a long time. Many wagons go by before I get up the courage to try jumping on one of them. I'm not only afraid of the guards, I'm also afraid to go into the market. What if somebody recognizes me, or just suspects that I'm a Jew? The German policemen are never far away. Finally, one of the Jewish guards notices that I'm standing there and hesitating, and he comes over to me and says, "You can jump on a wagon. Don't worry. I'll look the other way!"

That gives me the courage I need, and I jump on the very next wagon. On the other side, I run to the outdoor market on Starozakonna Street. It's the market where I used to go with Mama. At first, I'm afraid somebody will recognize me and know that I'm a Jew. But of course the people on the street realize that the children in the streets are Jews coming from the ghetto. After all, the Polish children are all in school. Only Jewish children walk around the streets during the daytime. And, anyway, you can tell by looking at us that we're Jews. We have no fur collars or muffs, and we're all wearing ragged, dirty clothes.

I try to watch the other children and do whatever I see them doing. I follow them to the place where the large outdoor market used to be, but it doesn't look anything like it used to look, with outdoor stalls for every kind of food. Now, there are no more stalls. People simply walk around the streets carrying whatever they have to sell.

Now, it's called the black market. I see children my own age buying food with money, or exchanging clothing or shoes or household
167

goods for food. The Gentiles walking around the marketplace are happy to trade with the Jewish children. They get good bargains.

The first person I see is a woman with two large jugs of milk. She puts the large, heavy jugs down and stands next to them, as if she's taking a rest. If a policeman comes along, she can simply pick up the jugs and keep walking, as if she's on her way home. When I go up to her and ask if I can buy some of the milk, she says, "Of course!"

"How much does a liter cost?"

"Seven marks."

I can't believe my ears! Mrs. Weinberg had thought a liter of milk would cost at least 15 marks, and she had given me 30 marks to buy two liters. When she sees me hesitating, the woman says, "Hurry up! We need to do this fast." I notice she has a strong Ukrainian accent.

I ask if I can taste the milk because Mrs. Weinberg told me that a lot of people water down the milk they sell. But the milk is creamy and delicious, and I buy four liters for the price of two!

I go back to the ghetto as fast as I can, planning a business scheme on the way. Instead of going directly home, I go to the street in the ghetto where milk used to be sold during the years I was growing up. There used to be a cow there that belonged to a Jewish family.

Mama had taken me there to buy milk for Emmanuel. Now, even though there's no longer a cow, people still go there to buy milk.

So I go there carrying my four liters of milk, planning to sell two of them. I go into a house
168

where I've bought milk for Emmanuel many times before. An old woman is living there now. I don't recognize her. I hesitate, wondering if this is the right thing to do, but I soon convince myself it's all right. Anyway, there are two younger boys there already, trying to sell milk to the woman. I listen to their conversation.

"What? How much do you want for a liter?" asks the old woman.

"Sixteen marks," says one of the boys.

"What? Sixteen marks? Impossible! I never heard of a price like that for a liter of milk! Is this the way you treat an old woman? I'll give you ten marks."

The boys start to walk away.

"Okay, I'll give you twelve marks a liter," the old woman calls after them.

"You can't buy milk for twelve marks a liter in the ghetto," one of the boys tells her, and they continue walking away.

"Okay, I'll give you another mark—another two marks per liter," says the old woman, "but this is highway robbery!"

The boys turn around, "We'll take it," they say.

They measure out six liters of milk and get ready to leave.

I watch the boys walk away, feeling totally confused, but go up to the old woman, determined to do the same thing. "Do you want to buy two liters of milk?" I ask her, hesitantly.

She screams at me, "No! Today I've bought enough!" So, without saying anything, I turn around to go away. But, then she calls me back, yelling, "Hey, you! Come back and show me the milk you've brought."

So I go back and she tastes the milk. She sees that it's creamy and hasn't been watered down.

"All right, I'll take it," she says. "And you can bring me more tomorrow—but the same kind of milk, do you hear?"

"I'll bring it!" I promise her, feeling happy and confident.

"How much do you want for a liter?" asks the old woman.

"Fourteen marks," I answer, hesitantly.

"All right," she agrees wearily, knowing that I had overheard the conversation she had with the two boys, "I'll give it to you."

She takes out twenty-eight marks from her drawer and hands it to me. I turn to go out and hear her say to nobody in particular, "Look at the salespeople we have today!"

In my hand there are now twenty-eight marks. I'm proud of myself and very satisfied. I decide to return two marks to Mrs. Weinberg, along with the two liters of milk. I'll take the money I earn and keep my business dealings to myself. Like everybody else, I've learned not to tell everything.

The next day, I promise myself, "Today, I'll go three times to trade for milk. I'll keep going back and forth and I'll sell milk to the old woman in the milk store in the ghetto twice before I bring two liters of milk home for Mrs. Weinberg."

Every time I cross the Peltevna Bridge, I can feel myself getting braver. But in spite of my ambition and my new-found courage, I only succeed in getting out of the ghetto twice. The third time I try to cross, there's a different man standing guard, and I can see that he's really serious about trying to keep children from crossing, so I'm afraid. I know I'll be in big trouble if he doesn't look the other way, like the other guard has done. I realize it isn't worth trying.

"Tomorrow is another day," I tell myself, holding tight the 80 marks I've earned from my business scheme.

The monotonous and frightening routine of my life has changed overnight! Even the atmosphere of misery in the Weinberg household no longer affects me like before. I'm spending more and more time outside, and I'm learning new things every day. Now, with the money I earn, I'll be able to buy and sell all kinds of foods in the ghetto. And other things, too—like a lice comb!

One day, I come home to an empty apartment. That's very unusual, since Mrs. Weinberg and Henrik almost never go out. I ask one of the neighbors if she knows what happened. There was a round-up, she says. She doesn't know if the Weinbergs were taken away, but they're gone. The empty apartment is silent.

Now, I'm terribly lonely again. But at least I've learned how to find food for myself, and how to earn some money. When the firewood runs out, it's just as cold indoors as it is outside. So I walk around the streets, and I go back to the black market as often as I dare to cross the Bridge of Death. Without the Weinbergs, I have no hot, cooked meals, but I have some of their clothing, and there's still some fabric that can be traded for food.

171

During the day, the ghetto is full of older people who can't work, and children who have been lucky enough to escape the round-ups. All of the healthy young men and women go to work for the Germans every day, and come back at night. That leaves only sick or disabled men, women with babies, the elderly, and children in the ghetto. So children and teenagers like me are the main source of trading and getting food in the ghetto. Maybe this has been true for a long time, and I've just realized it.

Once I get used to doing it, sneaking out of the ghetto is like a game. After I do it for a while, I'm excited by the challenge, and not so scared. It's certainly better than the alternatives: waiting in the ghetto to be taken away in a round-up, or starving to death! Crossing to the Aryan side to trade for food gives my life a purpose.

Now, my main concern is where to find food on the black market. There are many different kinds of foods for sale, but I have to be very careful not to be spotted by the German soldiers. The streets are very crowded in the old marketplace because so many people are out trading. Most of the people who have food for sale carry it around under their coats. They walk slowly and they whisper what they have to sell, and how much they want for it, as they pass me by. But they don't show their wares because that would be dangerous. It's winter and everybody is wearing long, heavy coats, so people can hide their goods under their coats, up their sleeves, or even in the hems of their coats.

Another way to find food is to follow people and listen to their whispered conversations. Sometimes, an "agent" goes out on the street looking for people who want to buy certain foods. He whispers to them to follow him and they go over to the entrance of the apartment building where the goods are stored. I have to be very alert in order to understand all the secret ways that people communicate with each other on the black market. I remember the strange things Mama used to do when the Russians were in control of Lvov—like going out in the middle of the night and standing in line to buy vodka so that she could trade it for vegetables at Lucia's garden. It's something like that. It's a different way of bartering, but it's still bartering.

I've also learned some new things about my neighborhood. The older people who are still here need food desperately, and they're willing to pay us kids to bring it to them, since they could never do what we're doing—cross the bridge of death and return without being caught. So when I go back to the ghetto with food, I walk home through my neighborhood and stop at some apartments where the people are happy to buy food from me. They're older people who have managed to escape the round-ups, but are too old to work for the Germans. They have no other way to get food for themselves. The younger people in their families go out each morning to work for the Germans and come back late at night, too tired to search for food. They're happy to buy whatever I bring them.

Another thing I have now is a fine-toothed comb to pick the lice out of my hair. I spent a great deal of money—70 Marks—for a "Hercules" lice comb. Everybody says that's the best kind, with the closest and strongest teeth. I use it every day to keep the lice out of my hair—not because I care about how I look, but because the itchiness drives me crazy. I might not be able to win the war against the Germans, but I'm winning the war against the lice! For me, this is something to celebrate.

But like everybody else in the ghetto, I walk around in ragged old clothing that I never change. I'm only interested in keeping warm. I really don't care how I look. Whenever I come across clean clothing that's in good condition, I trade it for food. I don't think of dressing better. Anybody who looks at me can easily see from my shabby appearance, that I'm a Jew. I wear an old, dark blue coat that reaches all the way down to my ankles. It has a black cloth collar, which was sewn on to replace the fur collar that originally came with the coat. My shoes are old and badly worn. I wrap my head in a warm, colorful wool scarf that I fold into a triangle, and then cross over my chest, and tie behind my back to keep the wind from blowing in.

As I become more involved with trading on the black market, I discover that there are a few bridges in Lvov: Zamarstynovka, Peltevna, Slonetchna, and Kleparovski. Each one has its special characteristics and its own dangers. The "bridges" at Kleparovski and Slonetchna are simply train crossings at ground level. But they're so far away that I never use them.

At Zamarstynovska, the bridge is located at the steepest incline of the embankment. In order to cross the train tracks, you have to climb up a very steep mound of earth. The bridge is only used for the trains. Underneath the bridge, where people and public transportation pass, the opening is very wide. Since the bridge is on the Aryan side of the ghetto, once I go through the hole under the fence, I can pass underneath the bridge without any trouble. But the hole under the fence is only a few meters from the bridge, and the policemen are always alert and looking for people trying to cross.

The Peltevna Bridge is a domed structure. It's as wide as the Zamarstynovska Bridge, and it marks one of the borders of the ghetto. On one side is the ghetto, while the other side is "Aryan." On the ghetto side, there are German policemen all of the time so it's impossible to cross through without a "life certificate." But there's an embankment on one side of the bridge that I sometimes cross. It's easier to cross there, since I don't have to go under the hole in the fence, but there are many more policemen at the Peltevna Bridge than there are at the Zamarstynovka Bridge. That's why it's called the Bridge of Death. On the other side of the embankment at the Peltevna Bridge is Poddembem Street, and the black market is near there.

The strangest thing about the Peltevna Bridge is the Jewish orchestra that sometimes plays music there. The orchestra is located on the Jewish side of the bridge. The Jewish "vol-

175

unteer workers" are supposed to march under the bridge on their way to and from work, in step with the music. It's a very strange sight to see.

With the Weinbergs gone, I'm spending a lot of time by myself again, walking around the streets. More and more, I wonder what's going to happen to me. People keep disappearing, and new families move into our building as fast as the others disappear. I don't even try to get to know the new families. I just ask them if they want me to bring them food, and if they do, I try to trade for it.

Alone at home, and walking around the streets by myself, I start having more conversations with my imaginary friends. They're not just conversations about the daily search for food. There are many other things bothering me, too.

"Is it right for me to be doing these things— taking money from starving people, to bring them food?" I ask them. "Will God punish me some day?"

Genia reminds me once again, "You need food. What good will it do Rosa if she comes home and you're too weak to help her? You need to take care of yourself right now."

Ivasyk has been my childhood hero ever since I can remember. And I realize that he did something terrible to Marisetchka—he killed her and cut off her breasts, in order to outsmart the witches who were planning to kill him and eat him. Ivasyk assures me, "When your life is in danger, it's all right to do terrible things, in order to save yourself."

But, there are other things bothering me:.

"What will happen if I survive the war?" I ask my imaginary friends. "Even then, I won't be really okay. I'll probably be an orphan. I may never see Mama again. Or Rosa. Or Emmanuel." Being orphaned is still the worst thing I can imagine. The boys from the orphanage whom I had befriended when I was in school had always been poorly dressed, and they never seemed to have enough to eat. It terrifies me to think that I'll be put into an orphanage and be as neglected as they obviously had been.

"But we were orphans, too," Heidi reminds me. "Remember that I made friends with Clara and Peter, and they became like family to me."

Yash and Malgosha had survived, too, even though their stepmother was cruel to them and turned their real father against them.

"It's terrible to lose your mother, but you can still go on," Yash tells me." You have your own life to live!"

"But after all of these crazy things that are happening to me, maybe I won't even be sane after the war," I tell them. "While I'm walking around the streets, I see a lot of people talking to themselves and doing things that seem very strange. Maybe I'll end up like that, too."

"But look at us," says the youth from the story of the golden spring. "We survived witches, and cruel treatment, and hunger, and imprisonment, as well as being orphaned. And we came out of it all right," he reminds me. "You should pay attention to the important things, like getting food every day," he says. "Don't be tempted to give up. Maybe your mother and your brother and your sister will come back some day. It could happen!"

And I believe him. After all, it did happen in his story.

Sometimes, when I'm cold and hungry and very, very frightened, I ask, "Maybe I should put an end to all of this misery, and just let the Germans take me away in a round-up?"

"Oh, no!" Ivasyk insists. "You still have enough energy to run and hide!"

And it's true. As long as I have enough energy to look for food every day, I know I won't give myself up. In spite of all my doubts, I know I'm not ready to die.

Mrs. Tepper had told me that I should do anything and everything I could to keep myself alive, and I'm doing all sorts of things that I would never have dreamed of doing before the German invasion. But these are strange times, and I'm all alone now, so I'm allowed to do illegal things.

"It isn't wrong, and you're not an evil person," my imaginary friends assure me. And that gives me the hope and the strength that I need to go out hunting for food another day in the ghetto.

Living with the Freiheiters

The fairy tale hero never sees himself as special; he just does whatever he needs to do in order to survive....

While the Weinbergs were living with me, I had become a skillful trader in the ghetto. I had started by going from door to door in apartment buildings where I saw people looking out of their windows. I would knock on their door and offer them food and they were happy to buy from me, since it was too dangerous for them to go out on the streets, and they had no other way of getting food. People in the ghetto came to know me, and waited for me to bring food and other things to their apartments, and take other items in exchange.

I've learned to charge very high prices for the foods I bring back to the ghetto, because I risk my life every time I go out of the ghetto. I've even made a profit. But, knowing that the people who buy from me are in danger of starving to death, my conscience bothers me. So if I see somebody who looks very near starvation, I sometimes just give the food away. But more often, I'm too worried about my own survival to worry about overcharging.

Since I've been crossing the ghetto fence every day to buy food and trade items, the Polish people on the "Aryan" side have also gotten to know me, and they ask me for specific things they want. I bring whatever I can find, and even when I bring things they haven't asked for, it's easy to sell them, because the Gentiles are always eager to buy things of such good quality so cheaply. Since most of the Jews don't have any money left, they give me their remaining household items to trade for food, such as clothing, shoes, embroidered tablecloths, sheets and blankets.

One day, I go to the apartment of one of my regular clients to do some trading. I knock on the door, but there's no answer. I knock again, and finding the door open, walk inside. The apartment is empty. I suppose the woman has been taken away by the Germans in a round-up. This is the first time I've entered an empty apartment. I feel terrified and leave quickly. But in the following weeks, I enter such apartments again and again, knowing that if I don't take whatever is there to sell, somebody else surely will. This is the only way to survive in the ghetto.

"What kind of a person have I become?" I ask myself. "I'm stealing from Jews just like me, who have nothing left, and nobody to take care of them!"

"But you're doing it to keep yourself alive!" Ivasyk tells me. "It doesn't make you a bad person. You're all alone in the world—you've lost your whole family. What else can you do?"

Ivasyk has always been my childhood hero.
If he tells me it's okay, then it must be true.

One bleak and lonely day, there's a knock on our door, and when I open it, I can hardly believe my eyes. It's Uncle Abraham!

We hug each other and start crying. I haven't seen any of the Freiheiters since before Mama went away.

"Where is everybody?" Uncle Abraham asks when he comes inside. The apartment is very quiet.

"I'm the only one left," I say. When I tell him everything that happened, he nods his head very sadly, and his eyes fill with tears.

"They took Shlomit, too," he says.

"I know," I tell him. "That was before Mama disappeared."

"Her husband keeps coming around to ask if we have any news of her, but we don't know anything," says Uncle Abraham.

"I wanted to come to you after everybody was gone, but I didn't know where you moved to," I tell him.

"Our apartment isn't far from here, but it's on the other side of the ghetto wall. Now the Germans say we have to move into the ghetto," he says.

So now Uncle Abraham wants to move in with me—with his whole family! During my early childhood, it would have been unimaginable to think that they would someday live in our apartment. They were the rich relatives who I saw on rare occasions. And now they're going to live here, in our very plain and simple apartment! This is actually the second time they've moved in with us, but the first time they only stayed for a few days. Now Uncle Abraham says they want to live here permanently. Of course I'm happy to have them. Now I won't be alone anymore.

All three of Uncle Abraham's grown-up sons—Eli, Leibel and Herschel—work for the Germans. They go out early in the morning and come home late at night. Only Uncle Abraham and his wife, Minna, and their three-year-old son, Mendel, are home during the day.

Although it's very crowded with the Freiheiters living in our apartment, it's wonderful for me because they're so good to me—they're very kind and generous. I can feel their love and warmth.

When I tell Uncle Abraham how I've been trading on the black market, and how guilty I feel about charging high prices, he says, "Jewish law tells us that we need to protect our own lives, as well as the lives of others. You're doing the best you can, in these terrible, dangerous times. You're a good girl, and you're certainly not guilty of doing anything wrong!"

Now I understand why Mama always loved Uncle Abraham so much.

And the Freiheiters still have money, so we have enough to eat every day.

Uncle Abraham is deeply religious. He keeps kosher and he prays every day. He looks like an ancient grandfather with his long, very full beard streaked with silver.

Uncle Abraham had six children with his first wife, Malka, who died from a serious ill-

182

ness when she was still young. Their oldest son, Leepa moved to Canada before the Russian occupation, and their daughter, Nessia, got married and moved to Paris a few years ago. Their youngest daughter, Shlomit, is gone. Eli is about thirty, and he's married, but his wife was taken away by the Germans in a round-up. Leibel, in his late twenties, is the next oldest. He's very quiet and it's hard for me to talk to him. He's never been married.

The youngest of Abraham and Malka's children is Herschel. He's very tall and thin. He's only about sixteen, but he looks much older. I guess that's why he was able to get a job at the airport with his brothers. I like Herschel a lot— he's easy to talk to, and he's not much older than me. Now that they're living here, we've become good friends. When the brothers come home at night, Herschel always has something to tell me—about work, or the Germans, or the way the neighborhood is changing.

Abraham's second wife, Minna, is much younger than my uncle. I remember Mama once told me that Minna had been a beautiful woman when she married my uncle, but now she looks awful. She wears dirty clothes and she never combs her hair. Their little boy, Mendel, seems to cry all of the time. Minna's whole life seems to revolve around Mendel, who she calls, "Munjo." Minna is always playing with him, or talking to him, and taking care of him.

Eli, Leibel and Herschel are forced to work for the Germans at the airport. They have special passes allowing them to leave the ghetto to work. They dig trenches and do other hard labor. But at night, Eli works with the Jewish Underground, forging documents.

Uncle Abraham's bakery must have been important to the Germans, because he and his family had been allowed to remain in their old apartment outside the ghetto, for a long time. The bakery was in the same building as their apartment on Grodetska Street. But now the fence around the ghetto is complete and Jews are no longer allowed to go outside it, except if they have a work permit—something we call a "life certificate".

On the day they arrive, Abraham's three older sons go around our apartment, looking very carefully in every corner, and discussing what they see.

"Since the apartment is on the ground floor, we could remove the floorboards and dig a hole under them to build a hiding place," Herschel explains to me. By this time, they're all experts at digging holes!

As soon as they decide to do this, they set about working on the project. In our salon, the beds stand along the wall farthest from the entrance. A floor-to-ceiling heating stove stands in the middle of the room. Between the stove and the beds there's a table with a small carpet under it. They decide to dig the hole beneath my parents' big double bed.

"That way, the hole can be very big, but if the German soldiers walk into the apartment to look for you, they won't stomp on hollow floorboards and discover where you're hiding," Herschel tells me.

184

The entrance to the hole will be beneath the table that's next to the bed.

Eli has access to secret storage rooms because he works for the Jewish Underground. He goes out and comes back with a saw to cut the wooden floorboards. Working together, the brothers saw a cut about two feet long, slicing through three floorboards. They make the opening about three feet wide. Luckily, our building has no concrete foundation. There's just compacted earth under the floor. Using a pickaxe, they take turns breaking up the hardened earth. It must be very hard for them to come home and start working, since they have to walk a long way to their jobs at the airport and home again every evening; and they work very hard all day long. But they don't complain. They just discuss what they have to do, and get right to work.

In order to remove the earth from our apartment without attracting attention, they take turns digging, and load a backpack with the soil they remove from under the floorboards. They take turns going out late at night, carrying the backpack to the garbage dump, which is a short walk from our building. They work very fast and complete the hiding place in a few evenings. Then they put two stools inside the hole and it's big enough for Abraham, Minna, Mendel, and me. They take the floorboards they removed and nail them together and put a wooden handle on the underside, so that we can open and close it easily from inside. Finally, they nail the small carpet onto the top side of the floorboards, so that it will hide the cut in the floor when we climb inside. It seems like they've thought of everything!

During the day, Eli, Leibel and Herschel are gone. They tell us to get into the hiding place any time we hear the engines and the horns of the German patrol cars. Now, there are round-ups almost every day, and the Nazi soldiers have started coming into people's homes to take them away. So the hiding place is ideal.

But there's one problem that can't be solved. Mendel is terrified of the darkness in the hole and he's too little to understand why we have to sit there. He screams and cries the first time we go into it. Luckily, the German soldiers don't hear him, and they don't enter our apartment this time. But we're worried about what Mendel will do the next time.

The next day, while we're outside, we hear people screaming on the street. Then we hear a loud voice announcing over a loudspeaker, in German, "*Raus! Schnell!* Everyone out into the streets!"

People are running in every direction, trying to hide from the Nazis. Luckily, we're close to home and we manage to get back to our apartment before the Germans arrive in their cars.

We all run to the hiding place, but little Mendel starts to cry when he sees where we're going. Minna says, "You hide. Go on! I'll take Munjo upstairs, where the Nazis won't see us. If we stay here, he'll just cry and they'll find us all."

There's no time to discuss it. So I climb into the hole with Uncle Abraham. There's the usual noise of the German patrol cars honking, and
186

the sounds of guttural voices yelling *"Raus! Schnell!* Everybody out into the street!"

Soon, we hear a loud banging on the door. Then we hear the door fly open and there are loud footsteps on the floor. The German soldiers walk through our apartment, moving furniture and kicking things with their heavy boots. I'm shaking the whole time. It's probably only a minute, but it feels like hours! Finally, they leave, slamming the door behind them.

It's a while before we're brave enough to come out of the hiding place. We're both shaking from the experience. We wait for a while, and then go outside to look for Minna and Mendel, but we can't find them. Hours later, when Eli, Leibel and Herschel come home, we tell them what happened. Of course, there's nothing they can do about it. Uncle Abraham is very quiet. He's been praying all day, and crying.

When people are taken away by the Nazis, we don't know where they go, but we hope that they'll escape—like Father did—or be returned some day. But there's no news—only rumors—and nobody knows the truth.

I have no time to worry about what happened to Minna and Mendel. We need food in order to survive. So the next day, Uncle Abraham gives me money and I decide to go back to the black market. The problem is that it's even more difficult to cross the Bridge of Death, now. The guards are much more watchful than before. Eli has told me to run in zigzags, not straight. This way, if the Germans shoot at me, they won't know where to aim, but I'm too frightened to try crossing.

The Freiheiter family

I decide to walk over to the second bridge—the one on Zamarstynovska Street. It's called Zamarstynovska Bridge. When I get there, I see that some children about my age have dug a hole under the fence a few meters from the bridge. I see children crawling through this small opening to get to the Aryan side of Lvov. I watch from a distance. Some children are coming out of the ghetto that way, and others are returning with food. This looks a lot less dangerous than trying to cross the Bridge of Death, so I go home to tell Uncle Abraham about it.

"Don't try it unless you're sure you can get in and out safely," he tells me. "I don't want you to take any risks."

But how can I get in and out of the ghetto without taking any risks?

"I'll be okay," I tell him.

After that, Uncle Abraham gives me money every day and I take a basket and go back to the opening under the fence near the Zamarstynovska Bridge. I don't talk to any of the other children who are doing this, because we're in competition with each other. We all keep our secrets and try to avoid looking straight at anyone on the street. It's been like this for a long time.

I use the money that Uncle Abraham gives me to buy whatever food I can find: mostly milk, bread, potatoes, eggs, and butter. I buy everything except meat, since Uncle Abraham won't eat anything that isn't kosher.

"What would we do without you?" Uncle Abraham asks me every time I come home with food.

"You're feeding us all, while all I can do is pray," he says, sadly.

It's illegal and very dangerous to trade on the black market. But there's no other way to get food. The poorer Gentiles come to sell food, and to buy the goods that the Jews have to offer at bargain prices. If a German soldier comes anywhere near the market, a warning is whispered from mouth to mouth, and people walk away as fast as they can.

Now I have a wad of bills from all the trading I've been doing. Eli tells me I need to be very careful with the money.

He says, "When you go out trading, put some of the money that you carry in one of your socks, and keep some of it in a bag around your neck. Tuck the bag inside your sweater. That way, if you get robbed, the hood-

189

lums won't find all of the money." He gives me a small bag to hang around my neck.

During the long days of wandering the streets by myself, I discover many strange things. It may be hard to believe, but even after the ghetto fence is completed, there's still one real bakery operating inside the ghetto! In fact, it's right on Kressova Street in a private house. The couple who lives in that small house—the Schlechters are professional bakers, and they make the most wonderful, aromatic varieties of pastries and cakes. I don't know how they get all of the ingredients to make cheesecake with raisins and cream cakes and Napoleons, but they're obviously dealing on the black market as I am. I take my earnings there and buy myself cakes and pastries every day. They have doughnuts filled with jelly, tortes, cream cakes, cheesecakes and other delicacies, too. Everything tastes so delicious that, once I start, I want to eat more and more. I think those are the most delicious cakes I've ever eaten.

But even while I'm eating these wonderful cakes and pastries, I can never rid my mind of the scenes of bitter poverty and the dreadful terror of our lives. With every bite, I wonder where Mama and Rosa and Emmanuel might be. And where are Minna and Mendel? I wrestle with my overwhelming desire to eat the delicious, cream-filled pastries, and my feelings of guilt and greed and corruption. Yet every day, my feet lead me back to the bakery against my better judgment. Of course, one day when I get to the bakery, the building is deserted. These days, nothing is permanent.

I meet many people at the market, and I even have some regular customers.

The Polish people realize that any child trading household goods and blanket covers for food must be Jewish, and I don't even try to hide my identity. Who would believe me if I did? I think it's only the German soldiers I have to watch out for. The Polish Gentiles seem friendly enough. I become friendly with a few of the Polish people I trade with, like Mama used to be with the people she traded with.

One cold day there's hardly anything to buy at the black market. Maybe it's just too cold for people to wander around. While I'm wondering what to do, a blonde woman comes up to me and asks, "Do you want to buy salami?"

I hesitate because I never buy salami, since it isn't kosher and I can't bring it home to Uncle Abraham. But I think probably somebody else in the ghetto will want to buy it from me. Finally, I decide to take a chance and I say, "Yes, I'll buy one kilo." I'm not sure what price is reasonable to pay for it, either.

But the woman says, "No. You have to buy all five kilos for 300 marks."

"I only have a little money with me. I'll have to go home and get the rest," I tell her.

"Okay," she says. "Follow me home and take one kilo now. You can come back later for the rest."

So I follow her to the corner building on Slonetchna Street. She knocks on the door, and when there's no answer, she starts to curse. She waits a bit and then starts banging on the door. Finally, the door opens.

Although it's the middle of the day, the apartment is dark—all of the windows are draped with curtains. Looking around, I notice one corner is lit by a red lamp. In that corner, is a bed and next to it, a chair with the jacket of an SS officer draped over it.

The woman must notice my terror, and she reassures me, saying, "Don't worry. They won't pay any attention to you."

She goes to the food cupboard to get the salami.

A woman is sitting on the bed, stroking the back of a man who is lying next to her. She asks, "What's new on the street?"

The blonde answers, "I found someone to buy our salami."

She hands me the salami and says, "Come back for the rest as soon as you can. And if you want to buy butter, bring enough money for that, too. But don't you dare tell anybody where you got it!"

She shoves me towards the door, saying, "Hurry back, I need the money right away."

As I'm leaving, the door opens and another woman walks in. Without even saying hello, she sits down and says, "I just heard the most terrible news! Last night they took some prostitutes from Lvov to live in Germany and soon, they're going to take the rest of us!"

"What's so bad about that?" asks the woman from the bed. "I'll have a nice vacation in Germany!"

I'm standing near the door, but I'm extremely curious to hear what they're saying, so I play with the buttons on my coat. Then the blonde says to me, "Hurry up, now!" and I have

192

no choice but to leave. I can hear them laughing after I close the door.

I guess the prostitutes must get food from the Nazi soldiers every day. Selling some of it is another way of making a living.

Like many other Gentiles, the blonde is happy to trade with the Jews from the ghetto. She asks me to bring her blanket covers and other household items in exchange for food. So I go back to her house a few times to buy salami and very expensive butter. We never speak about my being Jewish, but of course she knows. Only Jewish children come to trade on the black market.

I haven't seen the prostitutes again, and I suppose they must have gone to Germany. I guess the blonde isn't a prostitute, since she hasn't gone away.

Living with the Freiheiters, I have adult companionship, which is very important to me. But when I'm out on the streets alone, I am frightened of the dangers I face. I still turn to my fairy tale friends for advice.

As I walk around the streets, the imaginary conversations with my fairy tale friends start focusing on what I can say if I get captured by the Germans.

"You need to make up a believable story," they advise me.

So gradually, I piece together a story made up of bits of information about various people I've known inside and outside the ghetto, and the things that have happened to them from the time of the Russian occupation.

One day at the black market, the street is almost empty. I don't see anyone selling food and I begin to be afraid I'll have to go home empty-handed. But finally, I meet a woman who is very pleasant to me. She asks me if I want to buy eight kilos of porridge.

"Why not?" I say, and I give her the money.

I notice that she's looking at me with great interest. She asks me, "Are you going back to the ghetto?"

"Yes," I answer.

"Be very careful," she says.

She asks me if my family is waiting for me at home, and how we're getting along. I tell her the truth because she seems genuinely concerned.

She tells me her name is "Vitzmanova" (meaning "Vitzman's wife"). "That's a German name, isn't it?" I ask her.

"Yes, my husband was German," she says, "But I'm Polish."

She looks to be about my mother's age. Vitzmanova tells me that she lives on Poddembem Street—the first street after the railroad tracks on the Aryan side of Lvov—in the corner apartment building.

"If you ever need help, you can come to me," she says.

I answer her politely, "Thank you very much for your kind offer."

But in my heart, I think, "Who can trust the kindness of a stranger, when all of the people I thought were my friends have abandoned me?"

194

I'm able to sell the porridge grain very fast and after that, I go back to trade with Vitzmanova again and again. I don't write down her name and address, but it's easy to remember. Poddembem Street is right on the other side of the ghetto wall.

One day, while I'm crossing back into the ghetto from Poddembem Street, I see a cart piled high with frozen corpses. Some of them have their mouths open; some of them are missing shoes. It makes me nauseous just to look at them, and I think, "Today, it's them, but tomorrow it could be me."

Would Vitzmanova really try to save me from that tragic fate? Why would she risk her life for me? I don't believe she would.

Now that the ghetto wall is finished, walking around the streets on the Aryan side of Lvov has become more dangerous. If a German soldier should stop me, I would be in grave danger. I'm making up a story in case some German soldiers stop me and question me.

"My parents were anti-Communists, and they were taken to Siberia by the Russians during the Russian occupation," I begin. "And then what?"

"Tell them you went to live with your aunt," says Ivasyk. "Things like that really happened. And the Germans will like you better if they think your parents were anti-Communists," he adds.

But if I really want to be safe, I'll need an Aryan passport.

195

Eli belongs to the Jewish underground. He works with a group of young people at night. Through this group, he collects information about what the Germans are planning to do. Once he came home wearing the hat of a Jewish policeman—there's a Jewish ghetto police force, organized and controlled by the Germans—although he isn't part of it. Eli has to be very careful and he says almost nothing about his work in the underground. The only thing I know is that he forges documents.

One evening, Eli brings a beautiful young woman home with him. Although she's Jewish, she has long blonde hair and she looks like a Gentile. Eli moves his bed into the kitchen and his girlfriend comes to live with him. This is very difficult for Uncle Abraham because he's so religious. And our small apartment is getting very crowded—but only at night, when everybody is at home.

I like having Eli's girlfriend around. In spite of all the terrible hardships of our life in the ghetto, she takes care of her health and her looks. She takes a partial bath every day in a small tub in the kitchen. And now I know why her hair is blonde—she dyes it! She goes to work every day. I love to watch her put on lipstick and get all dressed up whenever she goes out. It's too bad she doesn't stay with us very long. She goes to live on the Aryan side of Lvov.

One night, Herschel comes home from work shivering. He seems to have a high fever. We pile a lot of blankets and coats on him, but he's still shivering. He tries to sleep, but he wakes up feeling hot and cold. Eli says it's obvious that he has typhus.

196

I love my cousin Herschel very dearly, and I can't stand the thought of seeing him die. So I make it my business to nurse him back to health. I've heard that in order to make a fever go down, you should take a wet sheet and wrap the person in it. So I wrap Herschel in a wet sheet, and I put cold compresses on his head, too. And this really does help.

Mama always used to say that chicken soup is a wonder drug. She called it "the golden soup." So as soon as the fever goes down, I go shopping for the ingredients to make chicken soup, and I cook it in a big pot on our kitchen stove. I sit by Herschel's bedside and feed him chicken soup and keep putting cold compresses on his head and chest to keep the fever down. I stay by him night and day, watching him sleep, or dozing off next to his bed.

Uncle Abraham tells me, "Nobody could do any better than you're doing."

While Herschel is sleeping, I say the prayer that Mama taught me, "*Shema Israel!*" over and over again. Uncle Abraham prays for Herschel all day long.

There are no doctors in the ghetto and there's no medicine. Many people have died of typhus in the ghetto, and we're all very scared that Herschel is going to die, too. There's nothing we can do but wait until the fever passes. Eli and Leibel still have to go to work every day, so Uncle Abraham and I take care of Herschel. And slowly, he recovers. He has to return to work as soon as he can, since the Germans are asking for him and running out of patience. But he's young and he's strong, and he gets up and goes back to work as soon as he's out of danger.

Eli tells Herschel, "Leibel and I will stay close to you all day, and help you if you're feeling weak." He tells Uncle Abraham, "Don't worry—we'll take care of Herschel," and they walk to work very slowly.

The ghetto has gotten smaller and smaller. Now, there are only three or four streets where Jews are allowed to live, and many apartments are empty because the Germans have taken so many people away in round-ups. Eli says that a lot of people have died, too—of hunger or typhus.

Not long after Herschel's illness, we have another problem. We have to move into a different apartment. Since there are now far fewer people living in the ghetto, the Germans have decided to reorganize it, according to professions. All of the people with the same jobs have to move into "blocks." The bakers have to live in one building, the tailors in another, factory workers in a different building, and the airport workers are being moved to Lokietka Street— the street next to Kressova. So we move into an apartment on 20 Lokietka Street, on the second floor. It's near where the barbershop used to be, but I haven't seen the barber for a long time.

When we move, we're not allowed to take everything—just our clothes and the few things we can carry. I have to leave my family photograph album in our old apartment, along with other souvenirs of my childhood.

Now, our most serious problem is that we no longer have a hiding place. Since we moved into a second floor apartment, there's no chance of digging an underground hiding place, like we did on Kressova Street. All day long, while my cousins are working and I'm crossing the ghetto wall to the Aryan side of Lvov to trade for food, Uncle Abraham is alone in the new apartment with no place to hide when there are round-ups. My cousins are very worried about him, and they talk for hours about what we should do. Eli thinks that he should cross the ghetto fence in the middle of the night and go to stay with the workers who are now working in his bakery. But Uncle Abraham refuses. He says "I won't leave my whole family to go and live with strangers."

So Eli insists, "In that case, you need to cut off your beard and come to work with us. If you don't, the Germans will surely take you away in a round-up, sooner or later."

Uncle Abraham is a deeply religious man and he doesn't want to shave his beard, but he can see that his life is in grave danger, so he finally agrees to do it. Uncle Abraham has always had a very long black beard with many strands of silver. It's so long that it looks like he's never cut it before. Eli makes him sit on a stool, and he takes a scissors and cuts off the beard. Herschel lathers his father's face with soap and shaves him with a razor blade. He shaves off the moustache and the sideburns, too. The sideburns are a special sign of religious faith in the Jewish religion, and Jewish men are never supposed to cut them! At first, Uncle Abraham is so ashamed and upset that

199

he covers his face with his hands and is afraid to look in the mirror. And when I see him, what a surprise! He looks a dozen years younger without the beard. If I passed him in the street, I would never guess that he was my Uncle Abraham!

Before the German invasion of Lvov, Uncle Abraham led a very comfortable life. I guess he's lost a lot of weight while living in the ghetto, but he doesn't look thin and weak. Even though he's never done any physical labor, he looks strong and healthy. But without a beard, he looks like an entirely different person. Now he goes to work every day with his sons.

Working for the Jewish Underground, Eli has a lot of connections with people and organizations, including the Nazi-controlled Jewish policemen in the ghetto. One evening, he comes home very late.

"Sonya, tonight there's going to be an *Aktzia* in the ghetto," he tells me. "The Nazi soldiers are going to come in the middle of the night, and go into apartments and round up all of the children and take them away. You need to leave as soon as possible!" he says. "With all of your connections outside of the ghetto, you'll have to find somebody to take you in."

I jump out of bed and get dressed as quickly as I can.

Cousin Herschel hugs me and tells me, "You'll be better off outside the ghetto, anyway."

Eli works as a forger of documents for the Jewish underground, and he has made me a false birth certificate. "Your name is no longer

Sonya Hebenstreit," he tells me. "Now, you are Zofia Zaborska." He hands me a birth certificate. "Sit and study this very carefully," he says. "You need to know every detail by heart. If the Nazis catch you, they'll ask you all sorts of questions and they'll check everything you say."

I study the birth certificate as carefully as I can, trying to memorize every detail. Cousin Herschel sits with me and helps me. From now on, I'm going to be Zofia Zaborska, the daughter of Michael Zaborski. Zofia is a real Polish girl, born in Sambour, a small city about a hundred kilometers from Lvov. Eli says "If the Nazis capture you and go to search for your 'family,' it will take them some time to find out that the birth certificate is a forgery." This would give me time to escape, if I should need to.

All the time I'm studying the document with Herschel, I'm worrying about where I'll go and what will become of me. I'm terrified!

It's after midnight when I put the birth certificate into the secret money bag that I carry around my neck, and load my socks with extra money that Uncle Abraham gives me. I bid farewell to the Freiheiters, who have been so good and kind to me, and who I've grown to love very dearly. We don't know if we'll ever see each other again.

I decide it's best to cross under the fence near the Zamarstynovska Bridge. But as I crawl out from under the opening in the fence, two strong Polish youths are waiting for me. They grab me, one by each arm, yelling "*Zhy-*

douvka! Dirty Jew! Give us all of your money, or we'll turn you over to the Germans!"

I know that even if I give them all of my money, they'll still turn me over to the Germans. The Germans pay two kilos of sugar for every Jew who is handed over to them—a very valuable reward in these times. If I take my money from the bag around my neck, they'll discover my false birth certificate and I'm sure they'll take it from me. They'll probably grab the whole bag. Then I'll have no chance to survive!

My heart is pounding and I'm terrified. I have to act fast and do something to save myself. So I scream, "Help! Thieves!" And I gather all my energy and pull first one boy's hand, then the other, to my mouth. First I bite one of them with all my might, and then I draw the other one's hand to my mouth and bite very hard. Both boys drop my arms and scream in pain.

As soon as they drop my arms, I run away as fast as my legs can carry me up toward the train tracks. I can hear a train coming, and I know it's very close, but I cross the tracks anyway. It's too dark to see, but I can feel the train approaching. Just after I cross the tracks, the train passes. To my great relief, that stops the hooligans from following me. I'm sure they can still catch up with me, if they try to. So I keep running, in case they decide to chase me. I run all the way to the corner of Peltevna and Slonetchna Streets. Crossing the wide boulevard, I run right into a drunken man, but I keep running. He's too drunk to follow me.

It's the middle of the night and, of course, very dark. But I know this neighborhood very well, since I go there every day to trade for food. I go to the corner apartment building on Pod-dembem Street, where Vitzmanova told me she lives. I hide in some large bushes that are not far from the building, wondering what I'll do if she refuses to take me in. It's the middle of the night and nobody is walking on the streets. I don't see the Polish boys who tried to rob me. I know I'm very lucky that the train was passing just at the right moment, and also that the coldest part of winter is over. I have a lot to think about during these lonely hours. This is the first time I've been so utterly alone. When I was orphaned, and Rosa was taken away in a round-up, I thought things couldn't get any worse in my life. But things *have* gotten worse! Now I've lost my whole family, the whole familiar world I grew up in—even my own identity! I'm no longer Sonya Hebenstreit, the daughter of Rachel and Israel. Now I'm Zofia Zaborska, a Polish girl, the daughter of Michael Zaborska— a man I've never even seen! I have to make up a whole life story about myself and my past, and I have nothing and nobody to turn to for help.

Things are changing all of the time. It's no longer safe to tell strangers that I'm a Jew. And now that I'm carrying a false passport, maybe I'm in even greater danger. I go over all of the facts about Zofia Zaborska again and again in my mind.

I don't know how many hours I stand there in the middle I of the night, waiting for daylight so that I can knock on Vitzmanova's door. But amid all the fear and apprehension, there are moments of relief.

"Don't be afraid" says Ivasyk "I'll be with you wherever you go."

"Me, too," says Yash."

"You'll never be alone with all of us standing right beside you," says the Little Match Girl.

"Remember the song: 'Round and round, hold your ground, the ball of life swirls round and round," says the youth from the story of the golden spring. "Don't forget that we all went through horrible and frightening experiences, and we all had the strength to find our way out of them. You will, too. We'll always be there with you!" he promises.

"Call on us when you need us. Listen for us when you need us."

"I will," I promise myself. "I will."

And very carefully, I go over the story I've been putting together to explain why I'm alone.

My parents were taken away by the Russians during the Russian occupation. I went to live with my aunt, but she was taken to work in Germany, so now I'm alone."

I repeat this over and over to myself, trying to make it sound like it's true. I think it's a believable story.

A New Name

I've been standing outside for hours, waiting for dawn. I don't want to wake Vitzmanova up in the middle of the night. That might make her angry with me. But I want to go to her very early, before people start walking around the streets, so that nobody sees me. Finally, after much hesitation when I see it's starting to get lighter outside, I decide it's okay to knock on her door.

I remember that Vitzmanova said her apartment was on the second floor. I go up the stairs as quietly as I can, and I don't meet any of the neighbors on my way. It's still too early for people to be going out. I find the apartment easily and I see her husband's name, "Vitzman," written on the front door. I know that her husband is no longer with her, but I'm not sure if she's a widow, or if he's just gone away. I hope I can trust Vitzmanova!

I knock very quietly and there's no answer, so I knock again and again, each time just a little louder, until I hear someone coming to the door. Finally, Vitzmanova opens the door.

"Oh, it's you!" she says, obviously surprised. She pulls me inside hastily, so nobody will see me.

She locks the door and asks, "Did any of the neighbors see you?"

That would put her in a lot of danger.

"No. I came up the stairs as quietly as I could," I tell her. "Nobody's awake yet."

"Good," she says, relaxing a little. "What happened? Why did you come here?" she asks me.

"Somebody told me there was going to be a round-up during the middle of the night and the Nazis were planning to take all of the children from the ghetto, so I ran away," I tell her. I don't say anything about Eli and the forged passport.

I can see that she isn't very happy to see me.

"I didn't think you would take my offer so seriously," she says. "But I'll try to help you. I can see you're desperate."

It's still very early in the morning and her children are sleeping, so we talk very quietly. Near the front door, Vitzmanova has a large chest that holds blankets and bedding. She opens it and takes out a thick blanket for me to sleep on. She takes out a few other things, too, in order to make room for me to hide in the chest if somebody should come to the door. It's comfortable, and I'm exhausted from staying up all night, but I'm so terrified that I can hardly sleep. The danger of my situation is very clear to me.

"We can't tell the children that you're Jewish," she says.

206

"That's okay," I tell her. "I have a passport with the name Zofia Zaborska. I'm going to pretend I'm a Polish girl with no parents," I say.

"How did you get a passport?" she asks me.

"I bought it on the black market," I tell her. I don't want to tell her about cousin Eli. Of course Eli had given me the passport for nothing, but I know that a false passport would have cost me hundreds of Marks on the black market.

When her children wake up, she tells them that I'll be staying with them for a few days, and they go off to school without paying too much attention to me. That's a relief!

I know I'm lucky to have a safe hiding place, but there are a lot of problems. First of all, if a neighbor should come into the apartment, I'll have to hide. And another problem is Vitzmanova's children. Her daughter is about six years old, and her son is about eight. The little girl is very friendly and nice to me, but, the boy is older and he suspects that I'm Jewish. He says so in a very nasty way, calling me *"Zhydouvka,"* even though Vitzmanova insists, "She's Polish, not Jewish!"

If he tells anybody about me, the Germans will come and search the apartment.

From my experience, I already know that any "solution" is never permanent. Every success is short-lived, and usually ends up creating another problem. A stranger like Vitzmanova might offer to help me, but the kind of help she offers me could easily turn into a fight for my survival. If the wrong German asks me the wrong question, they might find a weak spot in my story, and turn me over to the Gestapo. So I expect that staying with Vitzmanova might end in disaster. I know that I have to be ready for unanticipated problems.

I walk around the streets practicing what I'm going to say if the police catch me. "My name is Zofia Zaborska. Do you want to see my passport?"

No, they'll probably ask me for my passport when they stop me. I'll just say, "My name is Zofia Zaborska." Then I won't say anything else. I'll just answer their questions.

Vitzmanova wants me to go into the ghetto in the daytime and bring her blanket covers, which are very much in demand in the Aryan section of Lvov. In order to find blanket covers, I have to go into the abandoned apartments of people who have been rounded up and taken away by the Germans. I have to take the goose feather stuffing out of the blankets because the blankets are too bulky to carry with the stuffing in them. I do what I've seen other children do—I wrap the empty blanket cover around my waist. Bringing blanket covers for Vitzmanova is clearly the price I have to pay in order for her to keep me.

So I go back into the ghetto and find a blanket cover in an empty apartment. But it's too bulky, even after I take out the stuffing. When I wrap it around my body, I can't crawl through the opening under the fence near the Zamarstynovska Bridge. So I head for the embankment behind the "Bridge of Death" (the Peltevna Bridge). It's bitter cold, so of course I'm wearing my muff. Inside the muff is a photograph of my family. Approaching the Bridge
208

of Death, I can see German soldiers with rifles standing on the ghetto side of the bridge, near a small military booth. So I decide to go across at a distance, where the embankment is much lower. That's where Poddembem Street is, on the Aryan side.

Other children are also trying to cross over to the Aryan side, and the German soldiers see us. One of them shouts "Halt!" and starts shooting in the air. We all run as fast as we can, scattering in different directions. When I see the guards running in another direction, I take my chances and cross. Luckily, nobody stops me.

But, on the other side of the railway line, on Poddembem Street, I have a terrible surprise. A gang of Polish boys is hanging around there. I'm sure they've seen what happened. They catch me and one of them punches me in the head. Another one pulls my muff from me and pushes me down. Luckily, most of my money is in the bag hung around my neck and tucked inside my sweater, and of course the boys don't know this. With my muff in their hands, they turn their backs on me and walk away. I call after them, "Keep the money and the muff, but give me back my picture!" They don't bother to answer, but just keep walking.

I stop a man on the street and ask him to help me. I tell him what happened and point to the gang of teenage boys who are walking away. At first, the man looks at me without saying anything. Then he makes an ugly face and says, "Get away from me, you dirty Jew!" He spits at my feet and walks away very fast.

My head hurts, and I'm miserable about losing the photo of my family, but at least I still have most of my money. I decide to go straight back to Vitzmanova and on my way, I meet some German soldiers searching people in the street. Of course, they stop me and question me, too. But, because my Polish is perfect, they believe me when I tell them I'm Zofia Zaborska, as most Jews speak Polish with a heavy accent—like my father did. They don't even ask to see my passport. If the German soldiers had found me with my muff and searched me and found the picture of my family, they would have known that I was Jewish, and taken me away. So I guess the robbery was a fortunate thing, after all.

I take the blanket cover to Vitzmanova, and tell her what happened. I try to make light of it because I don't want Vitzmanova to see how close I am to getting hysterical. She says, "Here, sit down and have a cup of soup. You look cold. You can stay home for the rest of the day."

But she still wants blanket covers! So the next day, I go back into the ghetto, searching for blanket covers. Luckily, I find a good one, and I'm able to get out of the ghetto and back to Vitzmanova without anything happening to me.

Every day I stay with Vitzmanova, I go "hunting" in the ghetto. This means I walk around the streets and listen for any noise or voices coming from inside the buildings in the ghetto. Most often, it's deathly still in the daytime because everyone who's left in the ghetto is working for the Germans.

I go into an apartment building and stand near a door, listening for anybody moving around inside the apartment. If it's quiet inside, and it usually is, I knock very softly on the door. If there's no answer, I knock again, a bit louder. Finally, I try to turn the door handle. Many people have been taken away very suddenly, either in daytime round-ups or in the middle of the night, so many doors have been left unlocked. I even find doors standing ajar sometimes. The people who are still living in the ghetto keep their apartment doors locked, and I never try to enter a locked apartment. But there are far fewer people living in the ghetto now, and many apartments are empty.

Once inside an apartment, I look around to see if there's anything useful that's small enough to carry. I open drawers, take blanket covers from beds, and I even search for food. Sometimes the apartments have been searched before I get there, maybe by the German police or by other children like me. Sometimes, drawers have been pulled out and emptied on the floor, and things are left lying wherever they've fallen. It gives me the shivers to go looting like this, but the only other alternative is to starve to death. Anyway, that's what I tell myself in the endless dialogues that I conduct with my imaginary companions whenever I start feeling guilty about what I'm doing—and that's all of the time!

"Is it really okay to be stealing from people?"
"How else can you keep yourself alive?"

"But stealing is wrong!"
"In times of war, you're allowed to save your own life!"

Whatever I find, I trade for food, and I continue bringing food to the Freiheiters, too, while I'm staying with Vitzmanova. As long as I'm in the ghetto, I figure I may as well go to the apartment on Lokietka Street. But of course, none of the Freiheiters are home during the day. I also use some of my money to buy Vitzmanova and her children gifts. I buy her clothing for herself and her children. One day I bring my old pink dress for her daughter.

"I can't wear it in this freezing winter, and the way things are going, I may not even live until next summer."
"Don't give up yet. The war may end soon. Concentrate on keeping yourself alive!"

Vitzmanova is delighted with the gifts I bring her. But it soon becomes clear that I can't stay with her very long. I feel like I'm caught in a trap. If I go back to live with the Freiheiters in the ghetto, I'll be in danger of getting captured by the Germans during a round-up in the middle of the night. But if I stay with Vitzmanova, I'll be in danger of having her son tell the neighbors about me. I have to do something, but what?

One morning, while the children are at school and Vitzmanova is cleaning the apartment, there's a knock on the door. From where I'm standing, I can't get into my hiding place in the chest without being seen by whoever's at

212

the door, so I run into the salon and close the door behind me. Vitzmanova opens the front door, and I look through the keyhole. A man is standing there in an SS uniform! Somebody must have reported Vitzmanova to the police! I look around the salon for a place to hide, but there is none. Then I look out the window, which faces the street. Even though Vitz-manova's apartment is on the second floor, I consider jumping from the window. But I hear laughter coming from the next room, from a few different people, including Vitzmanova. I listen to them talking and they're speaking Polish, not German! Soon after that, Vitzmanova calls to me, "Zofia, come in here and meet these people!"

I'm very confused, and too afraid to move. Vitzmanova must have guessed my feelings. She comes into the room to talk to me, and says, "You have nothing to worry about. The officer is a relative of mine from Schlonsk. His name is Stach. He was drafted into the German army against his will, and now he's in the SS. He and his wife will only be here for a few hours. You can sit and visit with us. They won't do anything bad to you. Really, there's nothing to worry about."

Vitzmanova is certain that everything will be fine, but I'm not so sure. I'm afraid that her son will return from school and start calling me *"Zhydouvka!"* in front of the guests. What will I do if that happens? But I follow her back into the kitchen, hoping that everything will be all right.

Vitzmanova introduces me to the couple and we all go into the salon. I sit in the room

213

with them, but I don't talk. The young woman speaks only broken Polish, so they switch to German after a while. Vitzmanova has no idea that I understand German better than she does! I sit very quietly listening to their conversation, trying to look bored, as if I don't understand them.

Vitzmanova has told me that she's "Folkesdeutche,"—that is, "Ethnic German"—someone of German origin who lives outside Germany. There are many Folkesdeutche in Poland, and they have special privileges here.

Stach speaks both Polish and German without an accent. His wife is dressed in an elegant suit with a fur collar. The collar has a small fox head, and it reminds me of the fur-trimmed coat that Mama had once owned. From the way the couple are dressed, I guess they're not wealthy, but probably have enough money to live quite comfortably.

After a while, their conversation turns to the subject of household help. The young woman says to Vitzmanova, "I have such a large apartment in Schlonsk, it's hard for me to keep it clean. It's impossible to find servant girls in Schlonsk right now. Everybody there is wealthy now and nobody is left to work for us!"

I can't help but notice that she's looking in my direction a lot during that part of the conversation, and I understand that she's interested in having me work for her. But, of course, I don't react. I don't want them to know that I understand German. Vitzmanova pretends not to take the hint, either, and she says, "I'll look around for you. If I find someone, I'll send her to you."

214

Finally, the conversation passes on to other subjects and I'm relieved. After the couple leaves, I let Vitzmanova explain to me what they had talked about, as if I hadn't understood them at all. Actually, I'd been considering the possibility of working for them all along.

Vitzmanova says, "You made a very good impression on them. The young woman would like you to work for her, to help her clean her house. That could be a wonderful opportunity for you. If you move in with them in Shlonsk, nobody would know you there. You could start a new life, with plenty of food and good pay! What do you think about that?" she asks me.

When I open my mouth to answer her, my heart starts beating very fast. I don't know what to say. Of course, working for them would be the perfect cover. Working for a Nazi officer would mean that I would be safe and well fed. With my forged passport and my perfect knowledge of Polish, they wouldn't suspect that I was Jewish. Or, would they? And if they ever found out the truth, what would they do to me? As much as I might trust Vitzmanova to keep my secret, I know I can't trust her relatives. What if I said or did something that made them suspicious? As soon as they found out I was a Jew, I would be taken away by the police, and probably shot.

I realize how much I need to make up a story to explain how I came to be living on my own. I have to know everything about Zofia Zaborska, but I don't have a full story ready yet.

Also, I'm worried about Uncle Abraham in the ghetto. I'm still bringing food to the Frei-

215

heiters. What will they do without me? I feel as if I need to go back into the ghetto and keep bringing them food. And I want them to know that I'm still alive and all right. While I was living with them, I felt loved and protected. Now, I miss them terribly!

All of these ideas are whirling around in my head while Vitzmanova is talking to me. Finally, I decide to tell her, "I'll think about it. It sounds like a good idea, but I'm not sure. Maybe I'll go back to the ghetto in a few days."

"That's fine. You think it over and let me know," says Vitzmanova. She probably understands my confusion and my fear, and she doesn't bring the subject up again. Meanwhile, the couple leaves Lvov without making another offer. I recall how Stach was looking me over. I wonder if he suspected I was Jewish. I feel uncomfortable about this offer and decide to say no.

A few days later, Vitzmanova has another visitor. This time, it's her teenage nephew, Yusek, from a rural Polish village. His parents have sent him to stay with her. I think the boy realizes that I'm Jewish, but Vitzmanova says he can be trusted not to tell anybody about me. Actually, I'm a lot more frightened of Vitzmanova's son than I am of Yusek. I'm sure her son has figured out that I'm Jewish, but he might be too young to realize how serious an offense it is for his mother to be hiding me in their home. Vitzmanova assures me that her son won't say anything to anybody, but whenever he comes near me, he brushes past me and whispers, "*Zhydouvka!*" in a nasty tone of
216

voice, which makes me shiver. But I don't let him see how frightened I am. I keep weighing my options, and I decide it's best for me to stay with Vitzmanova for a few more days.

Every evening when I go to sleep, I take my money out of my sock and put it into the bag that I wear around my neck. I wrap that bag in my coat, which I use as a pillow.

One morning, Vitzmanova's daughter, Krisha, asks me, "Why don't you hang the money bag on that hook instead of sleeping with it under your head? It looks very uncomfortable."

I'm surprised that she's noticed my money bag at all, and even more surprised she has given it so much thought. She's too little to be thinking about such things. Instinctively, I feel that there's more to the story, and I'm reluctant to hang the bag on the hook.

"Would you like me to give you some money?" I ask her. I think that's probably what she's interested in. I like Krisha. Unlike her brother, she's always friendly and nice to me. "Here, take 5 Marks, and I'll give you 5 Marks for your brother, too," I tell her. "And here's 5 Marks for Yusek."

I think that the boys have probably told Krisha to ask me about my money bag. Krisha takes the money, but that evening she brings up the subject of the money bag again.

"Why don't you hang your money bag on the hook, instead of sleeping with it under your head?" she asks.

I know that the boys are behind Krisha's question, and I don't know what to do. If I don't give them money, they might report me to the police. So against my better judgment, I finally hang my money bag on the wall. But I feel that something bad might happen, and I'm right. When I wake up in the morning and check the money bag, 60 Marks are missing! I count my money over and over again, until I realize that the children must have stolen it.

Just then, the boys come into the kitchen and start teasing me and laughing at me. I turn to each one of them, asking, "Do you know what happened to my money?" But each one of them denies it, and they act as if this is great entertainment. Vitzmanova is out of the apartment right then. They wouldn't act like this if she was home, I think. At that moment, I realize that staying with Vitzmanova has become more of a problem than a solution.

The children leave for school and I wonder whether or not to tell Vitzmanova about the money. If she gets angry and yells at them, or makes them give me back the money, they'll resent me even more. I think maybe I should simply go back to live with the Freiheiters, but the ghetto is eerily quiet during the daytime. It looks as if everybody who isn't working for the Germans has been taken away in a round-up. So, I go back to the ghetto to "hunt" for more blanket covers and other things to trade, and come back to Vitzmanova that afternoon.

I've been thinking about the incident all morning, and when I go back to Vitzmanova, I tell her about the money. I can see that she's honestly furious with the children.

"Those miserable brats!" she screams. "Wait till they get home—I'll make them pay for what they've done!"

218

"No, please don't!" I protest. "What will they do if you punish them for the sake of a Jew?" I warn her. She realizes that I'm right. And not only that, but she says, "Now I bet they're going to tell the neighbors about you!"

We both know that it won't be safe for me to stay there any longer.

"I'll help you find another place to stay," she promises me.

And later that day, she comes up with a plan to help me. "Sonya," she says, "I've found a safe place for you! You can go to my friend, Zofia, who lives on the other side of Lvov. She's been living alone since her husband was taken into the Russian army during the Russian occupation."

What other choice do I have?

Zofia lives far away on the other side of Lvov, a long tram ride from Poddembem Street. Vitzmanova tells me that Zofia will come and take me home with her.

"Maybe you could give her a present, too. That would surely help," she suggests.

So I leave Vitzmanova's apartment and spend the night in the ghetto with the Freiheiters. I tell them what happened and ask them for advice.

"I'm not sure if Vitzmanova's friend will really be willing to help me. It reminds me of Michalova's promises to send me to her family in Tarnopol."

"But the ghetto is too dangerous now," Eli insists. "You can't stay here! With your passport and your story about the Russians sending your parents to Siberia and putting you in

219

an orphanage, you'll be better off on the Aryan side of Lvov."

So I decide to try Vitzmanova's friend.

The next day, on my way back to Vitzmanova's apartment, I buy an elegant pair of black high-heeled sandals for Zofia. That's what Vitzmanova said Zofia would want.

By the time I arrive, Zofia is already there. I get the feeling that I've interrupted an important conversation between Vitzmanova and Zofia, but Vitzmanova welcomes me warmly.

"Come in, come in," she says. "I want you to meet my dear friend, Zofia."

She introduces me to Zofia, who has swarthy skin, jet-black eyes and shiny black hair. She looks nothing like the typical blonde, blue-eyed Polish woman I was expecting. Later, she tells me that she's Ukrainian.

Vitzmanova and Zofia begin discussing my situation. Vitzmanova frequently turns to me and asks me questions.

"How long have you been living on your own?" she asks.

"A few months," I say.

"And what do you do every day?"

"I trade on the black market."

"Why don't you tell Zofia what happened to your parents?" she asks, and Zofia seems shocked when I tell her, "They were anti-Communists, and the Russians sent them to Siberia a long time ago. That's when I went to live in the orphanage."

But the conversation is mainly between the two of them, and it's all about the benefits to Zofia of taking me in, and the problem that Vitzmanova has with keeping me. They speak a lot about the "evil ones," but they never mention the Germans by name, as if even the walls had ears!

Finally, I tell Zofia how I met Vitzmanova. She's delighted when I show her the sandals I had bought for her, and she hugs me.

"What a dear child you are!" she says. Zofia is sympathetic and she agrees to take me in, just as Vitzmanova had said she would.

"Okay, you're welcome to come home and stay with me," she says. "Come, let's catch the tram. It's a long way home from here."

I'm grateful to have a new benefactor, and equally glad to be on my way before the children get home from school.

We sit next to each other on the tram, but Zofia doesn't speak to me. I guess she doesn't want people to see us together in public, and to think we're on intimate terms. I know that many people who look at me suspect I'm a Jew. I wonder if Vitzmanova has told Zofia the truth, but I certainly won't ask her! During the long ride to Zofia's apartment, I wonder what new troubles are waiting for me at her place. I wonder if I should go back to the Freiheiter family in the ghetto, instead of going home with Zofia. But meanwhile, the tram is taking us to the opposite side of Lvov—to a neighborhood where I've never been before.

I tell myself, "You don't know what's waiting for you. Be ready for anything. Keep on your guard."

When we get to Zofia's stop, Zofia touches my shoulder lightly and says, "This is where we get off."

Although it's beginning to get dark, I can see it's a pretty street.

I follow Zofia to her building. She says, "Wait here while I check to see if anybody is standing around."

There's nobody, so she motions silently to me and I follow her inside. Zofia lives on the ground floor in a tiny apartment. It's just one large room: a kitchen with a huge bed. There's only one window, which is very large. It looks out on the inner courtyard of the building.

"Usually, I don't keep the drapes closed, since the window faces the courtyard, but I think it's best to keep them closed while you're here," she tells me.

I say nothing, still wondering if I've done a wise thing in coming here.

Zofia puts a big pot of water on the stove, quickly peels some potatoes, and asks me, "Do you have any cigarettes? I have to have a smoke before I eat!"

I don't have any, so she asks me to go out and buy some for her.

"Three doors down from here, on the corner, there's a small shop. Here, take this and ask for Junake cigarettes. I'll cook dinner while you're gone," she says, giving me some money.

I really don't want to go walking around a strange neighborhood, but I feel her request is more like a command, and know I can't refuse.

When I leave her apartment, I'm full of dread. Will she put poison in my food before I return? Or call the police? Maybe I shouldn't go back at all? I could take the tram back to Poddembem Street and cross over into the ghetto. But when I remember the wagonload of naked, dead bodies in the ghetto, I decide to stay with Zofia. I'll stay there tonight, and tomorrow I'll think about what to do next.

I walk into the small corner shop feeling very intimidated because it's Aryan. I'm used to trading on the black market, and I've never entered an Aryan shop before! I buy the cigarettes and leave as quickly as I can.

When I get back to Zofia's apartment, the food is already on the table.

"Oh, I'm so glad you're back!" Zofia says. She takes the pack of cigarettes and lights one immediately, saying, "I have to smoke before I eat. Here, go ahead and start without me. You must be hungry."

I'm trembling with fear, but I take a spoonful of the stew, and it tastes quite good. I eat slowly, taking deep breaths between every bite. Meanwhile, Zofia paces back and forth while she smokes her cigarette.

"This is very good," I tell Zofia. "And you cooked it really fast."

"I'm a nervous person, so I do everything very fast," she answers. She's thin and she moves quickly, with very jerky motions. When she finishes her cigarette, she sits down and eats. By that time, I realize that the food isn't poisoned.

Gradually, I begin to relax. I look around Zofia's small room. There's hardly any furniture, but there are all sorts of knick-knacks and she has a gramophone (an old-fashioned phonograph). Zofia must notice that I'm looking around and she asks, "Do you want to listen to some music?"

I nod "yes" with my head, but in my heart, music is the last thing I want to hear! As I listen to the merry sounds coming from the gramophone, I hear the sounds of people crying in the ghetto, in my head. But Zofia's apartment is warm and comfortable, and I know that she's trying to be nice to me.

Zofia keeps her room spotlessly clean, and she's anxious to clean me up, too. As soon as we finish eating, she puts a huge cauldron of water on the stove and heats it up. She prepares a hot bath in a round basin which she uses for bathing and doing laundry. At first, I'm very embarrassed to undress in front of Zofia. I've been sleeping in my clothing for a long time, and I only change my outfit in order to get rid of the lice in the seams. But Zofia gently washes me and shampoos my hair. I haven't had such a warm and wonderful bath since Mama was with us, and it feels just magnificent. Of course, Zofia is only worried about lice, and she wouldn't have been surprised to find that I was full of them. But I show her my lice comb and tell her I have no more lice—that I check myself every day.

"You're a good girl," she says. "I think we're going to get along just fine together."

After that wonderful bath, Zofia takes out a large flannel sheet and wraps me in it. Then she nods in the direction of her bed and says, "Look, I have a big double bed that was meant for a married couple, but I'm all alone now. I'm a very small person—I don't take up very much room. There's plenty of room for both of us."

It isn't at all unusual for two people to share a bed, and it will be a lot more comfortable for me than sleeping across two chairs, or on a pile of clothing on the floor. I'm beginning to feel that I've made the right decision in coming here. And what a wonderful soft, warm goose down blanket she has! Lying in the safe, clean bed next to Zofia, I feel as if I'm in heaven. It's been a very long time since I've felt so comfortable. I had forgotten how good life could be.

I fall asleep easily. I'm curled up, facing the wall. There are tears in my eyes. How could I have suspected this wonderful, kind woman, of wanting to poison me? Here she is—a total stranger—taking care of me with greater kindness than anyone has done in a very long time! And sharing her very own bed with me! Maybe my luck is changing for the better. Maybe my whole life will be better now.

The next morning, I wake up with a start, not knowing where I am. In my dream, I was being chased through the streets. I feel very frightened until I realize where I am, and I smell the wonderful aroma of the breakfast that's waiting for me. Zofia has made toast with butter, sliced salami, and delicious, fresh coffee. I sit down to eat, and I start feeling at home. Seeing Zofia's apartment in daylight also makes me feel more comfortable.

Over breakfast, Zofia tells me a little about herself. "I'm living all alone now, and I'm very lonely. My husband was in the Russian army, and I haven't heard from him since the German invasion. I don't even know if he's still alive."

I nod in sympathy. This was what had happened to my mother's friend, Lucia, and I know it's a common story.

Zofia goes on, "At first, I tried to find somebody to live with me. A friend of mine sent me somebody—a young girl, like you—but she was very dirty and she ended up stealing from me. So, you came along at just the right time."

I can feel that Zofia is being honest and sincere with me, and I relax.

"I work in a cloth factory, and I have to be at work from nine in the morning until six o'clock in the evening. If you come here a little after six every evening, you can have dinner with me," she says, "and, now we have to leave. Look around when you come and go. The building manager is always snooping around here."

Unfortunately, the building manager's apartment is right next door to Zofia's apartment, and we have to pass by his door to get to the communal toilets. I know that could turn into a problem.

One morning, Zofia says, "Leave your dirty clothing here for me to wash today." She had found a louse in her bed, and she wants to scrub everything clean. I haven't done any laundry since Mama left, and I'm happy to have my clothes scrubbed clean. When I come back that evening, everything is hanging on a line in the middle of Zofia's room, and the smell of the clean clothes is almost as good as the smell of the dinner that Zofia has prepared. Zofia is a good cook, and she makes very tasty meals. I can see that I'm going to eat very well while I'm staying with her.

One evening, after dinner, there's a knock on the door, and Zofia motions to me that I should hide on the far side of the large floor-to-ceiling cupboard. She opens the door and talks

226

to the neighbor for a while. All the time, I stand rigidly stiff behind the cupboard, trying not to make a sound. I feel as if I have to cough, and I swallow desperately to keep myself from making any noise. It's only a few minutes, but it seems like forever. But Zofia isn't as afraid of her neighbors as she is of the building manager. Each morning, Zofia and I leave separately. I look carefully to make sure that nobody is standing around and watching.

While I'm staying with Zofia, I go back to the ghetto every day to get items to trade for food for the Freiheiters and my regular customers. Every evening, when I go back to Zofia's apartment, I bring food and a gift for her, which pleases her enormously. She's always glad to see me.

While I was staying with Vitzmanova, I saw the Freiheiters once. They were happy that I had found a safe place to stay outside the ghetto. But now that I'm living with Zofia, I can no longer see the Freiheiters, because they're all working during the day and I can't get out of the ghetto and travel to Zofia's apartment by tram at night. It's too far away.

Also, the danger to me in the ghetto is increasing, and the Freiheiters want me to stay out of the ghetto altogether. Things have changed so much, there's almost nothing left of the Lvov that I grew up in! Bit by bit, piece by piece, the city, my neighborhood, and my family have changed from the familiar and the comfortable into a nightmarish new reality. I can't even use my own name anymore!

The Freiheiters helped me create a believable story to tell people about my past, so I

227

could live outside the ghetto safely. And during the long, lonely hours that I spend wandering around the streets, I have endless dialogues with my imaginary companions about what to tell people.

"Hello, I'm Zofia Zaborska," I begin.

"And where do you come from?"

"I was born in Sambour, but I grew up in Lvov with my parents. But they were taken away by the Russians over a year ago."

"Why did the Russians take <u>both</u> of them? They usually took only the men, to go into the army."

"No, they didn't take my father to the army. My parents were anti-Communists, so they took them both to Siberia."

"Oh, I see. Poor child!"

"But I need more of a story."

"Okay.... And how did you live after that?"

"The Russians put me into an orphanage, here in Lvov."

"But you left the orphanage, right?"

"Yes. So what can I say next?"

"Tell them about your aunt."

"Okay...One day, my aunt came to visit the orphanage and took me home to live with her."

"That sounds okay."

"But what can I tell them happened next?"

"Tell them that the Germans took your aunt to work for them in Germany, so you were left alone in Lvov."

"Okay."

Slowly but surely, I'm weaving together the life history of "Zofia Zaborska"—a story that I think could carry me safely out of the ghetto and into the homes of Polish people who are strangers to me, but who might help me survive.

One morning, Zofia tells me that she's going to have visitors that evening. I understand that she doesn't want me to come back for dinner or to sleep there that night, and I say, "Okay, I'll sleep somewhere else tonight."

"Oh, no! That's not what I meant," she re-assures me. "They're good friends—two Italian army officers—one of them is coming with his girlfriend. They have to go back to the front very soon, and they're going to spend the evening here. You have nothing to fear from them. They're very good friends of mine."

I'm a bit afraid to meet them and spend the whole evening together with them in Zofia's small apartment, but I'm even more afraid of sleeping in the ghetto at night. Before we leave the apartment, I tell Zofia that I'll be back in the evening for dinner, as usual, but all day long I worry about it.

As it turns out, it really is all right. I've brought a salami with me. I always bring Zofia something to eat in the evening. Later, when Zofia's friends show up, they have wine and a cake. They've already eaten dinner, and they want to drink and dance to the music that Zofia plays on her gramophone. I watch them dance. When I get sleepy, Zofia makes up a place for me to sleep on a pile of clothing on the floor next to the stove. She and her Italian boy-friend sleep in her large double bed.

The next morning, Zofia sends me to the black market to bring back ingredients for a cake.

"The men are returning to the front tomorrow, and I want to make them a special treat," she tells me.

She also asks if she can borrow 500 Marks to give her boyfriend as a going away present. "I'll pay you back as soon as I get my paycheck," she promises me.

I think this is a very strange request, and I'm hesitant to give her so much money. But I don't see any way to refuse without insulting her. After all, she's saving my life by keeping me in her apartment, and endangering herself at the same time. Even if I never get the money back, I think it's safer to give it to her than say no and risk having her throw me out. So I give her the "loan" and I return that evening with the expensive ingredients for the cake, as well as food and the usual present.

But now there's a different problem. The building manager has seen me, and he warned Zofia that if he should ever see me again, he'll take us both to the Gestapo!

"I'm afraid you'll have to leave right now," says Zofia.

I plead with her, saying, "I'll sneak in through the window that leads to the courtyard."

But she's too afraid of what the manager might do. All of the presents, the food I had brought her, and the money I had lent her, meant nothing in the face of the danger of being questioned by the Gestapo. I leave, knowing I'll never see Zofia or my 500 Marks again.

230

During the time I stayed with Zofia, I kept trading on the black market as usual. Now I wander around the streets there, trying to make more friends. I'm walking around in a very bitter mood when I run into somebody I had met once at Vitzmanova's house. He's a friendly young man named Alexei Shum, who is very sympathetic to me.

"Sometimes a stranger is really an angel in disguise," my fairy tale friends remind me.

So I tell Alexei, "I was living with Vitzmanova, but her children figured out that I was Jewish, and they stole money from me. Vitzmanova was afraid they would report me to the police, so she sent to me live with her friend Zofia, on the other side of Lvov."

Alexei listens very sympathetically and asks a lot of questions. I tell him about what happened with Zofia, and how scared I am to go back into the ghetto.

"You *should* be scared," he says. "It's much too dangerous for you there, nowadays."

He tells me that he lives with his family on a street very near the black market. He points to an apartment building on Starozakonna Street and gives me his address.

Alexei says, "I'm on my way home right now. Why don't you come with me and meet my family?"

I go, feeling very safe with him.

Alexei and his young wife, Maria, are Ukrainian. They're dark-haired and dark-skinned, like me. Maria is petite and very

231

pretty. They have a little boy named Michael who was born during the Russian occupation. He must be around the same age as my brother, Emmanuel.

Alexei tells me that during the Russian occupation, he was a member of the "Militia"—that is, the local citizens' police force. After the Russians left, he moved to a different street, where nobody recognized him, because he was afraid of being arrested by the Germans. Now, he works as a trader on the black market, and there's always plenty of business.

Alexei's wife, Maria, welcomes me very graciously. "Here, why don't you sit down with us and have some *pierogi?*" she says "I'm just cooking it right now."

It smells delicious and I'm hungry, as usual.

From the moment I arrive, the Shums make me feel like a member of their family.

Alexei says, "Make yourself at home. You're welcome to eat all your meals with us. You can come and go at any hour of the day or night, and sleep here at night, if you like."

I can see that he and Maria are sincere about helping me, because they have other "guests" as well—mostly Jews like me who come and go, and use their apartment as a safe haven.

Alexei says, "You should stop trading on the black market and bring me all the clothing and bedding you have for sale. I'll give you a higher price for those things than you could get on the street."

"How can you do that?" I ask him. He and Maria laugh. "That's the business I'm in, and I have lots and lots of contacts!"

Maria says, "You need to be careful about who sees you here. We have people coming and going all day and night. It's better if you stay in one of the inner rooms in the apartment, not in the kitchen, near the front door."

The Shums have a very large apartment, with three rooms instead of the usual two. Maria makes up a makeshift bed for me. "I'm sorry I don't have anything better for you," she apologizes. "But I'll make it as comfortable as I can."

I'm quite small for my age, so I can sleep lying across two chairs, which she pads with some soft clothing. It isn't the most comfortable bed I've ever slept in, but it's a safe place, and the Shums are being exceptionally kind to me. I know I'm in good hands. I feel almost as close to them as I do to the Freiheiters. These strangers are risking their lives for me—and for other Jews, too, I can see. But I'm in grave danger on the streets, and it's getting worse and worse every day.

In the back bedroom, the Shums have another live-in guest—a woman who is obviously Jewish. Her hair is pulled back from her face and she has a long braid that she twists around the back of her head. Like me, she has lost everybody in her family, and now she's alone. When Maria introduces us, the woman immediately takes out a photograph and shows it to me.

"Have you seen my son?" she asks me. "He's just a few years older than you."

"No," I tell her, sadly. "I haven't noticed him on the streets."

The Shum family have many visitors, and every time somebody walks into the back room, this woman takes out her photo and asks if they've seen her son. But nobody has.

The Shum household is very lively, with people coming and going all of the time. I soon realize that the Shums are smuggling people out of the ghetto. Like my cousin Eli, they get false passports and help Jews escape from Lvov. Their apartment is always full of food, clothing, shoes and other valuable items. Polish and Ukrainian smugglers come frequently and I hear a great deal of bartering going on in their apartment. There is always plenty of food on the table. I wish I could go back to the ghetto and tell the Freiheiters that I'm all right, but Alexei says, "Please don't go there again after dark. It's just too dangerous!"

However, I do go back to 20 Lokietka Street during the day. The door to our apartment is locked, so I have good reason to believe that my family is still living there and working, as usual. I wish I could write them a note and push it under the door, but of course, I have nothing to write on and no pen to write with.

Alexei Shum has trade connections with people from Stalowa Wola, a village in the Polish countryside. He tells me there's a German munitions factory there. The traders from Stalowa Wola say that the Germans are guarding the area around the factory very heavily. The Germans have also established a forced labor camp in Stalowa Wola, we learn from some of

234

the people who come to the Shums. For some reason, the Jewish woman with the long, braided hair believes that her son might have been taken to that camp. She's been told that there are many young men from Lvov there, and she asks everybody who comes from Stalowa Wola to look for her son.

One day, a young couple and a single man arrive from Stalowa Wola. I'm in the back room with Maria, her son, Michael, and the Jewish woman, when they arrive. We hear them talking for a while in the front room, and then Alexei brings them to our room. One of the men approaches the Jewish woman a bit hesitantly and says, "I think I've found your son. He's in the labor camp in Stalowa Wola."

I can see that the young couple is looking at each other in a strange way, but I don't understand why. So many things seem strange nowadays.

The Jewish woman turns white and throws her arms around the man.

"My son! You've found my son!" she cries. "But what condition is he in?"

The man answers haltingly, as if he has a speech impediment. He says, "Your son, he's okay.. Really, he's fine... But he needs money... And clothes.... He asks you to send him pants...and shirts.. and boots.... If you can."

The woman starts crying, "My poor son! Of course he needs money and clothes. He left with only the clothes he was wearing. But where am I going to find boots for him? It's too dangerous to go back to my apartment with all the German soldiers in the streets, and I have no money."

235

She considers what to do for a while, and then decides, "I'll go out and sell my wedding ring!"

"Are you sure that's what you want to do?" Alexei asks her, anxiously.

"Of course!" she answers. "What good is my wedding ring if my son needs warm clothes?"

So she wraps herself up in her heavy wool scarf and leaves the house immediately.

The couple from Stalowa Wola stands and watches without saying anything. They've listened to every word, and they look quite disturbed.

When the woman returns, I'm in the apartment, and so is the young couple from Stalowa Wola, but the man from Stalowa Wola is out. The woman has sold her ring for far less than it's worth. But she's happy because she's bought warm clothing and boots for her son. Unfortunately, her happiness is very short-lived. As soon as she enters the room, the young couple speaks to her.

"We're so sorry," they say, "but we think the man who told you he's seen your son is lying. We couldn't say anything while he was here, because he's a very dangerous person, and we're afraid of making him our enemy. But we're almost certain that he didn't see your son. The camp is heavily guarded, and nobody can get in or out of it. There's no way of knowing if your son is there or not. And what's more, the way the Germans are guarding the camp, there would be no way for anybody to bring him anything."

The woman is beside herself. She sits down on the bed and puts her head in her hands and

236

sobs. Maria goes over to her and sits down next her. She puts her arm around her, trying to console her. But it's too late. The damage has been done.

The next day, the woman leaves. She says she's leaving Lvov to search for her son, herself. Alexei and Maria have done all they could to help her, but in the end, there was nothing they could do to help her find her son.

While I'm staying with the Shums, I'm busy all of the time. I run back and forth between the ghetto and the Shums, bringing everything to Alexei to sell for me. During that time, the Shums come to be like my family.

Zamarstynovska Street is a very busy, very noisy place. People are always out walking and shopping there, and the tram runs all day long. Since there's so much activity on Zamarstynovska Street, I can easily blend into the scenery with my baskets. That is, if I don't do anything unusual to attract the attention of the Gestapo.

One day, I'm returning to the ghetto with my baskets full of food to sell. When I get to the ghetto fence, I push the two baskets under the fence in front of me, as usual. Then, I get down on the ground and stick my head through the opening, as I always do before crawling through the hole that the ghetto children had dug underneath the fence. I look both left and right, and I see two Gestapo policemen walking toward me. I leave my baskets on the ghetto side of the fence and run into the hustle and bustle of Zamarstynovska Street. But the Gestapo policemen have seen me, and the baskets of food are clear evidence of who I am and what I'm doing. The two Gestapo policemen run to the fence and shoot their rifles into the air, yelling "Halt!" very loudly.

Naturally, that attracts a lot of attention. I'm the only person running on the busy street, and it quickly becomes apparent that they're after me. At that point on Zamarstynovska Street, the street inclines, so I'm running uphill, which slows me down. Hearing the shots and the cries of "Halt!" a group of Polish people on the street surround me and hold me until the German officers arrive.

When the Gestapo arrives, they disperse the crowd and shove me ahead of them roughly, back in the direction of the ghetto. I'm so scared I can hardly breathe. Are they going to shoot me? We walk through a "legal" passageway into the ghetto, to a small Gestapo office, where there are a few clerks. When we get there, they begin to interrogate me.

"Papers!" they shout at me, *"Schnell!"*

Of course, I'm carrying the birth certificate of Zofia Zaborska in the bag around my neck. I take it out and show it to them. But they ask me if I have other papers, too. Unfortunately, I do. I'm carrying some falsified documents—an identification card, a birth certificate, and a work permit that Alexei Shum had given me to take to a woman in the ghetto. This is the only time I've ever tried to do such an errand. I also have some money, but not very much, as I had bought food already—the food that was in the baskets I left at the ghetto fence.

"Where did you get these papers? " The Gestapo officer asks me, angrily.

"I found them on the street outside the Bristol Hotel," I lie to him. For some reason, that's the first thing that pops into my mind. I've seen the Bristol Hotel on Legionov Street, a short walk from the Theatre Vielki near the park where I used to go with Mama in the afternoons.

"And what were you going to do with them?" he asks.

"I was going to give them to a police officer I know, so he could return them to their owner. Surely somebody is looking for them!" I say, as innocently as I can.

The Gestapo officers look at me, trying to decide whether or not to believe me. They look over my birth certificate and shout at me: "You're Aryan! Why were you going into the ghetto?"

I answer, "I make my living by selling to the people in the ghetto."

"That's illegal!" they yell.

"I know," I say, "but I have nobody to take care of me."

"Where are your parents?" they ask.

"In Siberia," I say. "The Russians took them away because they were anti-Communist."

As terrified as I am, I know the right thing to say. I've practiced it enough on my long, lonely days of wandering the streets alone. The Nazis will like a girl whose parents were anti-Communist Russian prisoners. They'll think my parents were Nazi supporters, like many of the Poles of Lvov. I'm young enough for them to think that I couldn't make up such a story. and I look even younger because I'm so small for my age.

And the story works! When they hear about my parents, they start to act differently toward me. I've managed to make a good impression on them. The officer in charge tells one of the policemen, "Take her to the Aryan side. This is a case for the Polish police."

So another policeman takes my money and my documents and marches me back to the Aryan side of Lvov, into another Gestapo office, where Polish people are questioned by the Gestapo. There, they ask me the same questions and look over all of my papers very carefully. They also make me take off my coat and my dress, so that I'm standing only in my underwear, shivering. They carefully examine my outer clothing and check the linings to see if anything is sewn into the seams or if there are any secret pockets. That's what many Jews do, nowadays. But there's nothing hidden there. They must believe that I really am Zofia Zaborska, and that my parents really have been taken to Siberia, because they stop questioning me.

Finally, the officer in charge of the interrogation asks me, "Where do you live?"

I answer, "Near Lyczakov Station," because I know that's the last stop on the tramline, and I think it might be too far away for them to bother checking.

The officer in charge tells another policeman, "Take her home on the tram."

So the Gestapo policeman takes me back to Zamarstynovska Street, where we get on the electric tram. It seems like the ride will last forever, because Lyczakov Station is so far away. Meanwhile, it's getting dark outside, and I'm very worried. What will I do when we get off the tram? I've practiced my speech about my parents and my background, but I've never thought of what I would do if I was in this situation. On the outside, I behave very calmly, but on the inside, I'm in turmoil. I'm beginning to believe that this might be my last night on earth. Finally, we arrive at Lyczakov Station, the last stop on the tram, and everybody gets off. By this time, it's twilight.

"Take me to your house!" the policeman commands in a mean tone of voice.

"I don't really live here," I tell him. "I have no home, I don't live anywhere," I say, and I shrug my shoulders. "You have a gun, go ahead and shoot me, if you want to," I tell him. "I'm just a poor orphan, with nowhere to live and nobody to take care of me. Every night I sleep somewhere else, with anybody who will take me in. That's why I sell food in the ghetto."

He slaps me hard across the face. "Dirty Jew!" he shouts. "Now you going to die!" he growls at me, in broken Polish, "A not nice death!"

I say nothing. He grabs my arm and pushes be back onto the tram. We ride all the way back to the center of Lvov in complete silence. I wonder what's going to happen to me, and I try not to show how frightened I am, but I feel very dizzy on the way back.

By the time we get back to the interrogation booth, the officer who was in charge this afternoon is gone, and the one who had taken me on the tram ride now puts me in a small isolation booth. This room has sturdy stone walls, with one tiny window high up on one of the walls. There's a narrow cot bed, and a potty, too.

I don't know how many hours I spend there, worrying about what I'm going to tell the German police officer the next morning. I call on my fairy tale companions to help me. Over and over again, we rehearse what I'll say.

"Hello, I'm Zofia Zaborska."

"And where do you come from?"

"I grew up in Lvov, with my parents, but they were taken away by the Russians over a year ago."

"Why did the Russians take <u>both</u> of them? They usually took only the men, to go to the army."

"But they didn't take my father to the army.

My parents were anti-Communists, so they took them both to Siberia."

"Oh, I see. Poor child!"

"And how did you live after that?"

"The Russians put me in an orphanage. I lived there while the Russians were in Lvov."

"And when the Russians left, where did you go?"

"My aunt took me to live with her, here in Lvov."

"So where is your aunt now?"

"The Germans took her to work in Germany, so now I'm all alone."

"Don't you have anybody else to go to?"

"Not here in Lvov."

"Poor child!"

The next morning, when the officer returns, he questions me again.

"Why did you lie? Where do you live?" he shouts at me.

"I have no place to live," I tell him. "I have nobody to take care of me."

I've spent the whole night rehearsing my story, and I tell it to the Nazi officers. The combination of my story and my documents is so realistic that the officer in charge believes me! The policemen talk to each other and I listen, pretending not to understand their German.

"This is a case for a social worker!" the officer in charge declares. "These stupid Pollacks don't even know how to take care of their own children!" he says.

He sits down with his secretary and dictates a letter to her, a letter introducing me to a Polish social worker. In the letter, he repeats all of the details of the story I've told him about Zofia Zaborska. When the letter is ready, the junior officer takes me to the office of the social worker. Of course, my documents and my money remain at the German police booth. I'll probably never see them again.

At the social work office, the manager in charge reads the letter telling all about "Zofia Zaborska." She takes one look at me and says to the German policeman, "What's wrong with you? This is obviously a Jew!"

The officer answers her, "If you can prove that, then send her back."

Meanwhile, I listen to them talk without saying a word. I'm thinking that if the manager wants to prove I'm a Jew, all she has to do is to ask me to say a prayer. I don't know even the simplest Christian child's prayer, and I vow to myself that if I should get out of here alive, the

243

first thing I'll do is learn some simple prayers, just in case I'm ever caught again. Frightened that the social worker will start to ask me questions that I won't know how to answer, I quickly say to her, "Please, Pani Social Worker, if I'm going to stay here, I need to go to the people I trade with, because they owe me a lot of money."

Of course, when she hears about the money, her eyes light up and she's happy to let me go.

"All right," she says. "Go to your customers and come back with the money as soon as you can."

Free again, I decide to go straight to Alexei Shum and ask him to teach me some simple Christian prayers. Then I'll go back to the social worker and "prove" to her that I'm really Zofia Zaborska!

At Alexei Shum's apartment, Maria and Alexei are very happy to see me.

"We were very worried about you. What happened?" they ask, "Why didn't you come back to sleep here last night?"
I tell them everything that happened.

"Now, you must teach me a child's prayer. When I learn the prayers, I'll go back to the social worker and prove to her that I'm a Christian!"

But Alexei shakes his head and says, "Poor, innocent child! Do you think that a prayer is going to help you? You're in greater danger than ever before. If you go back to the social worker, she'll just take your money and turn you over to the Gestapo again. And by the
244

time you get back there, they'll know the documents you gave them were falsified. You can't go back there at all."

"But what can I do?" I ask him. "I gave the Gestapo my documents and my money. How can I earn a living if I don't keep on trading? My baskets of food are gone, and I owe you money, too. How am I going to pay you back?"

"Never mind," Alexei assures me. "The only thing that matters now is that you're still alive. I'll give you some food to trade in the ghetto and you can pay me back when you earn some money."

And for the next few days, I go back into the ghetto and trade. But every time I have to go under the ghetto fence, I'm afraid that the Gestapo will catch me again. And if they do, I know they'll never let me go again. I walk around terrified of what might happen to me.

Several days later, I'm on my way back to the ghetto with my two baskets full of food when I see that something unusual is happening. Polish people are standing all along the length of the ghetto fence, looking through the wooden slats and talking excitedly. Even from far away, I can see the smoke rising up over the ghetto, and I can smell it, too. As I get closer, I hear somebody chuckling and saying, "Now those vermin are getting what they deserve!" When I realize that the ghetto is going up in flames, I know I can never go back there. I quickly turn around and walk away, heading straight for Starozakonna Street, and the Shum's apartment.

Alexei tells me, "Sonya, it's too dangerous for you to continue living in Lvov. You can't go back into the ghetto again, and it's very dangerous for you to stay with us. Yesterday, the Gestapo went into the apartment of one of our neighbors and shot the husband and wife who were hiding a Jewish man. Now, the Gestapo knows all about you. They recognize your face. If you wander around the streets, they'll pick you up sooner or later. And next time, they won't let you go. You need to leave Lvov and find a safer place to live."

I can't imagine leaving Lvov. I wouldn't know where to go, and I have nobody to go to. I haven't heard from my relatives in the village of Rava Russka at all since the Germans came to Lvov. They don't even know that Mama is missing, or that Father has died. They might be in Siberia or in German labor camps or even dead, for all I know. Where can I go?

Fortunately, Alexei has a plan for me. "You can find work as a servant girl in a Polish village," he tells me. "The people in the countryside grow their own food. They always need somebody to help around the house or in the fields. It will be safer for you if you leave Lvov."

What can I say? I know he's right, but I'm terrified at the thought of leaving Lvov and being all alone.

Alexei takes care of every detail. His son, Michael Alexandrovich Shum, is about three years old, so he isn't required by German law to have a birth certificate. He was born during the Russian occupation, so his birth certificate is written in Russian on a Russian document. Alexei goes to a pharmacy and buys chemicals that erase ink. He obviously has a lot of experience with falsifying legal documents. After he

246

erases Michael's name and all of the details about his birth, he writes in Russian letters, "Replacement Birth Certificate," as if the original birth certificate has been lost or stolen.

Alexei asks me, "What name would you like to use?"

I know it would be wiser to make up a new identity for myself, but I say, "Zofia Zaborska."

"But the Gestapo already know that name," Alexei gently reminds me.

"Yes," I say, "I know. But since my cousin Eli gave me Zofia Zaborska's birth certificate, I've memorized everything about her. And I spent a long time making up a convincing story about her background. With so many changes in my life, I need something familiar to cling to. I can't start making up a whole new story now. It's confusing enough, as it is!"

"I understand," he says.

"And anyway, I'm leaving Lvov."

"Okay," says Alexei. "It'll be all right."

When the birth certificate is ready, Alexei goes to the train station and buys two tickets.

"I'll take you to the countryside on the train," he tells me. "I need to go to Stalowa Wola, anyway."

Meanwhile, at home, Maria is preparing a small green suitcase for me. She packs some warm clothes and a few pairs of socks. Along with that, Alexei gives me some money. Then, he hands me my train ticket and says, "We'll leave for the train station separately, because it's too dangerous for me to walk with you with the Gestapo patrolling the neighborhood. When we get on the train, take a seat somewhere near me. We won't be able to talk, but I'll let

247

you know where to get off. Don't worry," he assures me, "I'll take you all the way to Stalowa Wola. It's a small town, not too far from Lublin. There are many, many small farms there, and some family will certainly want you to help them with the housework."

Everyone who gets on the train has to go through an identity check. When I give the German official my birth certificate, I'm afraid that he'll look at me and say, "Stop! You're a Jew!" Or maybe worse, he'll know my name from the time I was caught, just a few days ago. Maybe I should have asked Alexei to give me a new name on the birth certificate, after all. But there's no problem; no questions are asked.

I get on the train before Alexei and he sits down not far from me, in a seat where we can easily see each other's faces. Most of the seats in the train are taken, but not all. As the train moves out of the station, I look out the window, trying to take note of as many things as I can and to remember them for later, in case I need them sometime.

We pass Belzec, a town that people are talking about a lot in Lvov. It's a place where the Germans are taking the Jews they capture in their round-ups. There are terrible rumors about what the Germans are doing to the Jews there. When we pass there, I start to grieve for my family, wondering if any of them have ended up there. I try very hard to keep my face blank, so nobody will suspect me of being Jewish. I try to convince myself that it will be good me for to go and live in a village and work on a farm. It will be healthy and I'll finally be safe.

But I'll be alone—all alone, in a strange place. Except for my one short stay in Rava Russka, as a young child, I've never been outside of Lvov before.

"But you won't be all alone, Sonya. I'll be with you," whispers Ivasyk.

"And I will, too," says Yash.

"So will I" says Malgosha, and the little match girl, and the youth from the story of the golden spring.

I doze off to the sound of their far-away voices.

It's a very long trip, and as we travel, it grows dark outside. The train makes many stops along the way and I feel as if we're moving very slowly. By the time we arrive at the station in Stalowa Wola, it's well into the middle of the night. As the train slows down and pulls into the station, I stand up and look out the window. Alexei comes and stands next to me at the window. We both look out at the platform. It's crowded with German soldiers, I don't know why. Maybe they're waiting for another train. Anyway, Alexei whispers to me, softly but distinctly, "Don't get off here. We're going on."

So I sit back down and try to remain calm. This time, Alexei sits next to me. I'm very tired and I doze off with my head resting on his shoulder. By the time I wake up, it's beginning to get light. Outside, I can see fields stretching in every direction. We pass many villages with small farmhouses and barns. As it gets lighter outside, I notice some of the signs of early

249

spring: the snow is melting and there are tiny green buds on the branches of the trees.

When we get to a tiny "station" called Shastarka, Alexei strokes my hair and whispers softly, "Get off here, and may God be with you!"

I get off the train without looking back at him, holding my small bundle of clothing, and the train pulls away with Alexei on it.

Rural Poland

In a fairy tale, the hero often travels far from home, all alone, to seek his fortune...

When I get off the train at Shastarka, the "station" is empty. It's called a station, but it's really just a wooden shack with three sides and a roof to protect it from the snow and rain. It doesn't even have a bench or a chair. Nobody else is there, and it's too early in the morning to start knocking on people's doors. I feel very anxious. I've never been in the countryside, so far from Lvov, all alone.

"Where will I go first?" I wonder, and "What will I say when someone opens their door to me?" With these questions in my head, I'm in no hurry to move. I stand in the station and rehearse my speech:

"Hello. My name is Zofia Zaborska. I've just come here from Lvov. I'm looking for work."

No, maybe I should tell them I'm an orphan first.

"Hello. My name is Zofia Zaborska. I'm an orphan from Lvov. I've come here looking for work."

That sounds better. Maybe that will make somebody take pity on me and give me a job? But no! I shouldn't tell them that I'm an orphan. They probably know that most of the orphans in Lvov are Jewish children whose parents have been taken away by the Germans. I'll just tell them that my parents were taken away by the Russians for being anti-Communists.

I feel very reluctant to knock on the door of a stranger, but I know that I have to find a place to stay and that nobody will help me if I don't help myself.

As the sun starts coming up, I look out over the flat countryside. I see a few small houses surrounded by fields. The houses are not very far from each other, so I suppose that each family owns just a small piece of land. It isn't long before I see smoke coming out of the chimneys of several farmhouses. Slowly, I walk out of the train station carrying my small green suitcase. I walk towards the nearest farmhouse. I know that the people living in the house must be awake, but I knock on the door very quietly and timidly. The woman who opens it doesn't smile at me.

"What do you want?" she asks, looking me over suspiciously.

"Good morning," I say. "My name is Zofia Zaborska. I've just come from Lvov. I'm looking for work."

"I have nothing for you," she says, coldly, and closes the door in my face. I walk away, feeling very downhearted. I wonder if I should say something different at the next farmhouse.

"Good morning," I say. "I'm looking for work."

But I get the same cold response.

As I'm walking away from the house, along comes a neighbor woman. She knocks on the door and says, "Blessed be Jesus Christ!" when the door opens.

The woman who opens the door answers her, saying, "Amen!" and the two of them start talking. Now I realize this must be their way of saying hello—it's the greeting that's expected of anyone who comes to the door. I understand that I've insulted people by failing to bless them, so I walk away as quickly as I can. At least now I know what to say when I knock on a stranger's door!

So when a woman opens the door of the next house, I say, "Blessed be Jesus Christ!"

"Amen!" she answers, and even smiles. She's a young woman with blonde hair pulled into a knot at the back of her neck.

Then I say, "Good morning" and I introduce myself. "My name is Zofia Zaborska. I've come from the city of Lvov, all alone on the train. I have a little money to buy bread, but what I really want is to find work," I tell her.

She looks me over and nods her head. "I see," she says, pleasantly. "Wait a minute. I'll go talk to my husband."

As it turns out, they have a larger house and more fields than many of the other small farmers in the area. And Maria Mazur, who has a young child, needs somebody to help her with the housework. Her husband, Josef, comes to

253

talk to me and look me over. I guess they believe my story because it doesn't take them
long to decide that I can come and live with
them, as a servant.

But according to German law, I can't stay
here for even one night without registering with
the local government council. So after eating a
hearty breakfast in Maria's kitchen, I leave my
belongings with the Mazur family and I take off
for the village office, which is quite a distance
away. It takes me several hours to walk there.

Looking all around me in this rural setting,
so different from anything I've ever known, I
begin to feel much more optimistic. On the long
walk, I notice many signs of spring: the trees
have tiny leaves, there are some wildflowers in
the fields, and everything looks hopeful and optimistic.

I walk along thinking to myself, "This is the
start of a new life for me. I have a new name, a
new identity, and now I'll be safe. I'll have food
to eat and warm clothes, and I'll be living with
a family, so I won't be alone anymore." I think
of the young man from the story of the golden
spring. He walked through fields like these,
and, after suffering many hardships, he came
to the golden spring. And the stones came back
to life at the golden spring. I've suffered a lot of
hardships, too. Maybe my fortune is turning.
Maybe everyone in my family will come back
some day. These pastoral surroundings give me
more hope than I've had for a long time.

When I arrive at the village council office,
nobody else is there on business, so they turn
to me immediately.

"Where are you from?" the clerk asks me, "and where are your papers?"

"Right here," I say, taking out the birth certificate of Zofia Zaborska, written in Russian. Of course, nobody there can read a word of Russian except me, but it looks very formal and official, like an authentic document. So I tell them that this is my "replacement" birth certificate, because I lost my original birth certificate when my parents were sent to Siberia by the Russians for being anti-Communists. I tell them the story of the orphanage and my "aunt," and I explain that I left Lvov to look for work in the countryside.

It's a believable story: all of the things I claim have happened to me are things that really have happened to many children during the past few years. I look like many Polish people from Lvov: I have dark eyes and dark hair, and I speak Polish with the accent typical of a native of Lvov. So there's no reason for them to suspect I'm lying. Also, I probably look too young and innocent to be making up stories.

Finally, after much discussion about what to do, they decide to issue me papers saying that I'm a resident of the Mazur household, where I'm working as a domestic servant. For me, this is a great step forward.

It has taken me all day to walk to the village council office to register as a resident of Polichna—the village where the Mazurs live—and to walk back to the Mazur household. By the time I get there, it's evening and I'm very tired. I sit with the Mazurs and eat a hearty supper of *borscht* (beet soup) and potatoes. Maria says, "Don't be shy. Take as much as you like!"

When she sees me taking potatoes with a large tablespoon, she laughs and says, "What a comedian you are. You can just pick up the potato with your hands, like we do! And you can drink your borscht from your cup, too. You don't need a fork or a spoon to eat at our table!"

She makes me feel comfortable and relaxed with them right away. Alexei was right. The Polish countryside is the best place for me. But every aspect of daily life is so different in the village from anything I've ever experienced that I'll need some lessons in village manners. And Maria Mazur is very pleasant and patient in guiding me.

Early next morning, I start to work on the Mazur's small farm. One of my daily chores is to feed the cows. Of course, I'm a city girl and I've never even seen a cow close-up before! So Josef Mazur explains what to do: "You put the hay in front of the cows for them to eat, and the straw behind them, for them to dirty." He tells me that the dirty straw is very important. Later, he'll take it to the fields, to be used as fertilizer in the vegetable gardens.

Well, that seems easy enough. But as soon as Josef leaves, I become confused. "The hay looks black and dirty and it doesn't look like something anybody would want to eat," I think, "Not even a cow. On the other hand, the straw is clean-looking and golden. It looks much more appetizing than the hay."

And I remember how in the story of Rumplestilskin, the little man had woven straw into gold. So I think, "I probably didn't hear him right. I'll give them the golden straw to eat, and

256

put the hay behind them for them to dirty. It's black, anyway. That must be the right thing to do!"

A while later, Maria Mazur comes to check up on me. "You've been here a very long time," she says. "I wanted to see if everything is all right."

But of course, what she sees is far from okay.

"Oh, no! What have you done?" she cries. "You've given them straw to eat and hay to dirty! How could you do such a thing? Didn't you listen to Josef?"

I'm lucky that Maria is a kind and patient woman. She helps me correct what I've done and I promise not to make any more mistakes. But clearly, I'm cut out for trading in the market, not for working on a farm!

The next day, Josef tries to teach me a different chore. "This is easy," he says. "All you have to do is take the calf out to graze in the field."

They don't have a very large plot of land. I only have to walk from their pasture over to the neighbor's and back again with the calf, letting it stop along the way to graze. It seems like something I'll be able do without making any mistakes. But as soon as I'm out in the field with the calf, she becomes very frisky and she wants to run around. The calf is much stronger than I am, and it's all I can do to keep up with her! So I decide to take the rope and tie it around my waist. "If the calf runs away, at least I won't lose her," I think. But after a short while, I'm exhausted. And since the calf wants to run around in every direction, I soon become tangled up in the rope, and very dirty from be-ing dragged by her.

There are some children grazing their cows in a nearby field. They watch me from a dis-tance and they think it's very funny to see a girl being pulled by a calf. They're all looking at me and pointing.

"What an idiot!" they shout, laughing. "That girl tied herself to her calf!"

When I get back to the farmhouse, I'm ex-hausted and there are stains all over my skirt, from having been dragged through the wet fields. I can see from the way they look at me that the Mazurs are very annoyed, but they don't say anything.

For the next few days, they give me easier tasks. I have to peel potatoes, which is a chore I've done with Zoshka many times, as well as Jijova. But I've never been very skillful with my hands, and the potato peel is always too thick. Just as Jijova had been annoyed with me for peeling away half of the potato, so is Maria Mazur. So she gives me grain to scatter for the chickens, another very simple task. At least I can do that without any problem.

I wash clothes for the family, too. The first time I do this, Maria goes with me to show me what to do, and the other village women are there, too, gossiping. The washing is done out-side, beside a small stream that isn't far from the Mazur's farmhouse. I tie up the dirty cloth-ing in a bundle and tie the bundle on my back. With the dirty laundry piled up on my back, and a wooden paddle in my hand, I walk to the stream. There, I put the clothing down near a wooden board that has been left on the stream

258

bank permanently. I wet each piece of clothing in the stream. Then I take the bar of home-made soap and lather the clothes. Next, I take a paddle and beat the soapy clothing. After that, I have to rinse the clothes in the stream to get the soap off them. It's not very hard work, but I'm not used to doing it, and it takes me much longer than it takes the other women.

The tasks the Mazurs give me are the simplest household chores, but I'm not used to doing them. Everything I do takes a very long time, and I don't do a very good job. I'm constantly worried that I'll do something wrong, and I quickly lose my self-confidence.

Every night, I go to sleep feeling like a terrible failure. The Mazurs have been patient with me, but how long will they want to keep me? Not only am I failing to help them, I'm also causing them problems, and I'm eating their food, as well! I toss and turn on the little bed they've made up for me on a bench in the kitchen. I wonder what's going to happen to me, and if I'll ever learn how to work on a farm. I'm also worried that I might talk in my sleep, and that they'll discover that I'm really a Jew. It's especially hard to get used to answering to the name "Zofia." Living on my own, outside of Lvov, is not so easy!

After about a week, the Mazurs tell me, "We're going to have to let you go. You'll have to find work somewhere else."

Of course, I'm not at all surprised. I take my tiny suitcase and go on my way, feeling very downhearted.

"Will I ever learn how to work on a farm?"

259

"Look at the fields all around you with new leaves budding on the trees and all the wild-flowers in bloom. It's a beautiful world! And you've gained a lot in the short time you spent with the Mazurs. Before, you didn't have residence papers, but now you have an official document that says you're a resident of Polichna. That's the most important thing, to be sure! You've learned country manners, like how to eat at the table with a family. And you've also learned something about farm life and household chores. Now you know the difference between straw and hay, and how to graze a cow in the field. You won't tie yourself to a cow again! Now, you'll know how to watch the cow with the rope in one hand and a stick in the other. For a city girl who has never been on a farm before, you're doing just fine, I think."

I walk through the fields, not knowing where I'm going. I only know that nobody is waiting for me anywhere, and that every step I take carries me further away from the horrors of Lvov.

Finally, I come to a village called Potochek—which means "small stream" in Polish. There, I see an old woman sitting outdoors, near a farmhouse.

"Blessed be Jesus Christ!" I say, approaching her.

"Amen!" she answers.

I put my tiny suitcase down and start speaking to the old woman. I tell her that I've come from Lvov, where there's a shortage of food, and that I'm looking for work.

She looks me over carefully and says, "Wait a minute, I'll go talk to my daughter."

Her daughter, Yulia Rakosh, is a mature woman. She isn't married, and she lives with her mother in a house that has been divided in two. Yulia's younger brother lives in the other half of the house, with his wife, who is pregnant. Yulia has to do all of the housework and the farm work by herself, since her mother is too old to be of much help to her.

Yulka (the nickname for Yulia) looks me over and asks, "Have you ever done farm work before?"

"Yes," I answer, nodding my head.

"Okay, we'll try you out. I could use a helping hand."

In return for my services, they'll feed me, give me a place to sleep, and work clothes. That's the normal way things are done around here, and it's just fine with me.

The Rakosh family has two cows and a calf that need to be taken out to graze every day. Yulka's mother, who I call Grandma Rakosh, stays home and does the lighter household chores, while I take the cows out to the pasture. Now, my self-confidence is coming back. After all, I do know a little about farm work. At least I can pasture the cows without getting into trouble!

But I'm finding it hard to live in their household. They don't have the same comfortable style of living as the Mazurs, and Yulka is very stingy with everything. She serves tiny portions of food, and I'm always hungry after our meals. At the Mazur's, Maria had served heaps of food, and everybody took as much as

261

they wanted. I had never felt ashamed to help myself to more food. But Yulka serves each of us individually, and it's never enough for me. I'm ashamed to ask for more food and afraid that Yulka will be angry with me if I ask for more. She's a cold and distant person, and she seems to be angry with everybody, all of the time. I feel like she's always looking at me very critically. So instead of asking for a bigger portion, I clear my throat noisily.

"What are you squealing like a pig for?" Yulka snaps at me. She doesn't take the hint.

"Sorry," I say, and I stop. I walk away from the table feeling hungry and miserable.

But Grandma Rakosh understands what I want. After that, she hides pieces of bread in her pockets, and gives them to me when I'm on my way to the pasture with the cows, away from the house, where Yulka can't see us. She knows that her miserly daughter would be angry if she saw this.

I always thank Grandma Rakosh very sincerely, and I feel that not only does she understand me, but she also cares about me. Yet, she isn't a person I can confide in. I can't confide in anybody, and I feel very lonely. So I continue to have imaginary conversations with my fairy tale friends about the things that are troubling me.

"Will I ever see my family again?"
"Maybe."
"What will happen if they find out I'm Jewish?"
"But they can't find out. You have a passport with Zofia Zaborska's name on it and you speak
262

Polish just like a Gentile from Lvov. Nobody will ever know you're Jewish."

But I know.

And I think about it all day long, as I go about my chores.

Every Sunday, after our big meal, Yulka takes out her rosary beads and sits and prays. She says, "Hail Mary, full of grace." And then she whispers, "and the Name changed into a Body and the Body lives among us. I believe in Jesus Christ, our Lord."

I listen carefully and try to memorize every word she says, thinking that a Christian girl my age would be expected to know how to say her prayers. But of course, I don't know anything! I try to remember Jijova's stories about the paintings of Jesus, but that's all I know about Christianity, and I still don't know the prayers that a Christian child should know. This troubles me a lot.

But luckily, my life passes quietly during the spring months and through Grandma Rakosh's kindness, I somehow manage to get enough to eat. Then, one day, a young man passes through the field where I'm watching the cows. I'm sitting on a rock when he comes up to me and greets me very pleasantly.

"Hello, young lady," he says. "I wonder who you're working for?"

"I'm staying with the Rakosh family," I tell him. "You know—Yulia and her mother."

"I see," he says. "But you're not from around here, are you?"

"No," I answer. And, as he proceeds to ask me question after question, I gradually tell him

263

the story of Zofia Zaborska. I'm happy that I've rehearsed it so many times, because he asks me a lot of questions about myself and my family.

After I've told him my story, he says, "I'm from Potok—it's a village not far from here," and he points in the direction of his village.

I've seen the signpost that reads "Potok," and I know where it is, so I just nod.

"I'm a landowner and also a shoemaker," he tells me.

Here is a man with both a profession and his own land. That's unusual, and I'm very impressed. When we've finished talking, he says, "Goodbye, we'll meet again. I'm going to make a visit to the Rakosh farm."

After he goes away, I realize that I've told him all about myself—that is, Zofia Zaborska—but he's told me very little other than his name, where he comes from, and what he does. I wonder why he asked me so many questions. He seemed very friendly, but now I feel uneasy.

Later that day, I go home and tell Yulia that Angie will be coming to visit. I notice she's very excited to hear about it. Grandma Rakosh tells me that Angie is a widower with two young children. Surely, he must be looking for a wife.

"But, if he's looking for a wife, why did he ask me so many questions about myself?" I wonder.

Yulia's younger brother and his wife are excited, too. I hear them talking to each other, saying, "Look how excited Yulka is about Angie's visit! Who knows, maybe something will come of it? Let's hope so."

That evening, Yulia fixes herself up to look pretty when Angie arrives. She puts on a scarf that she usually wears only to go to church.

Angie and Yulia sit and talk for what seems like a very long time. While Angie is there, I leave the house. I'm afraid he's going to ask more questions about Zofia Zaborska, and I'm not certain that he believes my story. Something about the way he looks at me troubles me, although I'm not sure why.

Meanwhile, as the days pass, Grandma Rakosh tries to teach me to spin linen thread on her spinning wheel. But, like the other handicrafts I've tried, my efforts are in vain. I work awkwardly and the thread comes out uneven with a lot of lumps in it. It's obvious I'll need a lot of practice in order to learn to spin linen thread. But Grandma Rakosh doesn't have the patience to keep teaching me, and I suppose I'm wasting their flax, as well as her time.

In the next week or two, Angie comes several times to the meadow where I usually watch the cows. He says hello, waves to me, and smiles pleasantly. I think he must be courting Yulka. But, as it turns out, I'm the one he's interested in!

One day, Grandma Rakosh tells me, "Angie asked us if we could spare you for a while. He wants you to come and work for him. He needs somebody to take care of his children and the house."

I don't know what to say. I would like very much to leave the Rakosh household, because I feel so uncomfortable here. Yulka acts more and more unfriendly to me all of the time, and I always feel that she's looking at me as if I've done something wrong. And she's so stingy with food that I walk around hungry all of the time. Grandma Rakosh still gives me slices of bread in secret, but since I failed to learn how to make linen thread, I feel she's losing interest in me.

Also, I have a disturbing feeling about Angie that I can't explain. Something about the way he looks at me and speaks to me makes me sense that he wants something more from me. I can't explain why, but I'm afraid of him.

Day and night, I wander around, wondering what to do. With no adult to turn to, I ask my fairy tale friends for advice.

"Trust your intuition," says Ivasyk. "If something feels wrong, don't go."

"He looks at me very oddly. And he asks too many questions!"

"It feels wrong, so don't go."

"But I'm hungry all the time here!"

"Is it worth giving up what you have to go live with a strange man?"

"I don't think so."

So I finally tell Grandma Rakosh that I don't want to go to work for Angie. As unpleasant as it is to live with Yulka, at least I know what to expect from her. That's better than leaving the household and having to adjust to new people and a new situation, especially one that frightens me.

My daily life is very different in the village than it was in Lvov; not only because it revolves around farming, but for other reasons, too. We wake up with the sun in the morning and we go to sleep when it gets dark. And nobody talks about the date, so I don't even know what month it is. But as spring turns into summer, I know it must be getting close to June. The weather is warm and beautiful, and I'm enjoying the privacy I have, now that I'm sleeping in the hayloft under the roof.

Sometimes, Yulka's sister-in-law climbs up to the hayloft on her side of the house, which is next to where I have my bed. She's nearing the end of her pregnancy and every step she takes makes a loud thud. I like to listen to the music of her heavy footsteps, and I sometimes imitate her distinctive walk. It's a little game that I like to play by myself. But the noise that I make irritates Yulka terribly and she snaps at me, "I don't know what's gotten into you, Zossia! What's the matter with you? Are you as heavy as a pregnant woman? Why are you walking like that, with every step like the beating of a drum?"

Of course, I stop the "walking game" immediately.

I often feel that nothing I do is acceptable in Yulka's eyes. Since Angie came to visit and asked me to work for him, Yulka treats me with a lot of resentment.

I know that my birthday—June 16th—is coming soon, and I'm feeling very downhearted. It's not as if my birthday is a cause for celebration, but the date is a marker of time passing: time that has gone by without my knowing where my family is, when I might see them again, or when this terrible war is going to end. There's never any news in the village. I knew

267

more about what was happening in the world when I lived in Lvov.

I know I should be grateful for everything I have: a steady job, food to eat every day, a place to sleep, identity papers, and a safe place to hide from the Nazis. Yet, I feel very lonely and isolated. I wish I could leave the Rakosh household, but where would I go, and what would I do? Every time Yulka looks at me, I feel like she's searching for something to find fault with. And I'm still afraid that I might talk in my sleep and say something to reveal my true identity.

There's no way of knowing what the date is, but one day I decide that the next day must be my birthday. I feel that whatever I dream tonight will somehow be important to me, that it might give me a clue as to what I should do.

But that night, I have a nightmare. I dream that I'm out in the pasture with the cows, waiting for Grandma Rakosh to bring me a slice of bread. I can see her from a distance, coming toward me. But she isn't alone. Walking on either side of her are two strange men. When the three of them reach me in the field, the men address me angrily, saying, "Show us your papers!" When they see Zofia Zaborska's birth certificate they ask, "What language is this written in?" I tell them, "It's Russian. I come from Lvov." When they reply, "It's a forgery! Come with us!" I wake up, feeling terrified. This isn't the kind of guidance I had been hoping for in my dream, and it certainly doesn't help me decide what to do.

The next day, a very strange thing happens. I go out to the fields with the cows as usual. I'm

thinking, "It would be better if Grandma Rakosh didn't come at all, than to have her come
with two policemen!" Then, just like in my
dream, I see Grandma Rakosh approaching me
in the field, with two men walking beside her,
one on either side! I'm petrified. Who are these
men? Why did they come looking for me? Do
they know I'm a Jew? Were they sent by the
Nazis? I look around, but there's nowhere for
me to run and hide.

When they reach me, my heart is pounding
wildly. Just like in my dream, the men ask to
see my papers and I show them the documents.
But unlike the dream, they leave without making a scene, and Grandma Rakosh gives me a
slice of bread that she's brought for me. I'm relieved that the men have gone away without
causing any problem, but also very unnerved
that something from a dream should happen in
real life. Nothing like that has ever happened to
me before, and I hope nothing like it will ever
happen again! And now I'm even more confused about what I should do.

I walk around with terrible feelings building
up inside me, and nobody but my imaginary
fairy tale friends to talk to. Even in the ghetto, I
hadn't felt so lonely. At least, there I had my
family, the Freiheiters, and my friends, Genia
and the Shums. Back in Lvov, everybody knew
I was Jewish, and I didn't have to pretend all of
the time to be somebody I wasn't, answering to
a name that isn't really mine. It's an enormous
emotional burden for me to be in such strange
surroundings, so far away from everything and
everyone I grew up with, pretending to be
somebody I'm not.

"Don't give up," Ivasyk whispers to me. "Don't lose hope."

"Remember the golden spring," says the youth. "One day, you may see your mother and Rosa and Emmanuel again."

But I've reached my lowest point, and I've almost given up all hope.

In the fall, after the harvest has left the fields full of stubble and the leaves are turning colors on the trees, all of the bad feelings that have been building up in me finally come out. I've suddenly developed a very painful skin condition. Boils full of pus have come out all over my arms and legs. My feet are so painful that it hurts when I put my shoes on. When I take the cows out to the pasture, I take off my shoes to relieve the pain. There are other children in the neighboring fields, watching cows in the pasture. I've never made friends with any of them. On the few occasions when we've talked to each other, they've teased me about my strange Lvov accent.

With my shoes off, I lie down on a rock and I doze off in the strong sunshine. All at once, I awaken to the sound of laughter and I see one of the boys running away with my shoes! He takes them and throws them into a well, where I can't get them back. Now, with winter coming up, I have no shoes to wear. I go back and tell Grandma Rakosh what happened with the shoes, but what can she do?

"Why did you take your shoes off?" she asks.

"Because the boils on my feet hurt so much."

"Let me take a look at them," she says.

And I show her the boils on my arms, as well.

"I see," she says. "This is something we need to take care of. You should have told me about this before."

Grandma Rakosh helps me get rid of the boils. Since there's no possibility of seeing a doctor, she uses a Polish home remedy. She puts herbal poultices on my arms and legs until the pus drains out of the boils and they heal. This a terrible time for me, emotionally and physically. I feel that the whole Rakosh family is losing patience with me. Yulka's sister-in-law has given birth and Grandma Rakosh is always busy helping her with the older children. Grandma Rakosh seems less interested in me with every passing day, since I never learned how to spin and I caused her so many problems with my boils and the extra pieces of bread that she brings to me. So I'm not surprised when Grandma Rakosh says, "I heard about a place for a servant girl at a large ranch in Brzozowka. Maybe you would like to go there to work?"

What with winter coming up, and no shoes on my feet, and never getting enough to eat, and the feeling that Yulka only wants to find fault with me, and that Grandma Rakosh is running out of patience with me, I don't hesitate for a second.

"Yes," I answer. "It sounds fine to me."

Brzozowka is a village about three or four kilometers away. To work indoors as a kitchen

271

servant on a large ranch for the winter months sounds wonderful. I'll have a warm place to spend my days and, since kitchen servants sleep in the kitchen, I'll have a warm place to sleep. And if I'm working in a kitchen, I imagine I'll have plenty to eat, too.

Before I leave the Rakosh family, Grandma Rakosh sits me down and talks to me. I guess she realizes how little I know about country life.

"Do you know how to behave on the ranch?" she asks me.

Of course, I don't, and I shake my head.

"You must do everything to please your mistress so that she doesn't get angry with you and send you away."

I want very much to learn what to do.

"If your mistress wears a new dress, you have to help her smooth it down, and tell her what a pretty dress it is, and how good she looks in it."

I nod and say, "Okay."

"And they'll have to give you shoes, which you must take care to clean and polish every day. And don't take them off and lose them!"

I'm glad to have Grandma Rakosh's advice, and I look forward to going to the ranch. I'm not afraid of what might happen to me there. I'm getting used to answering to the name "Zofia," and to doing farm chores. It's sure to be better than living with the Rakosh family!

A few days later, a wagon driver with a ladder wagon comes to fetch me. As I sit on the back of the wagon, I smile and wave goodbye to the Rakosh family and their small farm. I'm happy to be starting something new.

Unlike the Rakosh farm, the ranch is large and impressive. The main building is very wide, with many windows, several doors, and a large enclosed patio. Instead of the packed earth floor at the Rakosh farmhouse, the ranch house has a wooden floor. There are also many outbuildings for the cows and horses, and storage sheds for the milk and the apples that they grow, and of course, an outhouse for the toilet. Beyond the outbuildings, there are many small huts for the hired workers and their families. All sorts of work tools are lying around, and the ranch is obviously very prosperous. I feel as if I've been given a wonderful opportunity.

I'm greeted by the house manager, Natalia, a tall, heavyset woman with a very pretty face and round, rosy cheeks. Natalia is no longer young, but she's not married. I suppose she must have a special relationship with the ranch owner, because she's in charge of the ranch while he's away in the army.

Natalia immediately questions me about what kind of work I know how to do, and I'm proud to tell her that I know how to clean wooden floors like the one in the ranch house. I also tell her that I can do kitchen chores and some farm work. My duties on the ranch are to wash the large kitchen pots, to clean the kitchen stove, to peel potatoes, and to keep the very large kitchen spotlessly clean. I also have to wash clothes. These are all chores that I've learned to do—after making many mistakes— and I'm confident that I'll be able to do all of my tasks without getting into trouble.

Since I'm walking around barefoot, Natalia gives me an old pair of work shoes with wooden soles. They're too big on me, so I stuff the toes with cotton, like I used to do as a child whenever I got new shoes.

Natalia gives me a bed in a corner of the huge kitchen, like all kitchen servants. That first night, in the middle of the night, I wake up, needing to use the toilet. Everything is new to me here. I've seen so many new things that day, and heard so much about my chores that I'm feeling very confused.

I can't remember where the front door is located and it's a dark, moonless night, so I can't see anything in the kitchen. I grope around in the dark, trying to find the door. Finally, I decide to skirt the wall, knowing it will lead me, eventually, to the door. I'm moving as fast as I can, because I'm afraid they'll send me away if I pee in my pants. I feel my way blindly along the wall, in and out of the corners, passing many obstacles along the way. Finally, I get to the door. But next to the door, at about eye level, there's a small shelf for keys, and as I move sideways to go out the door, I bang my nose against it very hard. The pain is so sharp that I almost fall down. I cross my legs to prevent myself from peeing. Covering my face with one hand, I open the door with the other hand, and make my way outside to the outhouse. My nose hurts terribly!

When I come back inside, I walk back to my bed very carefully, promising myself that I'll memorize everything in the huge kitchen so that this will never happen again. But I'm in so much pain that I can't fall back asleep. The
274

next morning, when Natalia sees me, she can't believe her eyes.

"What happened? Who did this to you? Your face is all black and blue!" she cries.

"I banged my nose in the middle of the night, when I got up to go to the outhouse."

There's no mirror for me to look in, but I can feel that my nose is badly swollen, and it hurts terribly. Even so, I start to do my chores. After all, what else am I here for? I don't want them to send me away for being lazy. So I go outside and peel potatoes on the patio. Whether or not I work, the pain and the swelling will go away sooner or later. I don't want to lose this job!

Gradually, the pain in my nose goes away and the swelling goes down.

Natalia explains to me that peeling potatoes for our meals is a very important job because a lot of people work on the farm and eat their meals there. She doesn't let me peel potatoes indoors, as it would dirty the kitchen, and she's very strict about keeping the kitchen clean. Right now it's fall, and the weather isn't very cold, so it doesn't bother me to work on the patio. But when winter comes, it will be very cold and uncomfortable to sit outdoors and peel the potatoes, I realize. Oh well, nothing is perfect—not even this job.

Every day, I peel potatoes for all of the workers who eat their meals in the kitchen, including myself. There's Natalia, Mr. Felix Kubitsky, the agronomist in charge of managing the farm, his assistant, Janek—who also lives in the big house, and often other people who happen to be there for various reasons. It takes me at least an hour to peel the potatoes every day. I'm still not very good with my hands. But unlike Jijova or Maria Mazur, Natalia doesn't look at the potato peelings and yell at me for making them too thick and therefore, wasting food. After all, it's a very prosperous household, and Natalia is much more concerned with how carefully I clean the pots. Anyway, one of my jobs is to collect the potato peelings to feed to the pigs, so Natalia doesn't inspect the peels. I'm usually the only one who sees them.

Under German law, it's illegal for Polish farmers to raise pigs for their own use. They have to give all the meat to the Germans. So on the ranch, we raise pigs secretly. One of my jobs is to feed the little piglets that are kept in an underground hiding place, so that if German officers should come to the farm, they won't see or hear or smell them. If we get caught raising pigs, I don't know what they'll do to us, but it's certain that the punishment will be very severe. So we all have to do everything possible to keep the pigs a secret.

Potatoes are our staple food and potato farming—planting, harvesting, and storing the potatoes—is a big part of our lives. It's the height of the harvest season now. The farm workers have already pulled the potatoes from the ground and now everybody on the farm is helping to store them for the winter.

Potatoes have to be stored very carefully. If they freeze, they'll become soft and rotten, and we won't be able to eat them. So the workers build special storage places outdoors, for the potatoes. First, they dig trenches in the ground.

Each one is a few meters long. Then, we all help pile the potatoes neatly and compactly in each trench, making huge mounds about as high as my shoulder. Next, we cover the mounds of potatoes with a layer of straw. On top of the straw, we put a thick layer of mud, completely sealing off the potatoes. During the winter, the mud will freeze, and the potatoes inside will remain cold without freezing. In order to remove potatoes from the mounds, we make a small hole in the side of the mound. The hole is covered with wooden planks, to protect the opening from the cold. When the weather gets colder, the snow will also protect the mounds and keep the potatoes from freezing. One of my jobs is to collect potatoes from the mounds in order to peel them.

The workers are also harvesting wheat now. I watch the farm hands at work in the grain silo, and I help with some of the work. The wheat is allowed to sit outdoors in the sun for as long as possible before the strong, cold rains begin. Then, it's cut down with scythes and tied into bundles called sheaves. The farm hands take the sheaves of wheat, put them on the floor of the grain silo and beat them with sticks, until the grains of wheat fall out. I watch them, and then I help collect the grains and put them into sacks. Some of these sacks have to be handed over to the Germans. The rest are stored in the grain silo. When we need flour, the grain will be taken to the mill and ground.

The farm has an orchard that produces many different kinds of apples, and there's a huge storage house for the apples, with a separate cubicle for each different variety. One of my jobs is to sort out the bad apples from the good, putting the rotten apples aside to feed the piglets. Of course, I can eat as many apples as I want while I'm sorting them out, and I enjoy that task very much!

Another advantage that comes with the job of feeding the pigs is that I have to pass the milk storage basins on my way to the underground hiding place. I love walking past the milk basins, because they stand uncovered and I can dip my fingers into the cream that collects in a thick layer on top of the milk. I stick my finger into the cream and lick the heavy cream off my fingers. With nobody watching me, I can dip and lick, dip and lick as much as I want to, every day. It's a real treat!

Under German rule, each farm has to contribute a certain percentage of its produce to the Germans. So one of the farm workers takes a large container of milk to the collection place in the center of the village every day. The Germans want the creamy part of the milk. They pour the milk into a machine that separates the cream from the milk and we're allowed to keep the thin, runny liquid that's left over. It's so thin that it's bluish-white in color and tastes almost like water. The Polish people are furious with the Germans for taking the best part of the milk, but they can't do anything because the German military establishment is so powerful. The Poles are learning to hate the Germans—but not as much as I do!

Most of my chores on the ranch are pleasant, but there's one job I hate: washing the cooking pots. The kitchen stove is a wood-
278

burning stove, and the bottoms of the pots become black from sitting over the fire every day.
It's my job to clean the pots until they shine. Of
course, I have to work outside, since cleaning
them would mess up the kitchen, and Natalia
is very strict about keeping the kitchen clean. I
rub the bottoms of the pots with sand in order
to remove the black charcoal stains. Of course,
I have to clean the insides of the pots, as well.
Natalia inspects them very carefully after I finish. I work very hard, but it's nearly impossible
to satisfy her. I have to hold up every pot for
her to inspect. She often looks at a pot and
says, "Go back and clean it again!" It isn't too
unpleasant now, but when the weather turns
colder, I'm sure it will be an awful task.

One day, Janek, Mr. Kubitsky's assistant,
comes out through the kitchen door to stand
on the patio. Janek lives in the ranch house
and I suppose he has some free time once in a
while. He's a young, good-looking man, and
he's used to having all the girls get excited over
him. He watches me working hard at scrubbing
the dirty pot, and he asks, How are you, my
young lady?"

I can tell that he wants to tease me, so I
keep my eyes on the pot and I don't answer
him. But he won't leave me alone.

"Why is your face turning red?" he asks.
"Are you afraid of me?"

I still don't answer.

"Come over here, I want to show you something," he says.

"I'm busy," I tell him.

"So take a break," he says.

I know he wants to play with me, and maybe to make fun of me, so I pick up the bucket of water that's sitting next to me and throw it at him. Janek laughs and goes inside to change his clothes. I hope he doesn't try to start up with me again.

After I've been on the ranch for a short while, Natalia tells me to go out to the woods to collect wild mushrooms and berries. There are big forests just beyond the apple orchards, and they're full of wild fruits. At first, I'm afraid to go into the woods on my own because I've never been in a forest. I remember how Little Red Riding Hood got lost in the woods. And Yash and Malgosha, even though they were together, had also gotten lost in the forest. Even worse, they had been caught by a witch. But I know better than to share my fears with Natalia. I walk away from the ranch, past the small huts where the hired workers live with their families, past the huge apple orchards, and into the dark forest.

I have to be very careful collecting wild mushrooms, since among all the different varieties of mushrooms, there's at least one poisonous kind. In school, we learned about this kind of mushroom. It's bright red with white dots on it. And it's so poisonous, that even touching it with your hand can be fatal. So, I'll have to inspect every mushroom very carefully before picking it.

The first time I go into the big forest, I'm very scared. I don't want to go alone, so I walk very slowly. I call on Yash and Malgosha to help me.

"Come with me," I say. "You know your way around the forest, and you can protect me from the wild animals and Babayaga, the witch."

"Don't be afraid," Malgosha assures me. "You don't have to go very deep into the forest to find berries and mushrooms."

And she's right. I can see the huts from inside the woods, and I can still hear all the sounds of the farm—the machines working, and the children playing near the huts.

Once I get used to going into the forest, I'm no longer so frightened of it. I dare to go deeper and deeper into the woods each time, and I don't get lost. In fact, I begin to enjoy my trips to collect mushrooms and berries. I take one pail for the mushrooms and another for the berries, and I eat my fill along the way. Usually, when I get back with my buckets of mushrooms and berries, Natalia looks at me and says, "From the color of your teeth, it looks as if you've eaten as much as you've picked."

I shrug my shoulders. Of course, she's right!

When I lived with the Rakosh family, I felt very lonely. And, here on the ranch, I can't talk to Natalia because she's the manager and she's too far above me. So I have many conversations with my imaginary friends. But I still crave the luxury of having somebody to talk to—a sympathetic adult, like my friend Genia, or the Freiheiters, or Alexei and Maria Shum. On my trips to the woods, I have to pass the huts of the farm workers. That gives me an excuse to stop off and socialize a bit. Gradually, I make friends with some of the children of the farm

281

hands who live in the small huts near the forest. Most of them are younger than I am. Sometimes, on my way back from the forest, I give them mushrooms and berries, so they like me. After a while, I start to invite them to go with me into the forest with their own buckets to collect wild mushrooms and berries. It's very nice to have other children for company, even though most of them are a lot younger than I am.

After I've made friends among the children of the ranch hands, I sometimes go to visit them when I have a spare hour for myself. Soon, the mothers and the grandmothers become friendly with me, too. I especially like one of the "grandmas" who I see a lot. She works outside, scattering grain for the chickens that her family keeps. She's very friendly and I like to talk with her.

The ranch is a very prosperous place and nobody counts what I eat. So of course, I eat as much as I want. But Natalia doesn't invite me to sit at the big kitchen table with her and all of the important farm workers and managers. I eat by myself, at a small table near my bed. And although Natalia doesn't abuse me, she isn't warm and friendly, and she certainly isn't a companion to me. She never talks to me, except if she needs to explain how to do some chore or other.

In the evenings, there's nothing to do on the ranch. Natalia and Mr. Kubitsky sit around the kitchen table while I sit in my corner, folding laundry or doing other small chores. Sometimes Mr. Kubitsky's assistant, Janek, sits with them, talking and joking. I always listen to their conversations, but I never join in. They don't pay any attention to me, and I'm glad of that. I wouldn't know what to say.

Sometimes they drink liquor, and sometimes they have company, too. A neighboring farmer, Ludvig, sometimes comes and entertains them with stories and songs in the evenings. He and Natalia and Mr. Kubitsky sit around the kitchen table, drinking straight from the bottle. Ludvig tells jokes and stories and sings songs about love and romance. The nickname for Zofia-"Zossia," or "Zosshu"—is very popular in Poland, and every time Ludvig sings a song about "Zosshu" he looks in my direction and winks at me. I never respond, but I blush every time. Thankfully, Natalia and Mr. Kubitsky don't pay any attention to me, and I try to keep busy with my chores.

One night, after we've all gone to bed, I'm awakened by the sound of the dogs barking wildly outside. That can only mean that a stranger is coming. I'm very frightened, thinking that it might be German soldiers, and that they might be coming after me! Soon I hear someone thumping on the walls of the house. When I hear men's voices yelling, "Open up and let us in!" I put my head under the covers, shivering and shaking.

Finally, Natalia comes running from her bedroom and Mr. Kubitsky comes, too. When they hear the men's voices outside, Natalia tells Mr. Kubitsky to go into the bedroom and hide. She doesn't want anybody to see him. When Mr. Kubitsky is in the bedroom, Natalia opens the front door and steps outside by herself. She comes back in almost immediately, followed by two tall, strong-looking men wearing fur hats and coats, and carrying rifles. These men stride into the kitchen and command her: "Load up a wagon full of food for us, right now!"

In a frightened voice, Natalia tells me, "Put food on the table for the men!" and I hurry to obey her. I notice they aren't wearing Nazi uniforms.

As I listen to their conversation, I find out that these men are partisans who are hiding out in the forest in our area. They might even be hiding near the place where I pick wild mushrooms and berries! Of course, I've heard of the partisans, but I've never seen any of them before. When I realize who they are, I look at them with great curiosity. I notice that one of them has taken off his hat. He has dark black hair. "Maybe he's a Jew" I wonder. I've heard that some of the partisans are Jews. I look at the other man, but he keeps his hat on and his skin looks very fair.

While the men are eating at the kitchen table, their wagon is being loaded with baskets of flour and sugar and apples and potatoes. As I serve them, I keep looking at them and wondering what to do. One of the men notices that I'm looking at him and asks, "What are you looking at? Why don't you go to bed?"

But I can't help thinking that maybe I should tell them I'm a Jew, with no family and nobody to take care of me. Then, they would take me with them and I could live in the forest, with the partisans, and not have to pretend to be Zofia Zaborska any more. I steal secret glances at the men the whole time they're here, trying to make up my mind. I know that some

Polish partisans who are fighting against the Nazis hate the Jews as well.

"What should I do? Should I tell them I'm a Jew? But I'm not sure they'll want to help me, even if they're Polish partisans. Some of the partisans are friends with the Jews, but others are anti-Semitic. How can I be sure?"

"There's no way for you to know," says Ivasyk. "Be very careful."

Finally, I decide it would be too dangerous to reveal, in front of everyone, that I'm a Jew, so I keep silent.

But after the men leave, Natalia turns to me and asks, very angrily, "Why were you looking at the men with so much interest? I've never seen your eyes light up like that. Why were you so happy to see them take our food?"

I don't know what to say, so I keep quiet and get back into bed. I try to go back to sleep, but I toss and turn for the rest of the night, wondering if I've done the right thing.

"Maybe I missed out on the only opportunity I'll ever have to join the partisans?"

"But you would have been in greater danger by telling Natalia that you're a Jew."

I imagine what would have happened if I had admitted openly that I was a Jew, only to find out that they were Polish anti-Semites. I might have been thrown out, right on the spot, or taken straight to the Gestapo, or even killed! Frightening fantasies fill my mind, and I can't fall back asleep for the rest of the night, even though I'm exhausted.

Since that night, I feel as if Natalia is always watching me.

A few days later, she shows me a torn old sock and asks, "Do you know how to mend this?"

One of the few chores that Mama did around the house was darning socks on a wooden "mushroom," and she taught me how to do it, too. I'm not very good at it, but I know how to hold the darning mushroom and how to weave the threads in the spot where the fabric is worn away. I haven't tried it for a long time, but I think I remember how to do it.

"Yes," I answer, without hesitating. Maybe, if I help her, Natalia will like me better.

"I can sew it for you if you have a darning mushroom."

Natalia takes out a pile of old, torn socks and gives them to me to darn. Since socks are very expensive, people don't throw away their old socks if they can be mended.

Although I'm not very good with my hands, Natalia doesn't complain. For some reason, she doesn't know how to mend socks, although she has a darning mushroom. I don't give it a second thought, but after watching me for a long while, Natalia asks, "Where did you learn how to do that?"

"My mother taught me," I answer.
Then she says, "I thought only Jews knew how to mend socks."

"That's something I've never heard before," I tell her.

286

But now I'm worried. Maybe Natalia and the others are suspicious of me? They never ask any questions, but sometimes they seem to be looking at me in a strange way, especially since that night when the partisans came.

In the few months since I came to work on the ranch, I've become more relaxed about calling myself Zofia Zaborska, but now, I start feeling nervous again. I feel that Natalia is suspicious of me. I feel she's watching me, waiting for me to make a mistake and reveal that I'm really not Zofia Zaborska, but Sonya Hebenstreit, instead.

Christmas is coming and it's very cold on the patio where I peel the potatoes every day. The snow is piled up high, and the workers have to use horse-drawn wagons with wooden planks instead of wheels. These wagons can plow through the snow, carrying apples and baskets of food on the wood planks. People ride in the wagons, too. When visitors come, they drive up to the ranch in the horse-drawn wagons with the wooden planks.

Natalia is making a huge Christmas feast for the farm managers, and Mr. Kubitsky has been riding around on a wagon to invite the important people in our neighborhood. During the week before Christmas, I peel potatoes for hours and hours every day. Natalia is busy in the kitchen, day after day, cooking and baking. She's making a famous Polish dish called "*bigos*," which is a mixture of cabbage and sausages. She stuffs ducks and geese, and cooks one of our hidden, illegal pigs. And of course, she bakes a huge variety of Christmas cookies and cakes. We store all the goodies for Christmas on the patio. It's very cold, and it's enclosed by wooden boards so that the farm dogs and wild animals can't get at the food.

Finally, Christmas Eve arrives, and the huge kitchen table is set for a feast. It's my job to welcome the guests as they arrive, and take their coats. One of their guests is a priest, and the others are very important people. One man gives me a tip when I take his coat, and I'm very pleased.

When everybody has arrived and is seated, I help Natalia serve the food. I don't sit down with the guests, but I enjoy the party just the same. The guests eat their fill and they're very merry. When they've finished eating, they sit around the table, drinking. After a while, their voices become very loud. Then the priest asks if they would like to sing Christmas carols, and he leads them in the singing. I recognize these songs from Lvov, where groups of Christian children used to wander around the streets singing Christmas carols every year. I remember that those children used to knock on people's doors and offer to sing, in exchange for money or something to eat. Mama didn't like it, but she used to give them coins, anyway.

"We don't want them to call us Christkillers," she told me.

I remember the Christmas carols, and I hum along with the company. First they sing,

> *On a silent winter night,*
> *Angels fill the sky with light.*
> *A heavenly chorus sings:*
> *"Come, all ye shepherds,*
> *Come worship the Lord,*

Christ the Savior is born!
Christ the Savior is born!"

On a silent winter night,
Angels fill the sky with light.
A heavenly chorus sings:
"Come all ye shepherds,
Hurry on your way!
Go to Bethlehem,
To worship the Lord.
Christ the Savior is born!
Christ the Savior is born!"

On a silent winter night,
Angels fill the sky with light.
A heavenly chorus sings:
"Glory to God!
King of the universe,
The one we've been waiting for
All of these centuries.
Christ the Savior is born!
Christ the Savior is born!"

And they sing other Christmas carols, too.

"Poor little baby,
born in Bethlehem.
Little Jesus lies naked,
crying from the cold.
Why doesn't his mother dress him
to protect him from the cold?
Because she's very poor,
and she hasn't any clothes.

Poor little baby,
born in Bethlehem.

> *Little Jesus lies naked,*
> *crying from the cold.*
>
> *Maria takes her warm scarf off,*
> *and wraps her baby son in it.*
> *Maria takes her warm scarf off,*
> *and wraps the Baby Jesus in it."*

I remember other Christmas carols that I heard every year in Lvov. The words are full of love and mercy for the poor little baby who was born in Bethlehem, and the songs give me a feeling of warmth and comfort.

But the guests soon run out of Christmas carols, and Ludvig begins to sing popular songs about romance and flirtation. Everybody sings along, and the atmosphere quickly changes. The priest excuses himself and leaves, wishing everybody a happy holiday. After he leaves, there's a lot of drinking and it looks like many of the guests are drunk.

It's very late when Ludvig suddenly approaches me. I can smell the liquor on his breath. He pushes me roughly against a wall and yells at me, "Haika! Your name is Haika!" he screams. "And your father's name is Sroulik! You're not Zofia, you're Haika!"

I'm shocked and I don't know what to say. Haika and Sroulik are nicknames for Chaya and Israel, Jewish names. Sroulik is my father's nickname. Mama always called him that at home. How does Ludvig know this?

"But my name is Zofia," I protest. "I have papers!"

"Who cares about your papers?" he yells at me. "Your name is Haika and your father's name is Sroulik!" he insists.

Of course, Ludvig is drunk, and Natalia and Mr. Kubitsky are, too. Mr. Kubitsky comes over to where I'm standing with Ludvig, and shouts, "What's this? Do you mean to tell me that I'm keeping a dirty Jew in my house—a lousy, filthy vermin who will bring other vermin into the world after the war?"

I'm on the verge of tears. "Mr. Kubitsky," I say, "I've been here for a long time. You know me. You've seen my papers. You know my name is Zofia."

But Mr. Kubitsky doesn't answer me. I don't think he's listening to me at all. He walks over to the door and yells to his wagon driver, "Harness up the horses, I'm taking this Jew-girl to the Gestapo!"

By that time, it's very late, and the guests all decide to leave. Nobody says anything to me. A few minutes later, the wagon-driver comes to the door, and says, "Panie Felix, your wagon is ready."

But Mr. Kubitsky is so drunk that, when he tries to walk to the door, he falls down. Natalia and the wagon driver carry him to bed and I'm left all alone in the kitchen that had been so lively just a few hours earlier. I sit, trembling, on the bed, not knowing what to do. Why has this happened? I wonder. Did Natalia suspect me of being Jewish because I mended her socks? Is it true that only Jews know how to mend socks on a darning mushroom? Are there other things about me that make people think I'm Jewish? I'm scared, but also very tired, and

291

it's so late and so cold outside that I don't want to leave. Yet, I'm worried about what's going to happen in the morning. I lie down in my bed, but I can't fall asleep that night.

The door to Janek's bedroom is right near my bed. A little later, he comes into the kitchen and comes over to my bed. He puts his hand under the blanket and starts to touch me. Without thinking, I cry out, "Get away from me!"

I must have shouted very loudly because Natalia comes running into the kitchen with a candle in her hand.

"What's going on here?" she shouts.

"Oh, it's nothing," says Janek. "I just came in to pat Zossia on the head, to calm her down a little."

"What?" screams Natalia. "You should be ashamed of yourself! Leave her alone and go back to bed now!"

So Janek goes back into his room and closes the door. I lie there miserably for the rest of the night, thinking that the next morning Mr. Kubitsky is going to take me to the Gestapo.

The next morning, Mr. Kubitsky comes into the kitchen and tells me, "I'm going to Lublin. When I come back, I don't want to see you here!"

I nod my head in silence and leave as soon as I can, carrying my tiny suitcase. It's very cold outside and fresh snow is hanging from the trees. With every step I take, I sink into the snow up to my knees. I have no boots, only shoes, and my socks are very thin. They've been darned in many places. The ranch isn't near any other farms, and I look around to decide what direction to go in. I decide to knock on somebody's door and ask them to take me in. The only houses I can see are the small huts of the farm workers, who live in a single room with their whole family. I walk to the door of one of the families whose children I'm friendly with.

The grandmother opens the door, and she invites me to come inside. I tell the family that Mr. Kubitsky had gotten drunk and thrown me out, but I don't tell them the whole story.

They're very sympathetic and say I can stay with them until the weather clears up. It's too cold and snowy for me to go looking for another place to stay right now. So that night, I sleep in the bed with all of the children. Although it's very crowded, their home is warm and comfortable. I enjoy the feeling of being with a family. But, their place is really too small for them to keep me, and I know that it will be a problem for them if Natalia or Mr. Kubitsky find out that I'm staying there. I'm sure they'll hear about it, sooner or later. After all, there were many people at the party, and everybody will be talking about it, I imagine.

The following morning the weather is clear enough for me to be on my way. I thank the family and they wish me well. As I walk through the snow carrying my tiny suitcase, I look for another farm where I might work. I see farmhouses with smoke coming from their chimneys in the distance, so I walk away from the ranch, toward the other farms.

It's very cold, even though the snow has stopped falling. With every step I take, my feet sink deeply into the snow. When I reach the first farmhouse, I knock on the door and greet the woman who opens it to me with the words, "Blessed be Jesus Christ!"

I come straight to the point, and tell her, "I'm looking for work."

But she answers me by saying, "When the hills become green again, we will need somebody to take the cows out to pasture. Until then, we only have enough food for our own family."

I continue going from door to door, but everybody has the same thing to say. Some people are very kind to me; others are abrupt. But nobody has work for me.

Then I come to the house of an older, childless couple who seem to be wealthier than the other families.

"We don't really need anybody," the wife says, "but as long as you're here, you might as well stay. We'll find something for you to do."

They give me work to do, food to eat, and a place to sleep. But after a few days, I can see that they really don't have anything for me to do. So I'm not at all surprised when they tell me, "We have no more work for you and we can't feed you if you don't work, so you'll have to leave."

With a heavy heart, I take my tiny suitcase and walk toward the few houses remaining in the village. At the next house, they don't need any help, nor do they need me at the house after that. I can see that there are only a few houses left in the small village. One by one, I knock at each door, but nobody needs a helper.

As I walk along, slowly and sadly, I wonder what I'm going to do. With each step, I sink into the soft, fresh-fallen snow up to my knees. I walk for a long time, thinking about the little match girl, and how she froze to death in the snow. Then, I feel something soft closing around the fingers of my right hand, and I look to see what it might be. "Hello," says the little match girl, in a whisper.

"Hello," I whisper back to her, and we walk along in silence for a while. It feels good to have her with me. Now I'm not as lonely as I was before.

After a while, she starts to speak to me. "You know, it doesn't hurt to freeze to death," she says. "You just lie down in the snow, and after a minute, you start to feel warm."

I think about that for a while.

"Thank you for telling me," I say. "It makes me feel better."

We walk along side by side for a long time, not saying anything. As we walk, I notice a small house off in the distance with smoke coming out of the chimney. It's probably the last house in the village. It will take about half an hour to reach it, I think.

"If they don't give me a place to sleep there tonight, I'll lie down next to you," I tell the little match girl. She squeezes my hand and we walk for a long time in silence.

I knock on the door of the last house in the village. "Blessed be Jesus Christ!" I greet the

295

young woman who opens it. I can hear a baby crying inside.

When I tell her that I'm looking for work, she asks me to wait while she talks to her husband. I overhear her saying, "If I had somebody to help me, I would be free to work. I wouldn't have to take care of the babies all day long."

When she comes back to the door, she invites me in. Their whole house is only one large room and I can see the twins in a cradle near the bed. She tells me that the babies are newborn. The boy is named Bolek and the girl, Grazhena. It would be my responsibility to take care of them while Maria helps her husband with the farm work.

"Do you think you can do that?" Maria asks me.

"Yes, I can," I answer. "I know how to take care of babies, how to change diapers and how to feed them. I have experience doing that."

Maria is obviously pleased, and she smiles at me.

I have a job! And a place to live, with food and company, and I'll be doing something that I know how to do, so I won't make so many mistakes.

The Brzuszkiewicz family is a very quiet group of people. They treat me kindly, but they hardly ever speak to each other and I have very few conversations with any of them. Their house is smaller than the other homes in the village: their one room serves as both kitchen and bedroom. One bed is for Maria and her husband, Zhislav. Another is for Granny B and Gramps, Zhislav's parents. The twins sleep in their cradle, next to their parents' bed. Zhislav has a younger sister, Yulia (Yulka), who isn't married. Yulka has a seven-year-old daughter, Wanda. Yulka and Wanda sleep together in the same bed. Since there's no bed for me, and no room for me to share a bed with anybody, they cover the top of the stove with straw and I climb a ladder to sleep on it every night. I have to be careful not to sit up in the middle of the night, or I'll bang my head against the ceiling.

The twins are only a few weeks old. Because they're so tiny, they're kept swaddled most of the time. I have to rock their wooden cradle whenever they cry, and Maria comes to nurse them every few hours, between tasks. I don't have much to do in order to care for them. I simply have to be near them, to rock them when they cry, change their diapers, and make sure nothing bad happens to them. Wanda is too little to care for them. She's only six or seven years old.

Since I have so little work to do, I'm able to help with some of the housework. I clean the cooking pots—just the insides, not the charcoal-encrusted bottoms, and I wash the clothes. There's no kitchen sink with running water, but they have a large tin basin that I use for washing the dishes and the clothes. To get water, I go outside to the yard with a bucket and draw the water from the well. Watching the babies and doing the household chores is very good for me because it keeps me indoors most of the time, in the warm house, during the bitter cold winter.

The family has a small chicken coop with about a dozen hens. Granny B feeds the chickens every day. Maria teaches me how to look

297

for fresh eggs, and shows me how to feel the hen and check if she's ready to lay an egg. Maria is patient and very kind to me. After I learn how to check the hens, one of my daily chores is to search for eggs.

While I'm taking care of the twins, everybody is busy doing their chores. Maria works in the barn with the animals. The barn is very small. It's attached to the house, sharing one common wall. The Brzuszkiewicz family has three cows, too: one is mature and gives milk, and it's Maria's job to milk her. The other cows are too small to give milk—one is a newborn, and the other is just a little older. Maria feeds the animals and clears away the straw they dirty. The family also has a horse, which they use for transportation. Mostly, we eat whatever the farm produces, and we give a percentage to the Germans. But once in a while, Zhislav hitches up the horse to the wagon and takes a trip to Lublin or Krashnik, the nearest cities, to sell eggs or potatoes or flour and buy supplies.

Gramps and Zhislav are professional blacksmiths, and they have a small blacksmith shop right next to the house. They also make small items out of iron, such as basins and pots, which they sell to the villagers. People from the village bring their horses to the shop to be shod. I sometimes worry that the villagers will recognize me and remember what happened on Christmas Eve at the ranch, but mostly I'm in the house taking care of the babies, so I don't see many people.

In addition to their blacksmith shop, the family has an illegal distillery, where they make vodka from grain. The Germans force the Polish farmers to give them a percentage of their farm produce—eggs, milk, potatoes, and grain. So the grain they use to make vodka should really go to the Germans. If the Germans ever find out about the distillery, I don't know what might happen to the family. Certainly, they'd be punished severely. Because of this danger, they hide the distillery in their blacksmith shop. That's a good place for it because the smell of the blacksmith shop covers up some of the odor of the distillery. One of my jobs is to stand guard outside the blacksmith shop whenever they make liquor and warn the men if I see anyone coming our way. Another of my chores is to watch over the pot when they boil the vodka. The steam is trapped in a tube, and it's supposed to drip slowly, one drop at a time. I have to make sure that the pot doesn't boil over. Zhislav and Gramps make the vodka in the early hours of the morning before the villagers start moving around, or in the late afternoon or evening hours. Those are times when people don't usually go to each other's houses.

In short, the Brzuszkiewicz family has different sources of income besides farming. Having me there to take care of the babies is very useful to them because they all have so many different jobs to do.

Granny B doesn't talk a lot—nobody in the Brzuszkiewicz family talks much—but she's kind and patient with me. She asks me if I know how to spin linen and I tell her that I've tried it, but I'm not very good at it.

So try again," she says, and she sits next to me to help me practice. Slowly, with a lot of help from Granny B, I learn how to spin linen thread on the spinning wheel. Eventually, I'm able to produce a thread that can be used to make clothing.

I also help Maria prepare goose down for stuffing pillows and blankets. This is easy, even for me! You have to hold the feather by its spine and remove the soft, fluffy part by running your fingers down the length of the feather. Then you throw away the hard, pointy spine. It takes hours and hours to make enough for a pillow, even a small one, so Maria and Yulka and Granny and I sit around in the evenings and work on it together. I'm very good at this work.

Even though I have to keep my many bitter secrets to myself, I'm enjoying the feeling of being part of a family. Gramps is very quiet, but he's pleasant to me, and Zhislav hardly talks to me at all, but that's because he's so busy all of the time. Maria talks to me more and more, and she's very kind to me. She never gets annoyed if I do something wrong. Yulka is pleasant too, even though we don't have much to say to each other. I notice that they don't talk to each other very much, either.

Wanda, who is seven years old, is the most talkative person in the household. She and I have become good friends. On Sundays, I like to watch Yulka curl Wanda's hair by heating a scissors and wrapping strands of hair around the hot scissors. I remember how Zoshka used to curl her hair on a curling iron, and how I used to love to watch her do it. Wanda has long hair and her curls hang down over her shoulders. She looks beautiful with her hair curled.

In this village, I've never seen anybody bathe— not even when the weather is warm! Nobody in the Brzuszkiewicz family ever takes a full bath. Before the big holidays, the men wash the upper part of their bodies with hot soapy water, but I've never seen a basin filled with water, or anything else that looks like a bathtub. Everybody in my family in Lvov used to take a bath before *Shabbat*. It makes me feel very uncomfortable to be so dirty. So I sometimes take a bucket of water and a towel into the barn, and wash myself there. I make sure to do this in secret because I think the Brzuszkiewicz family might feel insulted if they saw me bathing. I also wonder if only the Jews bathe, and if by bathing, I might reveal my Jewish identity to them. Maybe it's like mending socks on a darning mushroom—something that only Jews do?

I like to spend time with Wanda, even though she's so much younger than I am. She's such a cheerful girl. When I have some free time, I often go out to the fields with her. One day, Wanda and I see a pear tree that's full of ripe fruit. Wanda is faster at climbing than I am, and she's high above me in the tree when she suddenly says, "Look, Zosshu! I see German soldiers marching our way!"

I immediately jump down from the tree. "Wanda, get down, quick!" I cry to her. "Don't let them see you! Even from far away, they can aim their rifles at you and shoot you!"

The Brzuszkiewicz Family

Luckily, Wanda is young enough that she doesn't think my reaction is very strange. She climbs down quickly without questioning me. An older child might have asked me why I was so frightened of the German soldiers. Or she might have gone home and told the rest of the family about it. But Wanda doesn't seem to think this is strange at all. By the time we get

302

home, she's probably forgotten all about the soldiers. And they haven't come to the Brzusz-kiewicz farm, looking for me. I don't remind Wanda, or say anything to Maria.

Like every other household in the village, the Brzuszkiewicz family has to contribute a certain percentage of its farm products to the Germans. So we put milk in containers, eggs in baskets, and potatoes in sacks for Zhislav to take to the official collection station in the village.

Once in a while, I carry a container of milk to the collection place. The Polish clerk takes it and puts it in a machine called a centrifuge, which separates the cream from the milk. The clerk takes the cream for the Germans, and I carry the bluish-white liquid that is left back home. But the leftover milk is so thin that it's almost useless. It's tasteless and you can't make cheese from it. The Brzuszkiewicz family complains bitterly about the milk, but there's nothing they can do about it.

The office where I have to bring the farm produce is in the center of the village. In order to get there, I have to pass very near the ranch where I worked before. I haven't seen anyone from the ranch since I left. I'm afraid that if they find out I'm still in the village, they'll turn me in to the Nazis. So I avoid the ranch by taking a very long and roundabout route to deliver the milk.

I don't know what month it is, but I always know when it's Sunday, because Maria goes to church whenever the weather permits. Except for the Christian holidays, nobody pays attention to the date.

Maria is very religious, and she likes to go to church on Sundays. I've been here for a few months, and the weather is getting warmer. One day, Maria asks me, "Why don't you come to church with me? You're old enough to have taken communion, aren't you?"

I haven't told them much about myself until now, since nobody in their family asks many questions. They know that I took the train from Lvov after my parents disappeared and that I've worked on several farms in the area. But I'm afraid to talk about myself—afraid that I might reveal something that would make them suspect I'm Jewish—like knowing how to darn socks. But I have to tell them something, so I talk it over with my fairy tale companions.

"They'll believe you if you tell them that your parents were anti-Communists, and sent to Siberia by the Russians. They'll like you if you tell them that. Remember how much the Polish Gentiles hated the Russians."

So I tell Maria the story that I've made up and told many times before.

"I grew up in Lvov with my family," I begin. "Then, after the Russians took control of Lvov, they told us God was a lie, and they closed all of the churches. We weren't even allowed to pray in our own homes. My parents were anti-Communists, so the Russians sent them to Siberia, and they put me in the orphanage in Lvov. When the Germans invaded Lvov, the orphanage was closed down and I went to live
304

with my aunt. But then, she was taken to Germany to work for the Nazis, so I had nobody to live with. It was hard for me to take care of myself in Lvov, and a friend suggested that I should get on a train and go out to the countryside. She said I could find work on a farm. So I came here," I explain. "I never took Communion because of the Russians. And I can hardly remember any of my prayers, after all this time. I was very young when the Russians came and closed down the churches."

"That's a terrible thing!" cries Maria. "You're a good girl, and I know your parents would be proud of you. It's not your fault if you didn't take Communion."

Maria seems very touched by my story, and she decides to take me to the local priest. I'm a little bit afraid to talk to the priest because I think he might somehow discover that I'm really Jewish. I try to remember everything I learned from Jijova, from the stories she told me about the pictures of Jesus hanging in her little hut. But as it turns out, I have nothing to worry about. The priest is very pleasant and he doesn't ask me too many questions.

There's no church in the tiny village of Brzozowka, so we have to walk to the next village, which is slightly larger. It's far away, so Maria shows me a shortcut through the fields. Even so, it takes over an hour to get there.

The priest tells me that he's going to start a communion class later in the spring, and that I can join it. Maria is very pleased.

The next time I go to church is at Easter. I arrive after most of the other worshippers have already gotten there. By the time I enter, the

305

church is full of people praying on their knees. Being in church is, of course, an unfamiliar experience for me. There's so much to know, so many new things to remember that I become confused. I don't know that I'm supposed to walk up to the front of the church and kiss the statue of Jesus and then return to my seat, taking every step forward and backward on my knees.

I glance at the others, trying to figure out what I should do. I dip my fingers in the holy water at the entrance to the church, and walk down the aisle towards the statue of Jesus. As I'm walking down the aisle, a few people make gestures to me with their hands, but I don't understand what they're trying to tell me, and I don't pay attention to them. When I get to the statue of Jesus, I get down on my knees, make the sign of the cross, and kiss the feet of the statue. Then I get up, turn around, and start walking back to my seat. That's what I think I'm supposed to do.

But as I'm walking to take a seat in the back of the church, again I see many people making signs to me with their hands. I don't understand what they mean. Then one woman whispers to me, "Down on your knees!" Suddenly, I realize what I'm doing wrong. I'm supposed to be walking on my knees! And not only that, it's forbidden to turn your back to the statue of Christ. I'm supposed to back away from the altar facing the statue of Jesus, walking backward on my knees!

When I realize what a blunder I've made, I'm extremely embarrassed, and afraid that the people in the congregation might begin to wonder if I'm a Jew. So I decide not to go back to church until after my Communion ceremony.

In the late spring, I start going to the communion class with five or six younger girls, since the age of communion is nine or ten years old. Among the other girls is one named "Zossia," so they call her "Little Zossia," and I'm called "Big Zossia." I've always been small for my age, and this is the first time in my life that I've been called "big." It pleases me very much to be called "Big Zossia!"

In communion class, the priest teaches us prayers and he gives me prayer beads, so I can count how many prayers I say, because you have to say the prayers over and over again, many times. There's no reading or writing. I suppose that the village girls don't have much schooling. And since I'm the oldest one in the study group, and I've always been a good student, the priest tells Maria that I'm the best one in the class! Maria is very proud of me.

We also have to confess our sins to the priest. I like the idea of confession, and I would love to have somebody to tell my whole story to. But I can't tell the priest anything of real significance. How could I tell him that I'm really a Jew? He might take me to the Gestapo, like Mr. Kubitsky threatened to do. So I make up all sorts of silly stories to confess—like cursing at the cows in the field, or hitting them, or stealing food from the pantry. After "confession," the priest tells me to recite ten "Hail Marys" or ten "Our Fathers."

On my long walks to and from communion classes, I talk things over with my fairy tale companions.

"I'm not really converting to Catholicism."

"Of course not!"

"I'm just doing this because Maria wants me to."

"It's okay. You have nothing to be ashamed of."

"But will God think that I'm abandoning my family?"

"No, God understands. You're all alone in the world, and you need Maria and her family to protect you. God knows that."

"But will God forgive me?"

"God understands everything. Of course, God forgives you. He wants you to live."

"And does God know that I'm still a Jew?"

"Of course! God knows everything."

As soon as summer is over, it's time for the Communion ceremony. All the little girls get dressed up in white dresses and wear garlands of flowers in their hair. Maria has bought me a white summer dress, too. But she says I'm too big to wear a garland of flowers in my hair. So instead, I carry a bouquet of flowers.

At the Communion ceremony, the children line up and repeat the holy words after the priest. Then the priest puts the wafer on each one's tongue, and sprinkles holy water on their heads. I'm the last one in line, because I'm the biggest. When it's my turn to receive Communion, I say to myself, "This is my chance to become a real Christian, and then it won't be a lie when I say I'm not a Jew." But then I think it's better to lie than to deny who I really am. So when it's my turn to receive the Communion, I go through the outward motions, but I scream inside my head: "I am a Jew! I am a Jew! I am a Jew!" Three times I scream this to myself, to remind myself of who I really am, and of my family and my friends and the life I left behind in Lvov. I know that I'm only going through the motions of taking Communion. I'm still a Jew and will always remain a Jew! And God will forgive me for doing this.

After the Communion ceremony, Maria is very pleased with me. She goes to Lublin on a shopping trip and buys me a beautiful white woolen blouse to wear to church on Sundays and holidays.

This is my second winter with the Brzusz-kiewicz family. One bitter cold day, Zhislav goes to Lublin on a buying and selling trip. He has to get up very early in the morning to fill the cart with eggs and milk and other farm produce. He gets back from Lublin in the late afternoon, half frozen.

When he comes inside, he says, "I can't remember a winter this cold."

Wanda helps him take off his boots and Maria warms up a bowl of soup for him.

"I saw something very strange on my way," he tells us, and we all sit around him, listening to his story:

"On the road to Lublin, I saw a group of Jews marching along the road, dragging their feet, and stumbling along. All they were wearing was the striped pajamas of prisoners. The German soldiers were screaming at them to move faster, and striking them with whips all of the time."

309

Granny B says, "Those must be the last Jews left in the world!"

Maria asks her, "What makes you think so?"

Granny answers, "I'm sure they're the last ones! There are no more wild hens to be seen anywhere."

Maria asks her, "What has that got do with the Jews?"

Granny answers, "Do you mean to say you don't know the legend? For every Jew alive, there is a wild hen somewhere in nature. When all of the wild hens are gone, that means all of the Jews have died."

"I never knew that!" Maria exclaims.

Zhislav says, "That explains it!" and he shrugs his shoulders. After that, the subject is dropped, and everybody asks to see what Zhislav has brought back from Lublin.

But I'm deeply shocked. I've never heard the legend about the wild hens. Am I, then, the last Jew alive on the face of the earth? If so, how long will it be before the Nazis discover where I'm hiding, and come to take me away? I struggle to keep my face like a mask, without any expression, knowing it could be very dangerous if they should suspect that I'm a Jew. Meanwhile, my insides are churning. I continue rocking the cradle where the twins are sleeping, and I wait miserably for the hours to pass, wondering if the Nazis will come that very night to arrest me.

I toss and turn in my bed, getting very little sleep, thinking about what to do.

310

"A fairy tale hero is always good to those who have been kind to him," says a voice inside my head. "Do a good deed."

As morning approaches, I come up with a plan. As soon as the family awakens, I make an offer to Maria, saying, "Why don't I go down to the spring in the valley and bring back water?"

Naturally, Maria is very pleased with me for offering to go. This is the coldest winter that anyone can remember. The water has frozen in the well in our courtyard. In order to get water, we would have to melt snow, or someone would have to go to the spring. I see this as an opportunity to get out of the house and go off on my own for a while. So I carry two buckets on a wooden yoke across my shoulders, and take the long walk to the spring to fetch water.

I wade through the heavy snow, sinking into it up to my knees with every step. But I'm happy to be out of the house and on my own for a while. As I get nearer to the spring, I see footprints in the snow. They look like the footprints of some kind of wild birds. My heart starts beating faster. I haven't seen any wild hens, but I'm almost sure these footprints couldn't have been made by any other animal. For the first time since Zhislav returned from the market in Lublin, I feel a ray of hope.

The spring is bordered by many trees, and their branches are heavy with snow and hanging low. I lift up my eyes, and on the branches I see wild hens—not just a few, but many of them! I'm so full of joy that I begin to cry. It's almost as if I'm seeing my relatives from Lvov

311

again. Now I know that I'm not the only Jew left alive in the world!

As I fill the buckets with water, my soul is filling with hope and optimism. I stay for as long as I can to watch the wild hens before returning to the farmhouse with the water. For the next few days, while the well is still frozen, I volunteer to fetch water from the spring every day. And every day, I take the yoke and the buckets and set off to visit my companions, the wild hens—the representatives of my fellow Jews in the world.

When the water in the well unfreezes, I go back to dipping the buckets into the well in our courtyard to get water with a much lighter heart.

The Brzuszkiewicz Family House and Well

It's spring again, and I often go out to the pasture to watch over the cows. One day, I see a

312

few soldiers far off in the distance. They're wearing uniforms that are not the same color as the German soldiers' uniforms. "How can that be?" I wonder. Maybe they're German soldiers dressed up in the uniforms of Russian or Polish soldiers in order to trap somebody like me into revealing that they're Jewish? I keep my distance, lying down in the tall grass to make sure they don't see me. I'm glad that Wanda isn't with me, and I decide it would be best not to tell anyone in the Brzuszkiewicz family.

The next day, I see soldiers passing by again—soldiers who are dressed in different uniforms than the Germans. Something new must be happening, I think. That same afternoon, I hear airplanes. I look up and see them flying very low overhead. As they swoop down, they drop papers on the ground. I'm terribly curious, so I run to pick up one of the notices and, to my surprise, it's written in Polish, not German! The notice reads: "The Jewish Committee of Lublin is looking for Jewish children who have survived the war: from convents and monasteries, from villages, and from all other hiding places. All Jewish war orphans are invited to come to our office in Lublin" and it gives an address. "Please come and make yourself known to us."

What can that mean? A "Jewish Committee" in Lublin? Could it mean the war is over? I'm so excited I can hardly breathe. I haven't heard a word about the war ending from the Brzuszkiewicz family. Maybe they don't know yet. News travels very slowly in the countryside. And I'm sure it isn't very important to them.

But what should I do? I'm still afraid to tell them that I'm really Jewish. They think my communion was a serious commitment to Christianity. Only *I* know in my heart that it's not.

"And we know, too," says Ivasyk.
"We knew the day would come when the war would be over. Now you can go back to Lvov, and maybe find your family," says the youth from the golden spring.

"But should I tell them that I'm really Jewish?"

"Why should you tell them? How would that help you?"

While I'm thinking about what to do, I read and re-read the notice many times. I memorize the address of the Jewish Committee in Lublin and tear up the paper. On my way home, I think about ways to approach the subject of the war without attracting too much attention. When I get back to the farmhouse, I ask Maria, "Did you hear the airplanes today?" To see airplanes flying low over the fields in our area is a very unusual event.

Maria didn't hear the airplanes. However, she heard that the war had ended, but only in certain places. She isn't sure if it's over in our area or not.

"But what difference can it possibly make to us?" she asks me. "If the Germans lose control, then the Russians will take over. Nothing will change."

314

I don't say anything more, for I can see that nobody in the Brzuszkiewicz family is interested or even cares who has won the war. I don't want them to think that it matters to me, either. But from that day on, I have terrible trouble falling asleep at night. I toss and turn in my little bed on top of the stove, wondering what to do.

If the war is over and there are still Jews left alive in the world, I want desperately to get back home to Lvov. But how can I get there without any money? What can I tell the Brzuszkiewicz family?

After many sleepless nights, I figure out a way to approach them. I tell Maria, "If the war is over, then maybe I should go back to Lvov. It could be that my parents have returned from Siberia. I miss them so much!"

But Maria doesn't want to hear about me leaving. "No," she says, "don't leave us. You've been here so long, you're already one of the family. What will happen if you get to Lvov and you don't find your parents?"

"If I don't find them, I'll come right back," I promise her.

They begin to talk it over in the family. They come to the conclusion that maybe I should go back and look for my parents. But how will I get there? Lvov is very far away, and it costs a lot of money to travel by train.

The Brzuszkiewicz family has their farm and their blacksmith shop, but they have barely any cash at all. Yet they agree to give me a new outfit and new shoes with wooden soles,

315

since I have been working there for so long. So Maria decides to have a linen suit and a pair of shoes made for me. But without any money, what will I do? So I tell Maria, "I can still wear my old clothes, and the shoes that they gave me on the ranch, so you really don't need to give me a new outfit and shoes. Instead, why don't you buy me a train ticket and give me two kilos of tobacco leaves?"

I know that I can sell the tobacco to get the money I'll need.

That sounds like an excellent solution to them, because they'll have to spend a lot of money on my train ticket. Meanwhile, the wooden soles of my old shoes are coming apart, so Zhislav takes them to his smithy and puts iron reinforcements into them. Maria gives me an angora hat that she had gotten somebody to knit especially for me, and a sweater that she had bought for me. At least I'll be dressed warmly and selling the tobacco leaves will give me a good start in Lvov. They also give me some pocket money, and I buy a train ticket to Przemysl.

My Story Comes to an End

Many fairy tales end with the words: "And they lived in happiness until the end of their days." However, the hero who lives happily ever after is a person who has suffered greatly and undergone gruesome experiences throughout the story. For Sonya, even after World War Two ended, there were many difficult experiences ahead of her before she finally settled on a kibbutz in Israel, where she still lives today.

It may have been a good idea to take the tobacco leaves that the Brzuszkiewicz family gave me but the way things turned out, I never used them. You see, the world had changed again, and I didn't return to Lvov for almost 50 years.

On the train, I found out that Lvov was now part of Russia, not Poland, and that at Przemysl, I would have to change trains and cross the border. The station at Przemysl was very crowded. Most of the travelers were going in the opposite direction—from Russia to Poland. I would have to wait a few hours for the train to Lvov. So I wandered around, looking for information about what it was like in Lvov. I had been gone for about two years. I had no idea if anybody I knew was left in Lvov, or if anybody I knew was still alive.

At the train station, a handsome young man approached me and asked, "Why are you going to Lvov when all of the Jews are leaving Russia and entering Poland?"

Startled, I said, "What makes you think I'm a Jew? I'm a Polish citizen. Here are my working papers to prove it!" I also pulled out my communion photograph.

The man replied calmly, "Put your papers away, child. I don't need to see them. I am a Jew, too. And not only a Jew, but a rabbi as well. I'm the only rabbi from Lvov who is still alive."

When I heard those words, I broke into hysterical sobbing. All of the sorrow that had been building up in me over the years came out at once. I couldn't control myself, and people were looking at me and asking what was wrong. Rav Kahana put his arm around me.

"Never mind," he said, stroking my head gently. We've all been through the same war."

He told the curious people who were staring at us that he was taking care of me, and he stayed very close to me until I finally stopped crying.

"Tell me, do you have anybody in Lvov—anybody who you are sure is still there?"

I said, "I'm going to search for my family, the Freiheiters. They were in Lvov when I left. And maybe my mother has come home. My sister and my brother might still be alive, too."

"Come, sit down," he said, leading me to a bench. He took a long list of names from his

318

briefcase. "This is the list of Jews who are still left in Lvov."

There were about six hundred names on the list, but not a single one of them was a name I recognized. I read and re-read the list several times, not wanting to believe my eyes. After a very long while, I felt certain that nobody from my family or our neighborhood was on the list.

Of the 110,000 Jews who had lived in Lvov when I was growing up, only 600 were still there!

Rav Kahana said, "If you have nobody in Lvov, then there really is no reason for you to go back there."

I knew he was right.

"I'm going to Lublin to start an orphanage for children like you, who have survived the war and lost their families. Why don't you come with me?" he suggested.

Orphanage at Peterswald, 1945,
Sonia - center, in white

So I didn't go back to Lvov, but returned on the train to Lublin with Rav Kahana.

319

From that moment on, the weird fairy tale I had been trapped in disintegrated. Now I had adults to whom I could tell the truth about my identity, and who I knew I could trust. I still had a long journey ahead of me, but I was no longer traveling alone in a world gone mad!

My first stop was Lublin, where I went straight to the orphanage. Then I tried working as a servant in a private home, and then I returned to the orphanage in order to get a formal education. Many Jewish survivors wanted to rebuild their lives in Poland, but I had different ideas. When I heard about the pogrom at Kielce in 1946, in which forty-seven Jews who lived in one building were slaughtered by Polish men wielding axes and knives, I knew that Poland could never be my home. So I joined the Hashomer Hatzair underground, a group of Jewish youth who were committed to making "*aliya*," i.e., going to live in Israel. My aunts Devorah and Nechama—Mama's two sisters— had gone to live in Israel before the Russian occupation of Lvov. Maybe I would be able to find them, there.

But Zionism was illegal in those days—at least, it was illegal for Jews to immigrate to Palestine because the British were in control of the Holy Land and Jews were not allowed in. So the Zionist youth groups had to organize themselves secretly.

When the head of the orphanage, Mrs. Nathanblut, heard that some of the orphans had joined the Hashomer Hatzair, she gave us a speech telling us how foolish it was for us to leave the safety and security we had in Poland, in order to go to a dangerous, undeveloped land, illegally. When she finished, I stood up and made my own speech. I had never rehearsed it, but every word came directly from my heart. I said, "Every human being has a homeland, but what is our homeland? Is this our homeland, where we're called "Dirty Jew" everywhere we go, and where the children in my school point at me and make fun of me whenever I pass them? Is this our homeland, where we just buried 47 innocent people—slaughtered in their own home for no reason except that they were Jews? Is this our bright future?"

Mrs. Nathanblut was in shock and so were the other children. So I continued, "We also want a homeland of our own, so that when Jewish people die in a war, at least we'll know what they died for!"

In all, I had been in the orphanage for about a year and a half, during which time I finished my formal schooling and became the editor of the orphanage newsletter.

Soon after my speech, I left the orphanage and joined the underground Hashomer Hatzair youth movement. The State of Israel had not been established, and our future was very much in question. Yiddish was the language we used in the Hashomer Hatzair, and I spoke it more in those times than I had ever spoken it during my childhood.

I became a member of a group called Haviva Reich, where I learned a great deal about Zionism and the land of Israel. When our group made *aliya*, in 1948, we all received certificates in order to emigrate. Our boat docked in the port of Haifa on May 19th, 1948—just a few days before the War of Independence.

We stayed at first in one of the buildings of the Technion, Israel's most prestigious university, and we were given a real Israeli meal. That was the first time I had ever seen olives! Then we left for a tent camp, where the boys were taken away to go to the army. We girls also wanted to join the army, but we were assigned to a different war front: the kibbutz. There, it was our job to produce food for the men in the army. So we went to a kibbutz: Kfar Masarek, where we worked in the gardens.

In 1949, after Israel's War of Independence was won, our group-all of whom were Holocaust survivors—settled permanently on Kibbutz Ein Hashofet. There, I met Abraham Kalsky. Like me, Abraham is the sole survivor of his family from Lodj. Abraham and I got married in 1950. We have four children, all boys: Eyal, Amos, Zachi, and Ido. Eyal and Amos are married and each is the father of two children: a girl and a boy. Eyal's children are named Ilan and Jessica; Amos' children are called Ohr and Matan. Our two younger sons are not yet married. Today, we are still living on Kibbutz Ein Hashofet, surrounded by our children and grandchildren.

Naomi and Avraham

I never saw Mama or Rosa or Emmanuel again, or Uncle Abraham and his wife Minna, or their baby, Mendel, or the Freiheiter brothers, Leibel, Eli and Herschel. But I did meet the children and grandchildren of Uncle Abraham's eldest son, Leepa—who went to live in Canada before the German occupation. And I know that Nessia, Uncle Abraham's older daughter who moved to Paris during the Russian occupation, had a son who lives in Paris.

And I found my aunts Devorah and Nechama in Israel! In July, 2006, I went to the 100th birthday celebration for my aunt Devorah, in Petach Tikva.

In recent years, I've become a speaker to Israeli youth groups studying the Holocaust, and a guide to groups of Israeli high school students who visit Poland to see the concentration camps. I've been back to visit the Brzuszkiewicz family several times, and I remain in touch with Wanda to this very day! In 1997, I was a candle-lighter at the Holocaust Memorial Day ceremony at Yad Vashem in Jerusalem. At the Ghetto Fighters Museum on Kibbutz Lohamei HaGhettaot, there is a children's wing called Yad LaYeled, with the story of my survival on display.

323